The First Ashore

The Stories of our First Anzacs

Peter Burgess

The First Ashore
The Stories of our First Anzacs

First published in Australia by Peter Burgess 2021

Copyright © Peter Burgess 2021
All Rights Reserved

A catalogue record for this
book is available from the
National Library of Australia

ISBN: 978-0-6453620-0-8 (pbk)
ISBN: 978-0-6453620-1-5 (ebk)

Typesetting and design by Publicious Book Publishing
Published in collaboration with Publicious Book Publishing
www.publicious.com.au

No part of this book may be reproduced in any form, by photocopying or by any electronic or mechanical means, including information storage or retrieval systems, without permission in writing from both the copyright owner and the publisher of this book.

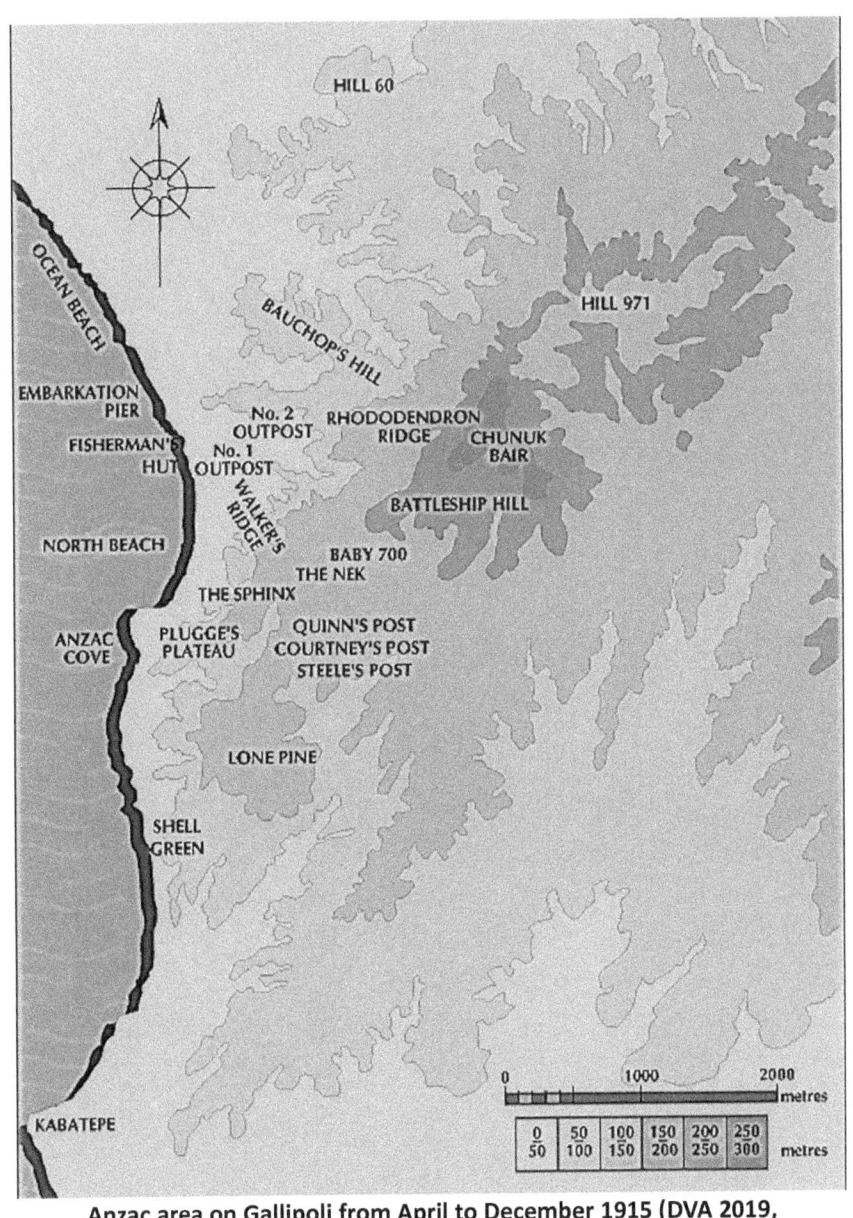

Anzac area on Gallipoli from April to December 1915 (DVA 2019, Maps of Australian locations on Gallipoli 1915, DVA Anzac Portal)

Introduction

On the 25th April, 1915, in the pre-dawn darkness, 36 landing crafts, carrying the first wave of the Gallipoli Campaign, moved slowly and silently towards the Turkish shore. Cramped tightly in the small lead row-boat of the No.1 Tow were approximately 30 fearfully anxious volunteer soldiers. These members of Queensland's 9th Battalion, A Company No. 3 Platoon plus a handful of 9th Battalion Scouts were the first Anzacs to touch shore on that fateful day.

Although no more gallant than the 16,000 Anzacs who landed after them, the men of the first boat provide a sombre microcosm of Queensland's tragic war experience. Three were killed on the first day and nine were wounded. Another three would later die on the Western Front. Those who survived returned home to face profoundly different lives. Disabilities, trauma, disconnection and unemployment made their repatriation a challenging struggle. Many lives faltered. However, for some the proud identity as first ashore 'Original' Anzacs inspired a unique strength. They became leaders in community and veteran affairs making significant contributions to the creation of the RSL, Queensland's first repatriation system and even the Commonwealth Police Force.

The first ashore Anzacs came from diverse backgrounds but war united them as Queenslanders and proud Australians. It also cemented their steadfast commitment to the Anzac values of mateship, duty and service.

This collection of stories honours their sacrifice.

Table of Contents

Identification	i
9th Battalion, A Company:	
Lieutenant Duncan Chapman	1
Sergeant Walter Edward Latimer	14
Lance Corporal James Claude Henderson	27
Lance Corporal Frank Loud	39
Private James Dundee Bostock	56
Private Eli Coles	65
Private William Arthur (Andy) Fisher	73
Private Frederick Young Fox	84
Private Harold Reginald (Roy) Hansen	97
Private Cecil Holdway	105
Private William Jarrett	116
Private David Kendrick	125
Private Benjamin Hugh Kendrick	133
Private Samuel Aubry McKenzie	144
Private Robert McNeil Crawford McKenzie	144
Private William Alexander Pollock	157
Private Archibald Henry Reynolds	163
Private William James Rider	173
Private James Roy (Scotty) Speirs	183
Private Frederick Thomas	191
9th Battalion Scouts:	
Lieutenant Frank Haymen	205
Scout Sergeant Fred Charles Coe (aka Kemp)	214
Lance Corporal Edward Teitzel	227
Private William Cleaver	239
Private Fred Uden	247
Private Alexander Kyle Wilson	256
Endnotes	261
References and Bibliography	287

Identification

Dr C.E.W. Bean, the Australian government's official war historian, made the observation that 'lots of people thought they were in the first boat.'¹ Although most life-boats used at the landing carried only about 30 troops, many more than that number believed they were first ashore. When writing his history, the plethora of claimants and the many conflicting eyewitness reports about who was first ashore perplexed Bean. He concluded the recollections of many soldiers were unreliable. The extreme confusion, the pre-dawn darkness and the geography of the peninsula made it difficult for them to report accurate details of the landing. Yet, despite this, after interviewing many veterans, it became obvious to Bean that almost every Anzac had a vivid recollection of his whereabouts when the first rifle shot sounded. The suspense during the long journey to shore had been unbearable. '*Every brain in the boats was throbbing with the intense anxiety of the moment.*'² As a consequence, the much anticipated first rifle shot brought blessed relief and became an almost frozen instant of time indelibly marked on every soldier's consciousness.

Using the rifle sound as his criteria, Bean believed it was possible to accurately identify the first boat ashore. After exhaustive research, he found there was only one group of soldiers who reported they were on the beach when the first shot sounded. Consequently, in the supplementary preface to the 3rd Edition of his Official History, he confidently declared Lieutenant Duncan Chapman, platoon commander of the 9th Battalion, was the first man to land at Gallipoli. '*Evidence worthy of attention has at last come to hand as to which was actually the first boat ashore. From the day of the landing tradition ascribed priority to the 9th Battalion, and evidence since available also points to this. ... there is ample evidence that, when the enemy shot was fired, most of the boats were at least some yards from the beach, and no other case has been*

The First Ashore

heard of in which a boat-load had then already landed and had began to throw off its packs.'[3]

Many accounts written soon after the landing supported Bean's conclusion. Private W.A. Fisher, a rower in Chapman's boat, in a letter dated 3rd May, 1915, wrote,

'The Queenslanders had the honour to be the first to land...... I happened to be one of the rowers in the first boat. We reached the beach about 4.30, and half of our chaps got out of the boat without anything happening. We were just beginning to think that the Turks were not there when one shot was fired.'[4]

A diary entry, dated May 1915, by Lance Corporal Frank Loud, a member of Lieutenant Chapman's No. 3 Platoon, was similar,

'Our boat was first to ground and 8 or 10 were already on shore. I was standing on the seat aft when the first rifle shot was fired. It hit the thwarts just by my ankle.'[5]

Also in 1915, Lieutenant Duncan Chapman explained in a letter to his brother from Gallipoli's trenches,

'No doubt you have read the various accounts of our landing here. To me was given the extreme honour of being the first man to put foot on the Peninsula.'

After the war, other soldiers added further testimony. Private Scotty Speirs, from No.3 Platoon, in 1934 recounted,

'A few strokes of the oars put the bow ashore. Lieutenant Chapman was right forward and hopped over and was followed quickly by the rest. Somewhere about 17 men were out of the boat before the first rifle shot rang out.'[6]

Private J D Bostock, the Lieutenant's orderly, recalled,

'I jumped into the water with Lieutenant Chapman and Sgt Coe ..... I know, and all of us who still remain of that first boat load, know that 'Chappy' was the first ashore and the 'Original Anzac.'[7]

Major Salisbury who commanded A Company, also firmly believed Lieutenant Chapman was first ashore. At the landing, Naval Lieutenant Waterlow's No.1 Tow guided the Major's rowboat to the beach.[8] Ahead of him, in the same tow, was Lieutenant Chapman's boat, the lead boat of No.1 Tow.[9] When the first Turkish shot was fired, Major Salisbury's boat was 20 yards off the beach[10] but, from this vantage point, he could easily discern that Lieutenant Chapman was first ashore. *'One of my subalterns, Lieutenant Duncan Chapman, was the first officer ashore.'*[11]

In 1941, the soldiers who landed with Chapman received some public recognition. Respected 9th Battalion historian, Norman K. Harvey, after interviewing surviving veterans, published a list of 18 names in his book, *'From Anzac to the Hindenburg Line, the History of the 9th Battalion'*. This list was extended in the 1950s when three more names were added by the 9th Battalions Association based on testimonies received and corroborated by other veterans.

HARVEY'S LIST[12]

1. Lieutenant Duncan Chapman	A Coy
2. Scout Sgt Fred Coe (aka Kemp) 1010	A Coy
3. Private James Dundee Bostock 1109	A Coy
4. Private Eli Coles 315	A Coy
5. Private William Arthur Fisher 362	A Coy
6. Private Harold Reginald Hanson (Hansen) 70	A Coy
7. (*Lance Corp Thomas Arthur Hellmuth 328*)	A Coy
8. Lance Corp James Claude Henderson 296	A Coy
9. Private Cecil Holdway 295	A Coy
10. Private William Jarrett 311	A Coy
11. Private David Kendrick 386	A Coy
12. Private Benjamim Hugh Kendrick 319	A Coy
13. Private Walter Edward Latimer 404	A Coy
14. Private Robert McNeil Crawford McKenzie 298	A Coy
15. Private Samuel Aubry McKenzie 292	A Coy
16. Private William Alexander Pollock 316	A Coy
17. Private William James Rider 317	A Coy
18. Private Frederick Thomas 388	A Coy

Additions made by 9th Battalions Association[13]

19. Private Frederick Young Fox 389	A Coy
20. Private William Cleaver 627	C Coy
21. Private Archibald Henry Reynolds 1171	A Coy

In 1954, Harvey also suggested that Colonel Butler, the Battalion's medical officer, should be added to his list.[14] Surviving accounts by the Colonel, however, clearly show he was not in the first boat ashore. In his 'Gallipoli Report', Colonel Butler wrote, *'other boats had got to shore sooner.'*[15] He also recalled his boat reached shore after the first rifle shot sounded. *'Four boats, including the one I was in, became locked together ...... progress was almost imperceptible .... In the meantime, the bullets were zipping into the water.'*[16]

Also, Harvey's inclusion of Lance Corporal Thomas Hellmuth appears to be incorrect. Statements made in 1915 by the Lance Corporal show he was distant from the beach when the first rifle shot was fired. In a letter to his mother, in May 1915, Thomas wrote, *'everything went lovely till near the shore and then one of the ropes from the pinnace broke and delayed us for a while. When we got about 50 yards from the shore the enemy opened fire on us and the fun started.'*[17]

While substantial documented evidence exists to support all other soldiers on Harvey's list, further research has added six more names to those who landed with Lieutenant Chapman. Each of these men has been identified as a member of the Lieutenant's No.3 Platoon or the 9th Battalion's contingent of Scouts. Their inclusion is based on compelling testimonies and/or corroborating evidence, directly or indirectly from at least one other source.

Recent Additions

Private James Roy Speirs, 364[18]   A Company
Lance Corporal Frank Loud, 348[19]   A Company
Lieutenant Frank Haymen, Scout officer[20]   C Company
Lance Corporal Edward Teitzel, 691, Battalion Scout[21]   D Company
Private Alexander Kyle Wilson, 616, Battalion Scout[22]   A Company
Private Fred Uden, 718, Battalion Scout[23]   B Company

Regrettably, some claims made by other soldiers remain uncorroborated. It is possible the following three Anzacs landed in the first boat, but because their proud recollections could not be verified by another source, they have not been included in this study.

Private Robert Sydney Davies, Service No. 1124, C Company. Robert maintained in a 1930s newspaper interview that he was one of a 'dozen picked men', scouts, in the first boat to land.[24]

Private Wyndham Drayton Jones, Service No. 376, A Company. In a letter to his parents, dated 30 June, 1915, he wrote, *'our boat hit the shore first … I scrambled over the side into the water up to my neck, and by the time I got out of the water … Bullets were flying all around me.'*[25]

Private Alexander Menzies Kippen, Service No. 145, A Company. Interviewed from his hospital bed, shortly before his death, Alexander proudly claimed he was in the first boat ashore.[26]

9th BATTALION, A COMPANY

Lieutenant Duncan Kenneth Chapman

A Company, 9th Battalion
(later Major, 45th Battalion)

Before war, Duncan Chapman's interests and hopes for the future were like those of most young men growing up in country Queensland. Physically fit and tall, with a lean physique, his passions were football and sport. As he grew into adulthood, an air of self-confidence set him apart from others. As a consequence, in war, the rank of Lieutenant was quickly achieved and, on the shores of Gallipoli, great fame was attained. Sadly, 15 months later, he lost everything.

Duncan's short life began in Maryborough, Queensland. Born on 15th May, 1888, he was the second youngest child in a large and loving family of 12 children. His father, Robert Chapman, was an industrious Scottish immigrant, and his mother, Maude Humphrey, was proudly Australian, born with a convict heritage. In 1887, the newly married couple arrived in Maryborough, where Robert attempted to establish a drapery business. A grand store was opened in Kent Street but, regrettably, within months the business failed.[1] Work was then found as a draper's assistant and later Duncan's father became head man at 'W. Adams and Sons', one of the largest drapery businesses in town. In Maryborough, they created a rewarding and prosperous life. The Chapman home, a large Queenslander on the corner of Fort and Walker Streets,[2] burst with people, energy and activity.

Sadly, in 1893, tragedy befell the family. Duncan was only five years old when his mother died unexpectedly due to complications incurred at the birth of her twelfth child. Crippled with grief, his father worked determinedly to keep the young family together. With much love, purpose and sacrifice, he raised 12 children on his own.

Duncan held great admiration for his father. Scottish values of hard work and thrifty enterprise strongly influenced his character and development. His father was also 'an intensely patriotic man'[3] whose colourful stories about Scotland and the family's very British history captured young Duncan's imagination. A favourite and often repeated tale was that the Chapmans descended from Bonnie Prince Charlie.[4] The family home in Fort Street was named "Glenfarg," after a picturesque glen near their ancestral village, and his father's landscape paintings of the 'old country' proudly adorned the interior of their Maryborough house.[5] His father's influence instilled a strong sense of duty, loyalty and belief in Empire. He and Duncan developed a shared sense of patriotism as well as many other common interests. They loved sports and together enjoyed shooting and fishing. In a letter, written 10 years after Duncan's death, Robert Chapman revealed the closeness of their relationship. He lamented that, above all his children, Duncan had been his '*sole support.*'[6]

Formal education for Duncan began at Maryborough Boys Central School (Central State School) where he proved to be a bright student who showed lots of potential. His name often appeared on school prize lists.[7] The special award received at the end of Year 4 for penmanship and the neatness of exercises was an early indicator of a meticulous and perfectionist nature. Academic prowess was also clear when, in 1903, Duncan received one of only three scholarships awarded to the brightest Maryborough students of that year.[8] This award enabled a high school education at Maryborough Grammar School, where Duncan was a student from 1903 to 1906.

Besides possessing scholarly aptitude, Duncan also was a keen and competent sportsman who excelled in a variety of sports. He was a capable gymnast, competitive rower, and loved football. Outside school hours, he played as a forward for the local team, the 'Thistles' in the district's rugby union premierships.[9] Duncan was also an active member of the Wide Bay Rowing Club, competing very successfully in 1905 and 1906 in Maryborough's annual Regatta.[10] Rowing was greatly enjoyed and, after leaving school, his involvement continued. In 1906, 18-year-old Duncan was elected as a young committee member of the Wide Bay Rowing Club.[11]

Although his many school and sporting commitments created a busy schedule, Duncan also found time to develop a keen interest in military matters. At Maryborough Grammar School, he joined the military cadets, a compulsory scheme that ran in every school throughout Australia. Like most teenage boys, he was enthused by the uniforms, the public parades, rifle teams, camps and competitions. Cadets became an exciting and popular part of his school life and, after leaving school, he chose to continue military training by immediately enlisting in Maryborough's citizens' militia, the Wide Bay Infantry Regiment.

Duncan's first job was in the office of Messrs Morton, Gordon and Morton, solicitors of Maryborough where he was employed as an article clerk from 1907 to 1908.[12] He enjoyed the work, and his integrity and quick mind made him a valued employee. It seemed a future career in law was inevitable. After completing two years' supervision as an articled clerk, Duncan successfully applied for a position as a law clerk with solicitors, Marsland and Marsland in Charters Towers.

Leaving Maryborough, family and friends was challenging and made more difficult by a recent family tragedy. Duncan's elder brother, Gordon, aged 21, had died 12 months before in a drowning accident.[13] It was with a heavy heart that, so soon after his brother's death, Duncan boarded the steamship "Bingera" for Townsville[14] on his journey to Charters Towers.

The move north marked the beginning of a new independence for the 21-year-old. He took up residence at Racecourse Road, Charters Towers and, with great diligence, proved himself to be a competent law clerk. A short time later, a new position with more responsibilities was gained in the office of Mr Newman Johnson. Local newspapers reported, by 1910, the young clerk was working independently in the Charters Towers Court, representing a number of his employer's clients.[15]

Although Duncan's career progressed well, he was restless. He missed his Maryborough life crowded with rowing, football, family functions, gymnastics, military camps and more. Life in Charters Towers was comparatively quiet. Social cricket matches partially satisfied his passion for sport. For instance, in 1910, the Charters Towers newspaper reported Duncan played for the Excelsior Hotel in a cricket match against the Exchange Hotel.[16]

However, Duncan needed to be busy, and he soon found other interests to dominate his life. In Maryborough, the volunteer citizen militia was just one of many diversions but, in Charters Towers, it became his sole focus. He joined the local Kennedy Infantry Regiment and, soon after, devoted all his weekends, holidays and after-work hours to the Regiment and its officer training programme.

In 1911, after gaining a commission as a Second-Lieutenant,[17] his ambitions and goals changed dramatically. War was on the horizon, and the army was offering adventurous opportunities for ambitious young men. As a response to Lord Kitchener's inspection of the country's defence preparedness, it was expected a full time Australian army would soon be formed. Enrolments in the Citizen Military Forces were rapidly increasing, especially in Brisbane where, between 1911 and 1913, there was a 50% increase.[18] Duncan astutely realized if he was to access career opportunities in this new evolving military, he needed to act quickly. At the end of 1911, he resigned his position as a law clerk and made the fateful decision to leave Charters Towers for Brisbane.

A room was rented at 'Clark's, Park Road, off Ipswich Road' at Oxley and a job was found as a payroll clerk in a city office, but his ambition was focused only on the militia. He transferred immediately to Brisbane's 9th Australian Infantry Regiment and, a few months later, in July 1912, moved to the 7th Infantry Moreton Regiment, D Company. Military training consumed all his energy and free time. There were parades, field exercises, rifle clubs, inspections, drills, medal presentations, military dinners and evening classes for officer training. Duncan worked diligently and, in 1913, newspapers reported he had successfully completed his officer examinations.[19] After receiving his second star, he was attached to the Kelvin Grove Company[20] and, in September, appointed 2nd Lieutenant to Lieutenant Chambers, jointly in charge of 46 men from Albion, the 7th Regiment's D Company.[21]

For an ambitious officer, position and social standing were important. To this end, Duncan moved from Oxley to the fashionable boarding house, "Whytecliffe" in Albion Heights. This beautiful suburban home, formerly the country estate of Brisbane's crown solicitor, boasted wonderful city and river views and was advertised as having 'balconies from all rooms, hot and cold baths, tennis and Clayfield tram at gate.'[22] It was an expensive abode for a payroll clerk but befitted a young officer's status and image. Duncan justified the move as a practical choice. Most of the men from his platoon lived in the surrounding suburb of Albion.[23] (Today, the elegant "Whytecliffe" stands restored at 469 Sandgate Road.)

Soon after arriving in Brisbane, Duncan acquired a circle of reputable social acquaintances. His Uncle James, a prominent Brisbane businessman, owned the city's largest drapery store and was able to provide important contacts.[24] Other influential introductions came through fellow officers of the citizen militia. With confidence and charm, Duncan soon became a popular figure in Brisbane's society. Strong friendships were established with influential citizens such as Mr Theodore Troedson, the Director of Queensland's Intelligence and Tourist Bureau, at whose wedding in November 1912, Duncan acted as best man.[25]

Duncan found these pre-war years to be exciting and most exhilarating. Yet when news was announced that the Empire, including Australia, was at war, he did not hesitate. He quit his job and residence, and, with great enthusiasm, joined the wave of jubilation that swept Brisbane's streets. With the other militia officers, he moved to Bell's Paddock at Enoggera where hundreds of volunteers were already busily erecting tents. Their arrival on 21st August heralded the beginning of Queensland's 9th Battalion.

Despite Duncan's young age, the army immediately enacted his commission. With military experience in short supply, Commanding Officer, Lieutenant Colonel Lee, realized the daunting task that his officers would face when training the raw volunteers into a disciplined fighting force. He therefore carefully selected his lieutenants. They needed to be experienced, firm, but not familiar, and have life experiences that connected them with their men. Duncan had served four years as a militia officer and possessed all these qualities. Lieutenant Colonel Lee readily appointed Duncan as one of two lieutenants in the 9th Battalion's C Company and, although Duncan was younger by seven years, granted him seniority.[26]

This appointment as senior lieutenant was more remarkable because Duncan did not fit the typical officer mould. Almost all officers listed on the 1914 Embarkation Rolls came from privileged social backgrounds. They were either wealthy landowners, lawyers, successful businessmen or university students.[27] In contrast, Duncan's father worked for wages, and Duncan was neither university educated nor did he have a profession. At the time of enlistment, he was a lowly paid payroll clerk. As well, the stain of a convict ancestry tainted him. His grandfather, Thomas Humphrey, was transported for life for sheep stealing and his grandmother, Miriam Houghton, received 14 years for robbing her master.[28] However, rather than these aspects hindering Duncan's military career, they enhanced the qualities that made him a popular officer. From Duncan's working class background and family history, he carried a sense of egalitarianism. Men serving under him observed he did not display the sense of privilege that many other officers carried. They described him as a *'well-made man, smart in his movements.... a good officer.'*[29]

With extraordinary pride and enthusiasm, Duncan embarked with the 9th Battalion on the "SS Omrah", the first troopship to leave Brisbane for war. The formidable task ahead could not daunt his eagerness. At their desert camp in Egypt, beside the Pyramids, for four months, Lieutenant Chapman engaged his men in a rigorous programme of intense military training. By the end of the third month, he was confident they were battle ready and eager to leave the desert. However, another month would pass before orders were finally received. In February 1915, enormously relieved, he marched his Company out of Mena Camp, eager to join the fight against the Germans. Their destination, the Greek Island of Lemnos, however, brought bitter disappointment and another long delay to participation in the war.

Upon arriving at Lemnos, while most Battalions remained on board their troopships, fortunately, Duncan's 9th Battalion was allowed to land. They set up a camp on the island where they were employed unloading supplies and constructing a jetty. As well, Duncan and the other officers began specific training programmes that focused on landing from boats and arduous climbs up hills with full packs. At the end of five weeks on Lemnos, the 9th re-embarked on another crowded troopship, where they waited impatiently for ten more days as over 200 ships gathered in the harbour.

Preparations were finally completed on 24th April. The 9th Battalion's A Company and B Company were transferred to the battleship "Queen" that would lead the invasion convoy. After a restless night, at about 1.30 a.m., disembarkation commenced. With meticulously well-rehearsed precision, the troops climbed silently down rope ladders to the row-boats waiting below. Duncan's No. 3 Platoon from A Company,[30] with several scouts from other companies, took their position in the lead boat of No. 1 Tow. At the bow on the starboard side sat the Lieutenant with his signaller, Private Bostock. Opposite were Lieutenant Hayman and his scouts.

Duncan described the landing as a *peculiar experience* marked by *'extreme suspense.'*[31] Not a word was spoken as the men anxiously searched the horizon for signs of the enemy. When the row-boats were within 50 yards of the beach, their steam tow-boat cast them adrift and the rowers in each boat took over. The silence was eerie. Even the muffled sound of the oars gliding through the water seemed strangely amplified. Duncan recalled as they approached the shore, his men crouched low in the boat, not knowing what awaited them. Fear and apprehension were overwhelming.

When his boat reached the beach, it seemed the Turks were not there. Duncan promptly gave the command, "All OUT!" A ladder was quickly put down from the bow and the Lieutenant was the first to jump into the waist deep water. With haste, he led the way to shore, followed closely by his runner, Private Bostock, the Scout Sergeant Coe and Lieutenant Hayman. Testimonies by Coe, Bostock, Spiers and other members of the boat confidently verified "Chappy' was the first ashore and the 'Original Anzac.'[32] Over half his men, approximately 17 soldiers, managed to disembark safely and were sheltering on the beach when the first single Turkish rifle shot pierced the silence. Some had already thrown off their water sodden packs and had commenced to fix bayonets.

Quickly, the gunfire intensified and, within moments, a rain of bullets hit their boat. As one of Chapman's soldiers stood, a bullet struck his cap, and he was thrown backwards into the water.[33] Another soldier narrowly missed a wound to his ankle when a shot hit the thwarts he was standing on.[34] The rowers were the last to make the frantic scramble ashore, but good fortune favoured them. All members of the boat reached the shelter of the sandy cliffs bordering the shore.

Within moments, the cove became crowded and chaotic. As boat upon boat came ashore on the narrow beach, platoons, companies and battalions were hopelessly mixed. Duncan attempted to gather his platoon, but it was impossible. In the crowded confusion, contact was lost and orders to form up were ignored. One of Duncan's men, Private James Spiers, recalled after landing that he did not see Lieutenant Chapman until four days later.[35] Even his signaller, James Bostock, whose duty was to stay by the Lieutenant's side in order to transmit messages, became separated.[36]

Waiting on a beach that was being showered with Turkish gunfire seemed senseless. Instead, pumped with adrenalin and reckless enthusiasm, soldiers answered the call, "Come on Queenslanders! Come on the 9th!" and rushed wildly up the steep slopes. Some from the first boat, including signaller Bostock, joined a charge led by 'Jock' Fletcher. Others followed Captain Butler. Scout Sergeant Coe left the beach with another group, as did Lieutenant Haymen. Initially, Duncan attempted to gain some order but quickly realized this was futile. With a group of Anzacs from various companies, he also charged courageously up the slopes.

He recorded his experience in a graphic letter to his brother from the trenches, nine weeks after the landing.

> 'Dear Charles,
> I can now have the pleasure of dropping you a few lines, as I have managed to "snare" some writing paper from one of our wounded officers, who has returned…
> Well, no doubt you have read and re-read the various accounts of our landing here, and a good many of them have given the facts pretty accurately. To me was given the extreme honour of being actually the first man to put foot ashore on this peninsula, to lead a portion of the men up the hill in that now historic charge. What a living hell it was too, and how I managed to go through it from 4 o'clock in the morning of Sunday, the 25th April, to Wednesday, the 28th, under fire the whole time, without being hit, is a mystery to me.
> We have firmly established ourselves now, and although the Unspeakable has made various attempts to dislodge us, and threatened to push us into the sea, his efforts have been abortive. He has come to respect the fighting qualities of the Australian, and is now resorting to defensive measures, which, performed under the guidance of German officers, are done pretty thoroughly.
> I was promoted Captain on 26th April, and put in charge of a full company of about 263 men. The responsibility is certainly great, especially as the lives of these men are practically given into one's keeping.

> *It is nine weeks since we landed here, and many poor fellows have tasted of the horrors of a campaign. Many noble acts have been performed, and courage is a quality that is not wanting among our fellows. In the Turk we have a truly obstinate fighter, and he has well earned the title of the "Fighting Turk"…*
>
> *Our battalion, the 9th, which formed the covering party, lost heavily, especially among the officers, who were spotted mostly by the snipers. The close shaves I had were remarkable, and if I am spared to get back I have a few curios of interest to show.*
>
> *Well, old man, the mail is closing shortly, and I have to censor a couple of hundred letters, so will have to close.'*[37]

Duncan's admission that his Battalion 'lost heavily' was much understated. The first day of the Gallipoli Campaign was a horrific disaster for the 9th Battalion. It suffered the heaviest casualties of any battalion, with the exception of the 7th.[38] At the first roll call, five days after the landing, from a landing force of almost 1000 Queenslanders, only 419 men answered the call. Duncan was devastated. Turkish snipers had carefully targeted his fellow officers. Over 65% of the Battalion's officers had been killed or wounded.[39]

Because of these losses, Duncan suddenly found himself promoted to Captain. Officially, his commission did not come into effect until the 7th June, but because of the desperate shortage of officers, he took up duties on the second day of the Gallipoli Campaign. For a young man, just six days off his 27th birthday, command and responsibility for more than 260 soldiers in the midst of an intense battle was a daunting task. In his letter home, Duncan had modestly informed his family of the promotion and revealed the heavy weight of responsibility that he felt, *'the lives of these men are practically given into one's keeping.'*[40] However, there was little time for self-doubts and, in his new role, he quickly proved himself an effective and popular leader. Men spoke of him with respect, fondly referring to their Captain as "Chappy."[41]

The benefits Duncan gained as Captain were quite dubious. He acquired his own headquarters, although he may have felt equally safe in the trenches. *'My headquarters in reality are a cubical cave dug into the ground 8 feet deep with some strips of galvanized iron and earth on top as a protection against bombs, shrapnel and stray bullets but I am beginning to doubt the stability of it as occasionally at night I hear suspicious little noises as of bullets striking the opposite wall.'*[42]

The strain of command was constant. During the first 22 days at Gallipoli, enemy fire did not abate. In a postcard to his sister, Duncan revealed that, after landing, he remained in the firing line for three continuous weeks.[43] The stress of such continuous duty and the heavy burden of leadership tested his strength and resilience. On 12th August, after three months on the Peninsula, weak and battle worn, Duncan succumbed to a severe bout of influenza. He was transported on the hospital ship, "Neuralia" to the 1st Australian General Hospital at Cairo and, from there, on 18th August, to the hospital camp at Helouan where he remained for three months. Although military records refer only to a diagnosis of influenza, such a long period of convalescence suggests severe sickness with perhaps complications related to exhaustion.

Duncan did not return to Gallipoli. He re-joined his unit on 19th November on Lemnos. His Battalion had arrived there two days before for a long-overdue rest period. Weeks later, the Gallipoli Campaign ended. Like the rest of the 9th, Duncan was pleased the ordeal was over but also disappointed not to be there at the end. With renewed energy, he looked forward to joining the war against the Germans.

However, more disappointment followed. Instead of France, the 9th was returned to the all too familiar deserts of Egypt, arriving there on 4th January, 1916. After three weeks at Tel-el-Kebir they marched, with a convoy of 80 camels, through soft sand to their camp at Gebel Habieta near the Suez Canal. It was a relief to not face the danger of active combat but, for the next few months, Duncan and his men endured great hardship. Their new orders were to construct trenches and fortifications on the Egyptian border. The desert heat and the frequent sand storms that filled trenches as fast as they were dug made their task almost impossible. Yet, the 9th persevered and three long trenches, each capable of holding a company, were built and consolidated.

While in Egypt, Duncan's proud connection with Queensland's 9th Battalion reluctantly ended. As part of a reorganization of the AIF, he was selected by lot for transfer to a new 49th Battalion. The move brought a promotion to company commander but, for Duncan, leaving the 9th was extremely tough. The Battalion's unique bond of comradeship and his identity as a '9th Battalion Original' were difficult to forfeit. With a heavy heart, he marched his new company out of the 9th Battalion camp on 26th February. A sorrowful silence made the poignancy of the occasion more acute as they marched without the usual accompaniment of a band to lead the way.

Duncan's time with the 49th Battalion was brief. Less than a month later, he was transferred to another new battalion, the 4th Division's 45th. Regrettably, this move further weakened his connection to Queensland, as the 45th was a N.S.W. battalion. The transfer, however, included promotion to Major, which was an amazing achievement for a 28-year-old. In the 18 months since his enlistment, Duncan had risen meteorically through the ranks.

In early June 1916, the 45th Battalion received orders to leave Egypt for France. Duncan was elated. At last, he would have the opportunity to participate in the 'real' war against the Germans. Their troopship "Kinfauns Castle" docked at Marseilles and, from there, the 45th travelled north by train on a three-day journey to the battlefields. Their destination was a flat swampy area close to the Belgium border near Fleurbaix, a quieter sector that would allow Duncan's men time to acclimatize to the new battle conditions. However, these plans were short-lived. Ten days later, the 45th was sent south to the Somme Valley to join a major new offensive, 'The Battle of the Somme.' The first phase had ended disastrously with over 60,000 casualties and now the Allied Command was mounting a desperate attempt to take the high ground around the villages of Pozieres and Thiepval.

On 14th July, Duncan and his men arrived at the village of Berteaucourt, 35 kilometres south of Pozieres, where they waited anxiously until needed. The first attack on 22nd-23rd July by Australia's First Division successfully captured the ruined village of Pozieres but, over the next days, the enemy mounted fierce counter-attacks. On 27th July, the Second Division moved in to take over. After an initial defeat, more German trenches were taken, but the Second's sacrifice was enormous with 3500 men lost in two days of fighting. Then, two weeks after arriving, it became Duncan and the 4th Division's turn to enter the bloodbath.

After leaving Berteaucourt on 27th July, as they marched towards Pozieres, they encountered the remnants of the 9th Battalion returning from the battle. Normally, Duncan would have been overjoyed to see his

The First Ashore

old platoon mates but, instead, he was shocked and dismayed by their desperate, haggard appearance. The 9th had entered Pozieres with 1016 men and were returning with only 623. Familiar faces of old mates were almost unrecognizable. *'They looked like men who had been in Hell... so dazed that they appear to be walking in a dream.'*[44] Duncan worried about the fate of the men he was leading.

For the next three days, while waiting orders, his Battalion bivouacked outside Albert, six kilometres from the front. The surrounding countryside, crowded with horses, wagons, guns, ammunition and wounded men, was a disturbing, chaotic scene. The constant sound of nearby artillery fire and the flash of explosions menacingly reminded Duncan of the job ahead. Sleep became difficult.

On 4th August, final orders arrived. The 45th Battalion was mobilized to a position just in front of Pozieres, in an area known as Sausage Valley, where they were to relieve exhausted battalions and consolidate the position that had been captured from the Germans that morning. From experience, Duncan immediately knew their task would be challenging. It was always easier to capture a position than to hold it afterwards.

The nerves of Duncan and his men were further tested when they departed Albert that night. As they began their march, German artillery launched a fury upon the town. Under a deadly barrage, the men bravely moved forward and, fortunately, incurred no casualties. The next day, passing above Sausage Gully, on the narrow roads to Pozieres, more mayhem greeted them. As they manoeuvred a path blocked by wagons, horses and men, coming in and going out, German artillery ploughed up the surrounding earth. The noise was deafening.

A somewhat shaken 45th finally reached Pozieres as the Germans began one of their largest and most deadly counter-attacks. As night fell, their horror intensified. Terrifying shellfire crashed in front, behind and above, as Duncan courageously directed his men along the trenches. The noise of approaching shells surrounded them and, in the darkness, each sound seemed larger and menacingly sharper than the one before. As the ground shook, lethal metal hurled in all directions. Everywhere, groans and cries of wounded soldiers filled the air.

By midday on 6th August, less than 24 hours after they entered the front, 32 men from Duncan's Battalion were dead and 70 were wounded. In the early hours that day, while Duncan was moving his men along a trench, another German shell exploded above them. This time it blasted the surrounding earth skywards. Many men were buried alive. Six were killed. It was said Duncan *'only lived a few minutes.'* Nearby soldiers reported Chappy *'was badly blown to pieces.'*[45] By his side, also dead, were his Lieutenant, his Sergeant and two Corporals. Their bodies remained unburied until the next morning, when graves were hastily made on top of the trench. A makeshift wooden cross bore three names–"Captain Drinkwater", "Lieutenant Draper" and "Major Chapman."

Tragically, Duncan had survived the horrors of the Gallipoli Campaign to die in the first hours of his first major battle on the Western Front. Youthful dreams and ambitions were gone forever, replaced by a never ending sorrow to be endured by his father, sisters, brothers and many friends.

At war's end, Major Duncan Chapman's body was exhumed from the battlefield and moved to his final resting place in the Pozieres British Cemetery. (Plot 3, Row V, Grave 22.)

Sergeant Walter Edward Latimer

No. 404, C Company, 9th Battalion
(later Lieutenant, 42nd Battalion)

Walter Latimer was an English-born patriot, a former British soldier and Boer War veteran. As one of the first volunteers in Australia's new army, he fought gallantly at Gallipoli and on the Western Front. Twice as a casualty of war, he was repatriated to Australia, but, with steely determination and a heroic dedication to duty, Walter returned to the front. Each time, his Australian identity grew stronger and the mental scars cut deeper.

Born on 8th January, 1877, his life began in the small picturesque English village of Corfe Mullen in Dorset. The setting seemed idyllic, but rural life in Dorset at the turn of the century was grim. Walter's father worked as a poorly paid farm labourer[1] and also as village watchmaker and clock repairer,[2] while his mother toiled long hours making dresses.[3] Insecure work forced the family to move home often. The first years of Walter's life were spent in Corfe, then in the nearby quaint hamlet of Woodlands and later in the even smaller hamlet of Pentridge.

Walter's father also served as a lay preacher and Walter received a strict Christian upbringing in the Methodist faith. He attended a Methodist Church school and also was a choirboy.[4] In later life, although not a regular churchgoer, Walter faithfully adhered to many Methodist doctrines such as abstinence from alcohol.

Upon finishing school, a job was obtained as a labourer on one of the district's large manor farms.[5] However, the drudgery of farm-work was not appealing to Walter, nor did he enjoy the long hours and low wages. Regrettably, for young Dorsetshire men, the only other options were migration or enlistment in the army. 18-year-old Walter chose the latter. In 1895, after his parents left Pentridge to live in Chilbolton, he travelled to Poole, where he signed up for a seven-year term in the British army. It was a momentous decision that changed his future forever.

With diligence and enthusiasm, he successfully applied himself to army life. However, Walter was also a daring opportunist who eagerly grasped any opportunities presented. After serving two years with the Dorsetshire Regiment in Londonderry and Enniskillen in Northern Ireland, he sought a change to the more prestigious Coldstream Guards. To achieve this, on 2nd December, 1896, he took the risky action of deserting his Dorsetshire Regiment.[6] Desertion was a serious crime and, in order to avoid severe punishment, an urgent change of identity was required. Using his mother's maiden name, Walter became Private Charles Holder, Service Number 708, C Company, 3rd Regiment.[7] It was a reckless move, but as a Coldstream Guard, Walter could pursue and develop his skills as a rifleman. He soon attained the 'marksmanship' badge of crossed rifles and became well known for his expertise at target shooting.

Eager to see the world, his first overseas posting was, in 1898, to Gibraltar and, a year later, to the Boer War in South Africa. He naively departed, unaware of the perils he would face in this deadly guerrilla war. In the campaigns in Belmont, Dreifontein and Modder River, Walter served gallantly but, sadly, in July 1900, he was evacuated home as a casualty. Doctors described his condition as, *'Disordered action of the heart and debility,'*[8] a major cause of soldier invalidity during the Boer War. Today it would be recognized as post-traumatic stress disorder.

Although his health gradually returned, he remained unfit for active service. Instead, a fortunate transfer was received. Because of his prowess as a rifleman, Walter was selected to join the newly formed "Imperial Representative Corps". This group of 1000 soldiers from the various branches of the military was carefully chosen to showcase the best of the British defence forces. Their mission was to represent Britain at the upcoming celebrations to mark the birth of the Commonwealth of Australia. British newspapers proudly boasted they were formed to *'lend lustre and significance to the historic ceremony.'*[9]

Walter and the Imperial Corps arrived in Australia on the 14th December, 1900, to a welcome that was truly spectacular. At their first port of call, Fremantle and Perth, the streets were ablaze with thousands of Union Jacks and Southern Crosses. Never had Walter witnessed crowds so huge or enthusiastic. Upon arriving in Sydney, the focal point of Federation celebrations, their reception was even more extraordinary. Their tour culminated on January 1st, the first day of the 20th century, at the birthday of a nation. The centrepiece of celebrations was Australia's "Great Inaugural Procession," a majestic parade through Sydney's streets that stretched for over five miles. Among the 10,000 people who marched, the Imperial Corps was the crowd favourite. Walter, representing the Coldstream Guards, was resplendent in his red tunic, brass buckle, gold buttons and tall black bearskin hat. At parade's end, a choir of 1000 voices opened the official ceremony at Sydney's Centennial Park. It was a visual spectacle that Walter would never forget.

For two months, the Imperial Corps continued their tour, attracting huge patriotic crowds wherever they went. At each city, Walter became more intoxicated by Australia and the optimism that was sweeping the country. By the tour's end, he was exhausted by the hectic schedule, but his attachment to Australia was strong. He hoped one day to return.

After arriving back in England, unfortunately, health problems associated with his Boer War service persisted. Walter was discharged from the army as medically unfit with a permanent disability pension of one shilling per day.[10] To be near family, he moved to the market town of Andover where his brother, William, had a shoemaking business. Walter learnt the trade and gained important skills he would later rely on.

Secure employment gave him confidence to propose marriage to Annie Elizabeth Potter, a girl he met as a soldier in London. They wed on the 8th October, 1902 at St Peters Church, Notting Hill, and, soon after, established a home in Andover. Within a year, their first child, Winifred Ada ('Ida') was born and a son, Frederic Philip ('Roger') arrived in 1905. Eager to provide for his young family, Walter fondly looked towards Australia. An application to join an assisted immigration scheme recruiting agricultural labourers for Queensland was successful and, on 14th June 1907, with much optimism and some sadness, Walter and Annie farewelled England, their parents, friends and siblings.

In Brisbane, a new rewarding life was established. Walter commenced work as a labourer and found comfortable lodgings in South Brisbane. The fourth house on the right from Cromwell Street on Ipswich Road became their home for the next 12 years.[11] They quickly became involved in the community. Walter was especially pleased to be accepted into Brisbane's volunteer citizen militia. The 9th Australian Infantry (Moreton) Regiment's colourful uniform with its white helmet, scarlet coat and blue trousers suited the ex-Coldstream Guard very well and prior military experience resulted in an immediate appointment to the rank of Sergeant (E Company).[12] Also, the opportunity to once again enjoy the sport of target shooting and its associated comradery was enthusiastically embraced. Walter became a competitive member of the Regiment's rifle club and, within a year of arriving in Brisbane, his name featured prominently in competition results. In 1914, he was elected captain of the city's Central Rifle Club.[13]

These early years in Brisbane were a happy time. Walter eventually gave up his labouring job and returned to the more profitable trade of bootmaker. A second son, Henry Edward (Edward) was born in 1910 and another daughter, Edna Sylvia, arrived in 1913. Later, Annie fondly reflected on these pre-war years and praised her husband's attributes, *'I can only add that before going to the war, my husband was good and kind and a good father, and very steady.'*[14]

Regrettably, war changed everything. At first, Walter hesitated to enlist. The trauma he endured during the Boer War still haunted him and, at 36 years of age, there were family responsibilities to consider. Yet the patriotic fever sweeping the country was hard to resist, and his military background instilled a strong sense of duty to Empire. Three weeks after enlistment commenced, Walter travelled to the new military camp at Enoggera and, on 12th September, joined Australia's new army as a sergeant in the 9th Battalion's C Company. Two weeks later, with some unease, he departed Brisbane on the troopship "Omrah". Unlike most of his fellow volunteers, Walter knew the reality of what was ahead.

Mercifully, the Australians' immediate destination was not the battlefields of Europe. Instead, they disembarked in Egypt where, for four months, an intensive programme of military training was carried out. A promotion to Sergeant Major saw Walter take a new role assisting in the discipline, training and welfare of A Company's 200 men. He missed his family very much and, although the workload was heavy, it pleased him to be kept busy. Like the rest of the Australian force, Walter was eager to fight the Germans so they might bring the war to a speedy end. When orders were received to leave the desert and move to the Greek island of Lemnos, instead of France, he felt bitter disappointment. Added to his frustration were seven more weeks spent waiting on Lemnos.

Finally, on Saturday, 24th April, operational orders were received. Walter's A company joined B Company on-board the warship, "HMS Queen", the lead ship of the huge invading flotilla that left Lemnos that day. About 1 a.m., the next morning, the troops were mustered on deck and, with great precision, began disembarkation. Walter's No.3 Platoon silently clambered down the rope ladders and took up positions in the three boats of No.1 Tow.[15] Connected to a steam pinnace, they were quietly towed towards the Turkish shore. As the outline of land became visible, Walter could sense the extreme anxiety gripping his men as he worked hard to hide his own feelings.

Their boat struck the shore and, incredibly, the beach remained quiet. It seemed they were about to land unopposed. Lieutenant Chapman gave the order, "ALL OUT!" Walter was sitting in the bow near the Lieutenant and was one of the first in the water. Still, there was no gunfire. He scrambled across the beach and began removing his pack. At least half, about 17 of the men, were out of the boat when it finally happened.[16] A single shot and then, with swift succession, the air filled with the sound of enemy fire.

Quickly, the scene on the narrow beach descended into chaos and confusion. Battalions, companies and platoons landed on top of one another and became hopelessly mixed. Contact with officers was lost. Then, the cry came, "Come on Queenslanders! Come on the 9th!" and Walter joined the scramble up the steep slopes. He attempted to follow original orders to move quickly inland to clear the way for others to follow. However, in the maze of gullies and ridges, communication was impossible. Walter's A Company and No.3 Platoon became scattered into small isolated groups.

Courageously, these groups pushed forward. By mid-morning, although many had reached far inland, their progress was being halted. Heavy Turkish gun fire sweeping from the bushes was increasing. Walter's group was forced to desperately dig in but, with each passing hour, the enemy's counter-attack intensified. By dusk, the onslaught was unbeatable. Retreat was their only option. Exhausted, the men made a frantic attempt to reach safety. As Walter rushed through the darkness, he failed to see the steep trench before him. Tumbling headfirst, a severe blow to his head left him unconscious. Mercifully, his life was saved by stretcher-bearers who were able to return him to the safety of the beach.[17]

After five days on a hospital ship, Walter was admitted to the Presidency General Hospital in Alexandria with a diagnosis of spinal concussion and paralysis. Despite almost seven weeks' treatment, he remained unable to walk or use his left arm. It seemed all feeling on the left side of his body was gone. He was then evacuated to England and, for the first ten weeks in hospital at Manchester, he did not move from his bed. At the end of two months, Walter could walk without assistance[18] but, in November, the medical board deemed him unfit for active service and recommended his return to Australia.

He arrived in Sydney aboard the "SS Runic", with 600 other wounded and sick soldiers, on Christmas Day, 1915. From there, a special train took the 9th Battalion men onto Brisbane where, on Central Station's very crowded No. 5 Platform, they were welcomed by a brass band, the Premier, Mayor, various dignitaries, 250 soldiers from Enoggera, and numerous overjoyed family members, including Annie and the children. '*Salvos of cheers broke forth as the men alighted – a little travel-stained and war-worn.*'[19]

A week later, Brisbane's Central Rifle Club honoured their ex-captain's return. Members gathered at the Grand Central Hotel in Ann Street to celebrate Walter with a joyful night of speeches, toasts and songs. He was pleased to reconnect with his old rifle club mates but this level of attention left him uncomfortable. Walter believed the real heroes remained on the battlefield and he constantly worried about their fate.

It took almost a year for Walter's body to heal. He returned to duty on the 15th March, 1916 as a Sergeant in the newly formed 42nd Battalion. For the next three months, he was stationed at Enoggera camp where he helped train and prepare volunteers. Finally, on the 5th June, his new Battalion embarked for war and, for the second time, with some trepidation, Walter farewelled his young family.

Their destination was England where another three months of crucial training was carried out at Lark Hill on the Salisbury Plain. Walter's dedication to duty was again recognized. He received promotion to 2nd Lieutenant. The additional responsibilities and the pressures of leadership were a heavy burden, but he left for the front in November 1916, feeling proud and confident.

The 42nd Battalion was deployed to the Armentieres area near Steenwerke. Despite menacing sounds of heavy artillery greeting their arrival, Walter and his men appeared undaunted. After such a long training period, they were better prepared than any previous Australian battalions. Their resolve and enthusiasm were only weakened by the onset of an extremely cold winter. The most severe weather in living memory was beginning and, in the exposed trenches, the men suffered terribly. During the night, blankets, food and water regularly froze. In these deplorable conditions, two weeks after arriving, Walter succumbed to influenza and was hospitalized for 10 days.

When he re-joined his platoon on 28th December, the horrendous weather had worsened. The severe cold of the trenches made his full recovery from influenza impossible. Added to this, German shelling and sniper fire were unrelenting and gas attacks were frequent. The Battalion lost more than 50 of its men in the first month. During this time Walter found the burden of leadership and responsibility for his platoon's welfare more exhausting. He struggled to hide his fears and feelings from his men.

In February, as the unbearable weather continued, the Battalion's position and strength became threatened. At 4.30 am, on the 14th February, in the early morning darkness, heavy mortar and artillery fire fell upon them causing significant casualties. As the Australian trenches crumbled, the Germans used the cover of an icy fog to launch an unexpected raid. Valiantly, the 42nd attempted to repel the advance but during the action, ten soldiers lost their lives, two men went missing and nine, including Walter, were wounded. According to the medical report, he was blown up by the bursting of a *'moaning minnie'*[20] (a noisy rocket explosion from the German Minenwerfer, a short range mortar). His Lieutenant-Colonel described the incident, *'On 14th February he (Lieutenant Latimer) was under a heavy minesweeper bombardment and was three times knocked over by the explosions.'*[21]

Although it took a few hours for Walter to regain his senses, he was returned almost immediately to the trenches. Twelve days later, there was another intense German bombardment leaving three dead and four wounded. More trenches were destroyed and Walter's nerves were further tested. The next day, the rain of bombs and artillery continued, with six more casualties incurred.[22] Walter was now struggling to carry on. His Lieutenant-Colonel previously referred to him as '*a dependable officer*' whose '*behaviour in trench fighting is cool,*'[23] but the stress of these unrelenting ordeals was taking a toll. Since the first terrible bombardment on the 14th February, Walter found it difficult to sleep and his head was aching constantly. Sometimes, he had no control over his body and often could not find words to express himself. In this state, it was almost impossible to function as an officer but, for two weeks, he made every effort to carry on, pushing himself to the edge of collapse. For ten nights, he did not sleep at all.[24] By 1st March, Walter was in a critical state.

The Medical Officer at the 12th Casualty Clearing Station urgently transferred him to the 7th General Hospital at Amiens, where doctors described a severe mental breakdown. '*Patient is an absolute wreck. When anything unexpected occurred, he started shaking and palpitations. War dreams, headaches, difficulty speaking, cannot remember things in last two months.*'[25] Six weeks' treatment at Amiens brought no improvement and, on the 18th April, Walter was evacuated again to England.

Shellshock (or neurasthenia) reached almost epidemic proportions during the war on the Western Front. Despite Australian field ambulances treating 7,205 cases,[26] the condition remained highly misunderstood. Military command was mostly unsympathetic and tended to link it to weakness and cowardice. Most treatments were also misguided and ineffective. Shaming, emotional deprivation and infliction of pain were commonly used.

In London, Walter was admitted to the 4th General Hospital, where patients received anaesthetic and electric shock treatments. It was believed electric currents applied to body parts would stimulate nerves and vocal chords. After two weeks of this torturous treatment, unsurprisingly, Walter's attacks of depression and apprehension did not abate. '*He complains of being depressed and troubled, is upset by anything unexpected such as a knock on the door. Worries much about his health – afraid abdomen pains are cancer.*'[27]

Fortunately, on the 4th May, 1917, a transfer was received to Craiglockhart War Hospital on the outskirts of Edinburgh. After the war, the work of this shell-shock hospital gained fame through poems, a film, stage-play and a series of books.[28] Its notoriety was chiefly because of the unusual treatment it gave to traumatized officers. Two of the War's finest poets, Wilfred Owen and Siegfried Sassoon, were also admitted to Craiglockhart in 1917. Their recorded experiences made the plight of shell-shock victims more visible and understood. In Sassoon's memoirs and poems, he described the daily suffering of Walter and other patients, the *'lonely victims of dream disasters and delusions.'* With graphic rawness, he wrote of their anguish and unrelenting torment, *'dreams that drip with murder', 'stammering disconnected talk'* and *'... by night each man was back in his doomed sector of horror-stricken Front Line, where the panic and stampede of some ghastly experience was re-enacted among the livid faces of the dead. No doctor could save him.'*[29]

At Craiglockhart, Walter was put under the care of the hospital's most progressive and controversial innovator, Dr W. Rivers who fortunately did not favour punitive treatments. Instead, his pioneering therapy involved a humane 'talking cure' based on soldiers confronting their painful memories and expressing their feelings. At a time when society expected men to keep a 'stiff upper-lip', the Doctor and his methods received much criticism.

But for Walter, the talking therapy was extremely beneficial. He arrived at Craiglockhart with a disheartening diagnosis. Dr Rivers wrote, *'He sleeps badly and has dreams from which he awakes suddenly with his heart beating. Both attention and memory are very defective. There is some tremor of the hands. Complains of attacks of pain ... but no abnormal signs can be detected, hearing is much impaired.'*[30] Five weeks later the Doctor's report was very different, *'continues to improve, active and cheerful. He is keen on going back to duty for which he should soon be fit.'*[31]

Walter left Craiglockhart on the 14th June feeling optimistic. He was returned to the Australian Hospital in London where the Medical Board deliberated on his condition. Although the improvements gained at Craiglockhart were obvious, medical officers deemed Walter remained unfit for duty. The diagnosis of severe neurasthenic (shell-shock) stayed and an immediate return to Australia was recommended.

For the second time, Walter arrived home as a casualty of war. With 156 other battle-scarred Queensland Anzacs, he reached Brisbane on 20th September. The city's Daily Telegraph made special note of his return, *'The well-known rifleman, Lieutenant Walter Latimer, is to be once more amongst us. He went away in 1914 with the first lot of Australians, was at the famous landing and was later invalided back here; on recovering, he went back to the front, this time in France where he won his commission, but in due course got hit again. His many friends will be glad to renew his acquaintance.'*[32] The real reason for his repatriation was not reported. Sadly, much social stigma surrounded mental illness and the condition of shell-shock.

Annie and the children greeted a thinner, haggard and somewhat 'different' Walter. His appearance and demeanour were worrying but, fortunately, the family's love and support again held extraordinary healing powers. Over the following months, his health gradually improved. The nightmares remained, but his sleep got better and he began to put on weight. In October, the Medical Board re-examined his case. Outwardly, Walter appeared well. Any mental scars were well hidden, and he gave testimony that he was *'keeping well and is pretty good.'*[33] Regrettably, the Medical Board deemed this was sufficient proof of an adequate state of health. An immediate return to active duty was recommended.

For the third time, Walter embarked for war. He left Australia on 2nd February, 1918, as a 2nd Lieutenant with the 42nd Battalion, 8th Reinforcements. Perhaps some consideration was given to his fragile mental state. Instead of a posting to the front, he was sent to the School of Musketry at Tidworth and placed in command of the sniper training wing. This posting suited the renowned marksman very well but, regardless, his mental demons soon returned. In early June, after weeks of severe abdominal pain, Walter suffered a bout of vomiting and stomach cramps that continued for three consecutive nights. Doctors diagnosed 'gastric neurosis', an anxiety disorder[34] and immediately classified him as medically unfit. He was again repatriated to Australia.

In October 1918, he returned to the familiar and unpleasant surroundings of Brisbane's military hospital at Kangaroo Point. However, unlike previous occasions, his stay this time was unexpectedly short. Only weeks after being admitted, peace was declared and, as a consequence, the hospital discharged Walter and many fellow patients almost immediately. He remained unwell but was eager to leave the discipline of the military hospital ward and desperate to put the war behind him. The termination of his commission on 28th November was greeted with great joy.

Despite the war being over, many of Walter's battles were just beginning. He left the army as a shattered man. He was unfit for work and his meagre 25% army pension was insufficient to support a wife and four children. The inabilities and inadequacies he faced compounded his anxiety. Annie desperately attempted to understand and assist but, like many veterans, her husband was unwilling and unable to share his anguish. The impact on the family was devastating. They tried to adjust to his sleeplessness and nervous disposition but it was impossible. Walter increasingly absented himself from his wife and children. He did not drink, but spent much of his time playing billiards in hotels in the Brisbane city area.[35]

In early 1919, a desperate appeal was made for a pension increase. *'I consider I am totally incapacitated for work.'* Callously, the application was refused. Six months later, Walter tried again. *'I declare my condition is worse than at the time of my discharge. I have had severe stomach trouble during the past five weeks and frequent vomiting attacks ... in consequence I am generally run down ... I have only been able to put in about three weeks work.'*[36]

As the months passed, anxiety and neurosis increasingly dominated Walter's life. He could not wait to learn the outcome of his second pension appeal. The pressure of family became too much to bear. The once popular and well-respected army officer, described before the war as a steady, kind and good father, deserted his young family. He disappeared into New South Wales in June, 1919.[37] Annie did not apply for divorce. Instead, to protect her family from the shame that surrounded mental illness, she hid her husband's disappearance with secrecy and misinformation. Younger family members came to believe Walter had died of war wounds in hospital after the war.[38]

For a time, Walter seemed lost as he wandered northern and western New South Wales in search of work. His life was in turmoil and he feared the isolation that was engulfing him. In a desperate bid to return to the person he used to be, he moved to Sydney. Utilizing skills learnt from his brother before the war, from a home at 56 Strathallen Ave, Northbridge, he advertised his services as a boot repairer. His determined and valiant effort to be self-employed achieved some success and provided a modest income.

However, the legacy of war remained and Walter's mental health continued to suffer. In October 1920, he was admitted to Sydney's

Royal Prince Alfred Hospital. After a long stay, he was discharged to "The Mill", a historic 1840s homestead in Moss Vale that had been converted into a convalescence home for damaged and disabled diggers. Run by the Red Cross, it housed only 18 diggers and, for the next two months, provided Walter with crucial comfort and care.

He left "The Mill" after Christmas and attempted to resume work as a boot repairer at Northbridge. Realizing his limitations, an assistant was employed but the extra cost made his business unviable. A medical report, dated 11th April, described Walter as '*nervous and frightened about himself.*' Almost all the next 12 months were spent in hospitals or institutions. In December, he was admitted again to the Royal Prince Alfred Hospital, where he remained until February. From there, he returned to "The Mill" for another three months. He left there feeling much improved and confident but, soon after, his mental health again deteriorated. By the 18th July, he was back in hospital, diagnosed as 'highly neurotic,' suffering 'frequent attacks of nausea and feelings of oppression in head.'[39] By the end of 1922, his doctors concluded further institutional treatment would be of no benefit.

Walter returned to his home at Strathallen Avenue and worked, when he could, from the boot repair shop set up at the front of the house. Mercifully, that year his life began to improve. A loving relationship developed with Maria Eveleigh, a nurse who worked at the Moss Vale Convalescent Home. She moved into Walter's Northbridge home and in September 1924, their first child, Edward Bruce, was born. With Maria's love and help, Walter's outlook and confidence began to improve. Although the symptoms of shell-shock continued, he no longer battled them alone. Walter became more outgoing and even joined the local rifle club at Rockdale and, later, became a member of the Western Suburbs Rifle Club. His former prowess as a marksman was gone, but competing in B grade shooting competitions brought him much joy. For the first time in many years, he felt content with his life.

Sadly, his ease did not last. Two years later, a heartbreaking tragedy struck. A second son, John, was born in December 1926, but complications during the birth resulted in Maria's unexpected death. The loss devastated Walter. She had been his sole support and source of crucial understanding. The prospect of raising two young boys without her seemed impossible. Walter's fragile mental state worsened. Three years after Maria's death, doctors reported he was '*suffering from poor sleep, no nerve, feels done.... markedly neurotic, introspective and despondent.*' Yet, despite this, Walter rose to the challenge. With the assistance of a housekeeper, he focused all his energy on the welfare of his two sons.

Throughout the Great Depression, Walter struggled to keep his small boot repair shop running. The stress increased his anxieties and contributed to a series of imaginary health concerns. Each seemed real and worrying to Walter, but they were always baseless. With little compassion, an exasperated doctor reported in 1935, '*Banging in head. Pains in stomach. In fact, he has almost everything including "verberrohoea"*.[40] The insensitivity of this remark typified attitudes in the post-war years. While great respect was accorded the limbless and disfigured casualties of war, shell-shocked veterans, like Walter, were treated very differently. Misunderstood, they often faced ridicule.

During his last years, Walter chose to isolate himself at his Northbridge home. Regrettably, a diagnosis of prostate cancer had been received in 1954. His mood afterwards was not good, described as often jumpy, depressed and irritable. In 1957, a Medical Officer bluntly referred to him as a '*sick looking old man, depressed and retarded.*'[41] Walter was admitted to hospital on 16th January 1958. Two months later, the suffering of this once dedicated and confident Lieutenant finally ended.

War had inflicted on him one of the worse kinds of disabilities. The skilled rifleman, Boer War soldier and courageous Anzac, described as 'cool in battle', became a nervous, depressed veteran plagued by neuroses and cruelly regarded as 'retarded'. Instead of the respect and the honour he deserved, he endured a life of stigma and misunderstanding. A once happy family was destroyed and, in Brisbane, friends and relatives were told the gallant Anzac hero was dead. Yet, Walter showed enormous determination and fought to re-establish his life. The inscription placed on his grave by his two youngest sons gives testimony to his character and strength.

"A Great Soldier, but an Even Greater Father."

Lieutenant Walter Latimer was buried on the 13th March, 1958, beside Maria Jane Latimer, at Macquarie Park, Randwick, Sydney. Grave D13, Plot 24.

Lance-Corporal James Claude Henderson

No. 296, A Company, 9th Battalion
(later Lieutenant, 1MD Ech & Rec)

Despite serving only one day on the battlefield, Lance-Corporal James Claude Henderson was one of Queensland's most gallant Anzac heroes. After landing with the first ashore, he fought fearlessly at Gallipoli. However, his most outstanding wartime achievements occurred on the home front. Through his dedication and tireless efforts, Queensland's first system of soldier repatriation was successfully implemented, and the lives of thousands of veterans and their families were improved.

Claude was a proud second generation Australian who descended from one of Brisbane's early pioneer families. He was born on 13th October, 1890 and grew up with his four siblings in the working-class suburb of Woolloongabba. His father, James Senior, was a hydraulic engineer who achieved a notable career as Queensland's Chief Inspector of Machinery.[1] By 1910, the family's improved circumstances allowed them to move from their modest home in Woolloongabba to a grand Queenslander, "Braeston", at 277 Annerley Road, Annerley. Claude admired his father's hard work and achievements. From him, he inherited a strong dedication to duty and public service.

Upon finishing school, Claude went to work as a clerk. Later, a job was gained as a salesman[2] but, like most young lads of the time, his strongest interest was in the military. Almost all his leisure time centred on the activities of the local citizen militia. Claude was an enthusiastic member of the Queensland Rifles and excelled at target shooting. In the annual musketry course in 1910, 20-year-old Sapper J. Henderson was listed as the best shot among the recruits.[3]

The First Ashore

When war was declared, he was one of the first Queenslanders to take the oath of allegiance. Two weeks after being appointed to the 9th Battalion's C Company, he enthusiastically departed for war. Like most volunteers, he was naively ignorant of the reality of what was ahead.

It was not until the Battalion reached the desert of Egypt that Claude's eagerness began to wane. For the next four months at Mena Camp, outside Cairo, he and the other volunteers endured a rigorous and repetitive routine of military training under a hot desert sun. As the weeks slowly passed, their impatience grew. Claude and his mates yearned for an active and meaningful role in the war and were frustrated by the delay. When promoted to Lance Corporal, A Company on 22nd January, his eagerness for battle intensified.

At the end of February, when orders were finally given to leave the desert, Claude expected their destination would be the war in France against the Germans. He was bitterly disappointed when, instead, the Battalion was sent to Lemnos, a Greek island off the Turkish coast. Five long weeks were spent on the island and another two weeks aboard a transport ship anchored in the harbour.

Finally, on Saturday, 24th April, to his enormous relief, the Australians were called into action. Claude's Company was moved to the warship, "HMS Queen" which would lead the invading armada. With all lights out, destroyers, warships, and transports travelled quietly through the night, towards the Dardanelles. Claude tried to get some sleep below, but it was impossible. At about 1.30 a.m., the 1500 troops on-board the "Queen", "London" and "Prince of Wales" were mustered on deck. Silently they disembarked, with well-rehearsed precision, into 36 life-boats. Then, in groups of three, the boats, towed by small steamboats, moved quietly towards shore. Lieutenant Duncan Chapman and A Company's Sections 13 and 14[4] plus some Battalion's Scouts took their position in the first of the three boats of No.1 Tow.

As the shore became more visible, daylight was almost breaking. Claude and the men in the first boat waited anxiously. Deadly rifle-fire was expected at any moment, but silence prevailed. The life-boats were unhitched from the pinnace and the order was given to 'Down Oars'. With just 50 yards to row before they hit the beach, Claude listened fearfully. Still, there were no bullets. He was beginning to think the Turks were not there. Lieutenant Chapman's voice broke the silence,

"All out!" First into the water was the Lieutenant, followed by his orderly, James Bostock, Scout Sergeant Coe, Lieutenant Haymen, Lance Corporal Teitzel and the rest of the Scouts. With heart pounding, Claude waited his turn. He leapt into waist-deep water and scrambled to the beach. More than half, at least 17 men[5], were out of the boat and on the shore when the cracking began. The air, suddenly, was *'thick with bullets, hitting and ploughing up the sand all about.'*[6]

Claude safely reached the beach. As he threw off his pack and commenced to fix bayonet, more and more men scrambled ashore. Platoons, companies and battalions soon became hopelessly mixed. On the narrow beach, efforts to re-group were impossible. As the confusion mounted, Claude joined a wild charge up the slopes.

Using bayonets only, the first line of trenches on the brow of the hill was quickly taken. It seemed at first the Turks were on the run. On reaching the plateau, later named Plugges Plateau, Claude and his mates paused momentarily and then continued their rapid advance onto the next ridge. However, their progress was quickly slowed by vicious Turkish counter-attacks. The fighting grew fierce, and deadly bursts of shrapnel increasingly filled the air.

Although Claude quickly became familiar with the long, devilish, hissing sound that preceded each explosion, he could not escape the shrapnel that burst upon him. It struck the left side of his body, tearing a piece from his shoulder while shattering his left wrist. The pain was excruciating. In shock and bleeding, he struggled back to the beach to join the hundreds of wounded waiting to be evacuated. Four days were spent on a hospital ship before he was admitted to No.1 Australian General Hospital in Cairo.

By then, this former Palace Hotel was overflowing with the tragedy of Gallipoli. Wards had to be hurriedly setup in the grounds of a nearby amusement park. Two operations to remove shattered fragments of carpal bones from Claude's wrist were performed in an operating theatre hastily constructed in the park's old ticket office. The procedures were successful but, almost six weeks later, his wound remained open and unhealed. The Medical Board noted there was much damage to the soft tissue and declared Claude permanently unfit for further military service.

The orders upset Claude greatly. He felt guilty for leaving the battlefield and despaired at the horror his mates at Gallipoli were still suffering. During the three-week journey home on the hospital ship, "Hororata" a mood of melancholy prevailed. The 523 other maimed, limbless, and blind casualties of war travelled towards an uncertain future. For Claude, the feelings of guilt and despair weighed heavily and would motivate his actions over the following years.

Because the "Hororata" was the first hospital ship to return to Australia after the Gallipoli landing, their welcome home was spectacular. In Perth, then Melbourne and Sydney, huge celebrations and street parades were held. When the Queensland contingent arrived at Brisbane's Central Station on 31st August, an estimated crowd of 8000 waited to greet them.

Claude was immediately admitted to the Military Hospital at Kangaroo Point where his disability was again assessed. Because of the tenderness of his wrist and its limited movement, a recommendation was made for his immediate discharge from the army with the allocation of a temporary pension. Bitterly frustrated, disappointed and ashamed of his inability to serve, he returned to his parents' home. Over the following weeks, to compensate, he desperately sought meaningful ways to contribute to the war effort and joined almost every wartime organisation and project that existed in Queensland.

On Wednesday night, 8th December, 1915, two weeks before his official discharge, Claude and a small group of returned wounded 9th Battalion men met at the Imperial Services Club in Ann Street. This historic meeting heralded the birth of today's RSL. The men met to form a 9th Battalion Reunion Organisation that would ensure the unique bond of mateship, which had been created at Gallipoli, was maintained and preserved.[7]

A week later, their first reunion was held at Café Majestic in Queen Street. It was mostly a light-hearted evening, but serious business also arose. Loud calls were made for the formation of a larger organization that would include all returned wounded soldiers. To this end, it was decided to convene a special meeting on 24th February at the Temperance Hall on Edward Street. Among the crowd of approximately 60 men who attended, Claude was a passionate participant. Unanimously, the meeting voted to form a 'Queensland Returned Soldiers' Association'[8] that would be non-sectarian, non-political and aim to foster patriotism, keep the memory of fallen comrades and promote the welfare of all soldiers. Major Walsh was elected President, while Claude Henderson and his good friend, William Millward were made provisional joint Honorary Secretaries.[9]

The Association grew at spectacular speed. Claude and the other honorary officers ensure the momentum was not lost by labouring long hours. The workload of the joint secretaries, in particular, was enormous. In the first three months, Claude and William Millward processed more than 600 memberships. They also organized temporary headquarters in offices at 282 Elizabeth Street[10] and, in April, helped prepare for Brisbane's first commemoration of Anzac Day. Claude soon found almost all his time was consumed by the many activities of the Returned Soldiers Association. He worried his other commitments to the war effort were being neglected and, as a result, after Anzac Day was successfully completed, he reluctantly relinquished his position as Secretary and took the less time-demanding office of Treasurer.

However, the extra time he gained was quickly consumed by the 1916 campaign for the introduction of conscription. Claude took a prominent role in the fierce political debate, attending numerous rallies and meetings. In a speech that he delivered on 3rd October, 1916, three weeks before the First Referendum, he promoted his stand as the soldier's viewpoint and stressed the urgent need for reinforcements. '*On the Peninsula, men were frozen to death because of lack of reinforcements; and they did not want this to happen in France.*'[11]

While juggling his time between the Returned Soldiers Association, the referendum campaigns and other volunteer work, Claude supported himself by working in the offices of the Queensland War Council. A month after his discharge from the army, he obtained the position of 'Clerk-in-charge' at the Council's Treasury Building office. The job suited his talents and provided another avenue for him to contribute to the war effort. As well as assisting recruiting and fundraising, the War Council also carried out soldier welfare initiatives through subsidiary bodies such as Medical, Employment, Land Settlement, Education and Anzac Cottages sub-committees. These were areas of work that Claude relished.

The job of chief clerk was incredibly busy. The weekly meetings of the War Council's five sub-committees generated a huge amount of paperwork. At the beginning of 1916, with a staff of just four typists,

Claude's office was processing 450 to 500 letters per day.[12] Yet, despite this immense workload, more responsibility was sought. Claude's dedication to the Council's work was extraordinary. One month after commencing as clerk, in February 1916, he added to his duties the unpaid position of Secretary of the Council's most important and busiest sub-committee, 'Employment'.[13] Over the next 12 months, his appetite for work did not diminish. By January 1917, Claude was Superintendent and Honorary Secretary of all War Council activities throughout the State.[14]

He gave his time gratuitously. Besides receiving his minimal clerk's wage, all of Claude's other roles in the War Council remained unpaid. To make ends meet, he relied upon his temporary war pension of £34 per annum, which the War Council Executive lobbied to be made permanent and increased to £1-14s per fortnight.[15] It was not until 1917 that the Executive Committee unanimously agreed that *'owing to the very great increase of work and consequent responsibilities that has fallen on his shoulders,'*[16] Claude should receive a pay scale that reflected his duties.

Under his stewardship, the Queensland War Council's achievements were significant. By July 1919, its land settlement scheme had placed 995 soldiers on farms. Sizeable areas were cleared at Sunnybank to create poultry farms and, at Beerburrum, a small township had grown to service the area's soldier settlers. An Industrial Arts and Crafts Soldiers Club, formed in 1917, became a centre for vocational training for disabled soldiers.[17] Also, more than 50 Anzac cottages were built for the homeless widows and orphans of Queensland's fallen soldiers. To finance these many projects, numerous fund raising enterprises were organized. Most notable were the profitable Golden Casket lotteries. All this important work fell under the responsibility of the War Council's Secretary and State Superintendent, Claude Henderson.

His enormous responsibilities were widespread, but he devoted his greatest energy to the Employment sub-committee. It was his firm belief that Queensland had an obligation to provide secure jobs for all veterans and, relentlessly, he pressed business and government to meet that obligation. Tireless work was carried out to ensure returning veterans were registered with the War Council for employment. Regular visits were made to hospitals where Claude personally interviewed returned men to ascertain their needs and employment requirements.[18] Collaborating closely with business and government agencies, he often travelled the State to procure jobs. The task was mammoth. Meeting minutes for March 1916 recorded 356 soldiers registered for work, but a year later, that number increased to 1,713 soldiers.[19]

Claude's name became well known to all returned soldiers. On their arrival home, they were advised to immediately seek out Mr Henderson. The Queensland Premier, in February, 1917, in his address to wounded and invalided soldiers, re-enforced this message, *'We in Queensland have a War Council, the Offices of which were situated in the Commonwealth Treasury Buildings. Mr Henderson, a returned soldier, was there to attend to (your) wants, to help (you) as the people of Queensland desire that (you) should be helped.'*[20]

Queensland's newspapers made sure Claude's efforts and dedication did not go unnoticed. The Telegraph in 1916 reported, *'Mr Henderson, knowing at first hand, the needs of soldiers is able to bring to his work a comradeship and a sympathy that no civilian, however eager to assist, could feel.'*[21] The Daily Mail published, *'Mr Claude Henderson, Secretary of the Council, I consider to be the very acme of courtesy and justice.'*[22] The Daily Standard referred to him as the *'popular assistant Secretary to the Queensland War Council,'*[23] while the Courier Mail, in 1916, reported that Claude *'has always been ready to give a helping hand in promoting the welfare of his returned comrades of Anzac fame.'*[24] Official military recognition came in September, 1916. For his War Council work and his role in the formation of the Returned Soldiers Association, Claude was made a Lieutenant, attached to the 9th Brigade.[25]

Besides the War Council's many initiatives, Claude was ever mindful of new ways to improve the lives of veterans. Throughout 1916, he lobbied strongly for the formation of a Returned Soldiers' Residential Club that would provide comfortable city accommodation for veterans discharged from hospital and those waiting to return to the front. He envisaged it as a place where comradeship could flourish, old friendships be renewed and mental damage be soothed. In June, Claude was elected to the four person sub-committee that considered various building proposals.[26] The following month, he took the position of Honorary Secretary of the Purchasing Building Committee, which gave him almost sole discretion to investigate a suitable building for purchase.[27]

Upon his recommendation, in August 1916, the "Corona" building on the corner of Wharf and Ann Streets was purchased.[28] It served as Queensland's Returned Soldiers' Residential Club until 1922.[29]

Amid an incredibly busy schedule, in 1916, Claude also found time to attend an important conference in Melbourne. He was one of five Queensland delegates selected to attend a meeting of the various returned soldiers associations that had arisen in each State. Unanimously, the meeting voted to amalgamate the state associations into a more powerful Federal organisation. A provisional constitution was drawn up and, on 3rd June, 1916, using the name 'Returned Sailors and Soldiers Imperial League of Australia' (RSSILA), the RSL of Australia was born. For their work, Claude and his good mate, Lieutenant William Millward were later made life members. (Newspapers in 1917 reported they were the only Queenslanders to receive this honour.)[30]

Claude was a passionate supporter of the new organization. As the Queensland branch grew, his role also expanded. At the RSSILA's first annual meeting in Queensland in 1917, he was elected branch vice-president and was also made vice-president of the Central Council.[31] In March, as a Queensland delegate, he attended the national Congress in Sydney. Claude's intense commitment sometimes was expressed in radical ideas. For instance, at the Sydney Congress, Claude proposed a controversial motion, *'That the Prime Minister be requested to give consideration to the immediate closing of stadiums and racecourses, believing that in so doing he will materially assist recruiting.'* The unusual proposition received support and was carried with 12 votes to 9.[32]

As the war progressed, Claude's attention turned more and more to implementing effective soldier repatriation. He became general Secretary of the War Council's newly formed Repatriation Fund Committee, also known as the Returned Soldiers Repatriation Fund.[33] Its primary aim was to help unemployed soldiers become self-employed and, under Claude's business-like approach, it achieved great success. By providing loans, introductions and personal assistance, many returned soldiers became market gardeners, motor transport drivers, milkmen and farmers.

The Repatriation Fund's effective processes and machinery became the model for other states. The Daily Mail in 1917 advised the Prime Minister that the problem of integrating thousands of soldiers into society had become critical and urged him to establish a Federal system of repatriation based on the Queensland model. It claimed Queensland was leading all the States in repatriation chiefly because '*it steered clear of political "ornaments" and appointed its Repatriation Fund Committee from businessmen, with Chairman John Macdonald and Secretary J. Claude Henderson.*'[34]

Claude was pleased Queensland's achievements in repatriation were being recognized nationally but he was not prepared for the Federal Government's response. In July 1917, the government proposed a new nationwide repatriation scheme that would take control from the states. Queensland's War Council feared their loss of influence and the imposition of an inferior system controlled by outsiders. Claude and Mr Langley Simmons were hurriedly dispatched to Melbourne to express the Council's concerns.

Unfortunately, their protests were in vain. In April 1918, the Federal Repatriation Act relieved the Queensland War Council of its responsibility for repatriation. RSSILA branches throughout Queensland loudly opposed the change, criticizing the centralization of power. Their hostile opposition threatened the functioning of the new system and the Federal Government wisely responded by appointing Claude as head of its new Repatriation Board with the title of Deputy Controller of Repatriation.

For the next four years, in this role, Claude faced many new challenges. He attempted to continue the effective administration of repatriation in Queensland, but the entry of politics placed restrictions and conditions on his work. Claude's popularity, which had previously seemed incontestable, began to suffer. For the first time, he became the target of overt criticism. The delegates at the 1918 RSSILA Conference noted that Claude, although courteous and considerate, now was too much under the thumb of the Federal government. When later reflecting on the problems of these years, Claude commented, '*politicians muddled around too much with things they knew nothing about.*'[35]

While these tumultuous changes occurred, Claude attempted to enjoy the first months of married life. On October 12, 1917, he wed Bertha Hamilton Neil, a twenty-five-year-old clerk who lived in his Annerley neighbourhood. Their large and notable wedding took place at St Philips Church of England, Thompson Estate, South Brisbane. It was a military service that reflected the extreme patriotism engulfing Claude's life. Officiated by army Chaplain-Colonel Rev. Garland, the church was heavily decorated in the colours of the original 9th Battalion. His best man and long-time friend, Lieutenant William Millward, proudly wore the Battalion uniform. As well as friends and family, the guests included many War Council staff and a large number of returned soldiers.[36]

Marriage brought new responsibilities. A home was established at 'Hillcott', George Street, Annerley and the following year, their first child, Jack James Neil Henderson, was born. Another son, Harold, arrived in 1920. Eager to spend time with his young family, Claude began to re-examine his crowded work-life. After six years of intense public service, he was weary of the relentless demands of repatriation and, in July 1922, he resigned from his position as Deputy-Controller[37] and embarked on a major life-change.

The family moved 100 kilometres from the stress of the city to the country town of Kilcoy. With no previous hotel experience, Claude purchased the town's Stanley Hotel. Managing a large country pub presented challenges, but Claude's temperament, popularity and business skills ensured his success. The pub was a busy part of the district's social life and, as a result, the family quickly became active community members.[38]

Sadly, as they embraced their new life in the country, tragedy loomed. At Kilcoy, Bertha's health suddenly began to decline. In 1926, her need for specialized medical treatment forced the family to move back to Annerley. Claude sold the pub and started a new venture as a city real estate broker. Regrettably, Bertha's health worsened and, only months after their return to Brisbane, she passed away.[39] Claude was devastated.

In the years that followed, he placed his two boys in boarding school and again allowed work to consume his life. His many connections throughout Brisbane meant his real estate business grew rapidly. From a small office in Brisbane Arcade, Queen Street, 'Henderson Real Estate' moved to the more prominent location at 270 Queen Street, opposite the GPO,[40] where it operated for more than a decade.

Some happiness returned to Claude's life when a friendship with a co-worker from his days in the War Council Office blossomed into romance. On the 21st December 1927, Claude and Florence Elizabeth Finch married. Together, they re-established a happy family life. Over the next decade, four daughters arrived, Claudia, Betty, Ann and Dell. With his family expanded, Claude again decided to move to the country. While retaining the real estate business, he purchased a tobacco farm on Mains Road at Sunnybank.

The timing was not good. His farming venture coincided with a downturn in Brisbane's real estate market that suddenly placed the father of six children under serious financial pressures. Sadly, a lapse of judgement brought unforeseen ruin. On Thursday May 9th, 1940, the Brisbane community was shocked when the afternoon newspaper revealed well known and highly respected citizen, Claude Henderson, had been arrested and charged with theft.[41] At 9.30 a.m., detectives raided his real estate office in Queen Street and, after confiscating business records, charged Claude with the theft of £280. In one day, his fine reputation and honour were destroyed. The court case found that, due to 'financial embarrassment,' money had been diverted for his own purposes from a trust account. Claude pleaded guilty. Describing the case as a very 'sad story', the judge convicted him with a 12 month good behaviour bond on the condition he made restitution.[42]

Unemployed, embarrassed and in despair, Claude withdrew to the family home, "Fassifern" at Hazelmere Parade, Sherwood. It took almost 12 months for him to find a new path. In 1941, at 50 years of age, he re-enlisted. With the rank of private, Claude was posted to the Records Office, where his clerical skills and years of experience in government administration made him a valuable asset. By Christmas, a promotion to Sergeant was achieved and, in November, 1942, Claude returned to the rank of Lieutenant.

The comradeship of the army was a wonderful healing tonic. When eventually discharged on 3rd April, 1947, he sought to continue his association by obtaining a job at the Wallangarra army depot, 200 kilometres from Brisbane, on the NSW border. The work suited him well, and he enjoyed living in the country. When Claude's wife, Florence, passed away in 1953, the close-knit Wallangarra community provided great comfort. He chose to remain at the Depot until his retirement in 1956.

Claude moved to the beachside suburb of Thorneside where a small cottage was purchased. Romance again followed when he met Vi Ghen, a widow who lived nearby. They enjoyed each other's company and, at the age of 66, Claude married for the third time. Final years were spent quietly at Thorneside with Vi. He died there in 1970 at the age of 79.

The legacy of Claude Henderson was immense. Through his work with the War Council, the RSSILA and the Repatriation Board, he had improved the lives of hundreds of veterans and their families. Although he humbly credited the successes of our first system of soldier repatriation to 'the tolerant spirit of the Digger', more accurately, it was because of Claude's determination, sacrifice and hard work. Under his leadership, outstanding achievements were made for Queensland's veterans. He devoted his life to the Anzac ideals of service and mateship. In a 1945 speech, Claude issued the following valuable advice to future generations, *'A spirit of tolerance in the whole of the community is necessary and all must help …. It will only be realized by the Anzac spirit.'*[43]

Lieutenant Claude Henderson was cremated at the Mt Gravatt Crematorium on 13 May, 1970.

Lance Corporal Frank Thomas Loud

No. 348, A Company, 9th Battalion

During four years of active war service, Frank Loud endured unimaginable hardship and ordeal. He suffered concussion, critical bouts of illness, was twice gassed and became a victim of severe shell-shock. In his Gallipoli Diary, Frank flippantly described his survival strategy was *'to lay still and trust to luck.'*[1] Fortunately, his luck prevailed.

Before the world descended into war, Frank led a privileged life. Born in 1891, he was the son of one of Melbourne's most successful citizens, William Loud, an ex-sea captain who, upon arriving in Australia in 1874, established a prosperous contracting business, "W. Loud & Sons". As the city of Melbourne grew, his business flourished and, for over 100 years, it remained one of Australia's most successful civil engineering companies. The family's home, "Granville," was located at 185 Beaconsfield Parade in the beachside suburb of Albert Park. This grand, elegant, nine-room mansion, with wide balconies facing the ocean, stands today as one of Melbourne's premier addresses.

The family's trappings of success surrounded Frank's upbringing. However, he was not spoilt by privilege. He was educated at the Middle Park State School, and continued his studies at the Gordon Technical College where he proved to be a capable student gaining credit awards for Arithmetic.[2] Physical fitness was always important. Living by the beach, he inherited his father's love of the sea and, with his brothers, William and Fred, Frank became an active competitor in the local yacht and rowing clubs. From their father, the Loud boys also learnt the importance of hard work and enterprise.

When Frank turned 21, he was keen to assert his independence. In an attempt to emulate his father's success, he moved to Mitchell in outback Queensland. Astutely aware of the district's booming demand for artesian bores on new pastoral leases, he attained an engine driver's licence[3] and, at remote Basalt Creek in 1913, set himself up as a contractor to bore artesian wells. With his services in high demand, Frank's future appeared very promising.

However, in early August 1914, life was upended. The small, patriotic Mitchell community greeted the news of war with unbridled enthusiasm. Believing the conflict would end quickly and that Mitchell's remote location would cause them to miss out, local lads rushed to enlist. In the first four months of war, 46 young men from the district's small population of approximately 1200 volunteered.[4] Frank was one of the first to join. On Thursday night, 27th August, with eight other local men, he left by mail train for the recruitment office at Roma. Before departing Mitchell Railway Station, the town staged a memorable send-off that began in the afternoon and went well into the night. After stirring speeches and much singing, a sovereign, generously donated by the local citizens, was presented to each volunteer.[5] Frank's pride and excitement were hard to contain.

Upon reaching Enoggera Camp on Brisbane's outskirts, the Mitchell men joined more than a thousand volunteers hurriedly being prepared for war. Frank was appointed to the 9th Battalion's C Company (later moved to A Company). Ten days later, with little time to adjust to military life, he left on the "SS Omrah" for overseas service. First port of call was Melbourne. This was a fortunate stop as their ship moored at Port Melbourne Pier, a very short distance from Frank's family home. During their three weeks' stay, every evening, he would flout the rules and swim ashore to spend time with his proud parents, sister and brothers at 185 Beaconsfield Parade.[6]

Despite a strong love of family, Frank left Melbourne on 19th October with little regret. His excitement at the prospect of an overseas adventure was immense. Seven weeks later, when Australia's First Expeditionary Force disembarked in Egypt, he was not disappointed. Cairo was both exciting and exotic. However, at their desert camp at Mena beside the Pyramids, the troops were engaged in a torturous regime of military training and, as the months slowly passed, Frank's high spirits began to wane. Although challenging, the training turned Frank into a truly tough and confident soldier. At the end of four months, he was ready for battle and extremely eager to the join the war. Another seven weeks' delay that followed on the Greek island of Lemnos caused much frustration.

It was almost eight months after enlisting that his Battalion finally received its operational orders. On the afternoon of the 24th April, 1915, Frank's company was moved onto the battleship "HMS Queen" for transport to the Turkish coast. The awful events that followed were recorded meticulously by Frank in his 'Gallipoli Diary'. This extraordinary document, donated by his daughter to the Australian War Memorial in 1989, survives as one of the most important and earliest personal records of the Gallipoli experience. Its original owner, Corporal Tom Ford, a Brisbane medical student, was killed on the first day of the campaign. Days later, while scouring the beach, Frank found Tom's abandoned pack and his unfinished diary. To honour Tom's sacrifice, he continued the diary.

The experience of the landing was vividly retold and includes a powerful testimony that Lieutenant Chapman's boat was the first boat ashore.

> *'It was rather a peculiar sensation steaming along slowly towards the shore expecting to hear the ping of a rifle every second. Each little movement in any of the boats could be distinctly heard and was quickly hushed. We got right inshore the pinnace let go and swung around so as to use her machine-gun. As we were directly behind the pinnace and our pinnace was slightly ahead of the other four, our boat was the first to ground and 8 or 10 were already on shore. I was standing on the seat aft when the first rifle shot was fired. It hit the thwarts just by my ankle. We waited for no more but made for the sides. I went to jump but tripped and hit the briny head first rifle, pack and full equipment. We only had our packs slung on our shoulders, so I quickly lost mine leaving it in the water. On reaching the beach, I quickly loaded and fitted the bayonet on my rifle while staggering across the 40 yards of sand.*
>
> *By that time there must have been at least 100 rifles cracking at us off the cliffs.'*

As boat after boat landed on the small crowded beach, confusion and disorder took over.

> 'Things seemed pretty lively and orders to form up in platoons on the beach were ignored and I think every man's only thought was to get to the top of that cliff.
>
> We must have been about two thirds of the way up the cliff before I saw the first man fall. Then Courtney of our Company whilst going over a bit of a spur was shot through the head and both knees.'

Frank's journey after leaving the beach was truly remarkable. Historian Bill Gammage noted his heroic advance was to 'a point which, although not the furthest inland which Australians penetrated on the day, was as far inland as any in his sector.'[7] Stubbornly and tenaciously, Frank held fast to the Battalion's original orders to advance at all costs. The objective was to clear the way for the main body and to secure the right flank on the 3rd Ridge.

Sadly, during the first hour of the advance, Frank was a witness to the tragedy of friendly fire.

> 'A little further on I reached another line of trenches ... we formed a firing line in it ... I am afraid then several of our chaps were shot by their own men as they pushed on ahead but of course there was such a mix up you could not tell as the scrub was full of fleeing Turks and their snipers were busy.'

Between 7 and 8 a.m., a lull in fighting enabled Frank to move a considerable distance forward. 'As things were now fairly quiet, I got a move on to try to re-join my battalion.' Upon reaching the 2nd Ridge, 'after a lot of scrub-dashing' he found some of the 9th Battalion digging in 'on the rise to my right so on re-joining set to lend them a hand.'

Soon after, the Turks launched a powerful counter-attack. In response, the men were ordered by Brigade commander, Colonel E. Sinclair-MacLagan, to leave the trenches they were digging and move forward across 400 Plateau.

> 'On our Brigadier arriving, we were ordered to advance and form a firing line apparently to hold the enemy in check while our reinforcements then landing would dig in behind us.'

The order proved to be a terrible mistake and a disaster for the 9th Battalion. Between 10 a.m. and noon, the men bravely moved forward in sections across 400 Plateau but, as each group reached the open area, Turkish machine gun fire swept the Plateau. Casualties were huge. Frank was lucky to survive.

> 'As soon as we lifted our heads and it seemed as though every second Turk had a machine-gun. I myself reached an old bomb proof shelter which had been filled in. There was a couple of feet of mud and water in the bottom of it. ... We were there some time, bullets whizzing all around us and shrapnel fairly screaming over us.'

Gammage concluded Frank reached a position somewhere near Mortar Ridge.[8] After miraculously surviving his epic trek from the beach, the Turkish counter-attack soon made this position untenable. Retreat across open ground, although extremely dangerous, became the only option.

> 'The word was shortly passed along that some of our chaps were holding a trench to the rear of us and to try and re-join them singly. Four of my mates went. One was hit in the neck but managed to crawl to shelter. I was just going to make a rush across the few yards of open ground when a shell hit and burst fair on top of our shelter ...
>
> The concussion knocked me out for a few minutes and gave me another ducking in the mud and water. When I regained my senses again, apparently only being stunned for a few minutes as I was not even bruised, my mate was laying dead just in front apparently killed by the same shell.
>
> A machine gun was raising the dust just ahead every few seconds so I just stood in the water and waited for close on an hour (it seemed like 10). I could not pluck up courage to make the dash, but when the fire slackened for a few seconds I made a dive for it. Never ran so hard before. I left my own rifle in the mud and grabbed another I saw laying outside. Luckily for me the average Turk is a rotten rifle shot or I would not be here now.'

The First Ashore

Incredibly, Frank arrived at the western edge of the Second Ridge where he joined one of the advance parties valiantly holding a depression at the head of Owens Gully known as The Cup. This position can be accurately identified by Frank's description of a battery of Turkish field guns captured by the 9th Battalion very early in the day.

> 'On reaching shelter in the shape of an old trench I followed it down and along another narrow communication trench I came upon a gun shelter... In all I think built for about six guns. The shelters and trenches were all well-constructed ... There were two field guns. One in the shelter and another with a couple of dead horses alongside a few yards from one shelter.'

Commanding the small group of soldiers at The Cup was Lieutenant Haymen, the scout officer who had also landed from Lieutenant Chapman's boat. The Lieutenant, with about 50 to 60 men, arrived at The Cup just before noon with orders to re-enforce a position 50 yards in front of the captured guns. However, as the day progressed, the Turks intensified their effort to recapture these guns and Haymen's group was heavily targeted. They suffered severe losses but, with tenacity and courage, held on.

> 'There must have been about 60 of our lads in the trench also a machine gun which was doing excellent work until put out of action by a shell.'

Frank's reference to a single machine gun 'doing excellent work' indicates he joined Haymen's men mid-afternoon. This gun had belonged to the 9th Battalion Machine Gun Section commanded by Lieutenant Costin which, throughout the morning, from a position above The Cup, bravely drew Turkish fire. Tragically, in the early afternoon, these gunners and their Section were destroyed. Sergeant Alexander Steele, the sole survivor, heroically carried the only remaining gun to Haymen's party at The Cup.

As the afternoon progressed, the fighting at The Cup became more brutal. Turkish commander, Lieutenant Sefik recalled the courageous resistance he met, 'Our skirmishing line had approached as far as our captured battery …. The enemy was not only stubbornly persevering in not … (giving) up the guns but they were also executing counter assaults.'[9]

By late afternoon, Haymen's men were exhausted, thirsty and bewildered. In his diary, Frank revealed their terrifying reality. His acceptance of the horror is unsettling.

> 'We were there the whole afternoon under a hot fire coming from three directions. Several of our lads were killed around me and a few wounded. It was sickening to watch but one soon gets callous and takes no notice of wounds. One man on exposing himself to get a shot had his jaw shot away – you could see the bone hanging from the flesh…..Whilst another while helping me drag a man hit in shoulder, into shelter, was hit in the back. On examination we found the bullet had only gone through the muscle on one side of the small making a clean flesh wound while still another was hit in the cheek four teeth smashed and out the other side, without touching the jaw bone.'

At about 4 p.m., after an hour of very intense fighting, Lieutenant Sefik successfully recaptured his lost guns. The Turkish Regiment's war diary recorded, *'The enemy were not able to take cover from our firings here; they could not hold this precipitous slope so they retreated via the southern edge path of Kanlisirt (Lone Pine) using scrub as cover. They left behind a considerable number of corpses.'*[10]

Frank and his mates were the last courageous defenders on the edge of the 2nd Ridge. *'Just on dark we could see the Turks coming over the next hill in swarms so left the trench and lay behind the mound.'* With the Turks all around, it seemed the game was up. *'One of our officers was shot just then through the chest. He was standing up and fell on top of me. Shortly after a bullet took the front sight off my rifle. This was about the closest shave I had.'* (Although Frank did not name the officer, official histories and unit diaries record Lieutenant Haymen was the only officer killed in that area, late that day.)

A safe retreat seemed almost impossible. Support lines on 400 Plateau were almost a kilometre away. Also, soldiers refused to leave their wounded mates behind. Sergeant Alex Steele recalled the withdrawal took almost three hours.[11] Three parties were formed - two protecting parties and a party for carrying the wounded.[12] Frank was assigned to one of the protecting parties but, heroically, he also helped carry one of the wounded to safety.

> *'Although dark, one had plain evidence of the havoc wrought by the enemy's shrapnel as I saw heaps of our dead just in the track we took. Also several wounded were discovered.*
>
> *About half way in one poor devil called out to me not to leave him and on my calling for a hand, a NZ and an officer came back (we were in the last of (the) covering section) and while considering the best way to carry him 5 Turks ran up to us, jabbering and laughing to themselves… The officer with us got 2 of them and when I fired another fell. You can guess we were not long in picking the wounded man up and by keeping in as thick scrub as we could find making a bee line to the beach which must have been 1 ½ miles away. I guess we covered ½ mile, considering the weight we were carrying, in record time as bullets were flying fairly thick.*
>
> *… We met a party of about 14 men guarding some wounded and they told us that the line of the trenches had been constructed about 300 yds ahead so (we) made for them.'*

Upon reaching these trenches, they spent the rest of the night digging in. Over the next three days, there was no time for rest or reflection. Desperately, Frank and his mates held on. No place was safe.

> *'There was constant rain of shrapnel rifle and machine gun bullets all day Monday. We were kept busy improving our trenches …… No one slept as things were still very lively and it was also very cold without overcoats.'*

By the fourth day, Frank was mentally exhausted, hungry, thirsty and suffering from lack of sleep. When the 9th Battalion was called to muster on the beach, he straggled back, desperate for rest and eager to find out how his mates had fared.

> *'It quietened down during the day and I found one of the 9th men (the first I had seen since Lieu. Hayman was shot on Sunday) and on hearing that our Batt. was mustering on the*

> beach we left the trenches about 5 p.m. and re-joined them. There were then only 380 of the old battalion but stragglers kept arriving up till Saturday who brought our total up to 420 so considering we landed 1000 strong our loss was heavy. I had my first food and drink of tea since leaving the Queen. I also went and found a dead man's pack and replaced my haversack and mess tin lost in the fray.'

The Battalion's rest was brief. On Saturday, 1st May, the 9th was sent back into the firing line, taking a position on the extreme right flank, in a trench running up from the sea facing Gabe Tepa. Frank, however, received a temporary reprieve from the dangers of the front line. A water spring had been discovered in a gully just behind the Battalion's new position, and Captain Butler, the Battalion's Medical Officer, recognized its importance and insisted it be guarded.[13] Frank was fortunate to be chosen and, for the next three weeks, he enjoyed the relative quietness of this special duty. A week after his return to the trenches, his good fortune continued. Water shortages began to occur, causing an annoyed Doctor Butler to quickly demand a return of the old water guard. Frank suddenly found himself back at the spring for another six or seven weeks. Guard duty was preferable to the trenches, but there were dangers.

> 'We then spent a dreary six or seven weeks with nothing to do bar dodge shrapnel which began to sweep down the gully we were in pretty persistently and I had many a narrow shave from being hit.'

Frank eventually gave up his guard post as a favour to his mate, Private Ben Kendrick,[14] another member of the first boat ashore.

> 'About July 12th one of my old mates arrived back from hospital he had been hit the day we landed the bullet passing through his thigh bone without breaking it and after a couple of days spent in the trenches the bone began to ache so (I) suggested he should take my place and take things quietly. So I returned to the trenches.'

By mid-August, conditions on Gallipoli were deplorable. As well as lice, flies, heat and the stench of death, a lack of sanitation and clean water in the trenches caused sickness to spread. Like many others, Frank's mental and physical health began to suffer. He resigned himself to an uncertain fate and clung to dreams of home.

> *'I notice even the toughest amongst us are beginning to show signs of nerves and everyone is heartly sick of the game of war. I myself if ever I get back think I will take up a small block of orchard land and take things easy but am afraid it will be sometime if ever I see Australia again.'*

The steadfast pride that he felt for his fellow Anzacs and what they had achieved became a source of comfort.

> *'In case there is a bullet with my name printed on it and so never see the big island again I would like to say that taking them on the whole the lads are excellent and what I have seen I think they are far superior as soldiers to the home country men...'*

Frank endured almost four continuous months on the Gallipoli Peninsula. On the 16th August, he succumbed to acute diarrhoea, an illness that was spreading rapidly through the trenches. He was evacuated to one of Malta's large convalescent camps. Four weeks later, his condition remained poor and, on 26th September, he was moved to Egypt's Mustapha Convalescent Camp for another five weeks.

When orders were finally received for him to return to Gallipoli, good fortune again favoured Frank. He reached his unit on the 17th November, the day the 9th Battalion left the Peninsula for its long overdue rest period on Lemnos. Weeks later, the Gallipoli Campaign ended.

The 9th left Lemnos on New Year's Day, 1916, and were returned to Egypt. For the next three months, in harsh isolation and soaring heat, they laboured in the desert, building trenches and fortifying the defences near the Suez Canal. During this time, Frank became increasingly frustrated and dissatisfied with his life as an infantry soldier. With Bill Cleaver, another mate from the first boat ashore, he transferred to one of the Battalion's new machine gun companies. This relatively new weapon in the war fascinated him, and he also believed dugouts and conditions for gunners were better than those suffered by infantry soldiers. Unfortunately, he would soon discover unique dangers and the casualty rates for gunners were often extremely high.

Upon joining the new 3rd Machine Gun Company, Frank earnestly began training. The heavy Vickers Machine Gun required skilled operation and, in Egypt, for three weeks, he attended daily gun drills, lectures and tactical exercises. There was also a period of intensive training when the Company arrived in France.

Frank's first battlefield experience as a gunner was in the Petillion area, south of Fleurbaix. From mid-May until early July, gunners provided crucial support to a series of diversionary infantry raids. The most brilliantly executed of these occurred on 2nd and 3rd July when Frank's old 9th Battalion mates, led by Captain Wilder-Neligan, successfully raided German trenches near Fleurbaix. The 3rd Machine Gun Company's support contributed significantly to the raid's success and gained them much acclaim.

With boosted confidence, Frank then moved with his Company to the bloody fields of Pozieres. In this new action, the gunners' role was to support the 9th Battalion infantry as they attacked the ruined village. The battle raged for four days and nights, and Frank endured horrors he could never have imagined. The enemy's unrelenting artillery explosions rocked the ground constantly, destroying trenches, mangling bodies and burying groups of men alive. Everywhere, the haunting groans and cries of the wounded filled the air. Soldiers went mad with their nerves destroyed. The 1st Division lost 5000 men at Pozieres. Thirty-eight of Frank's mates from the 3rd Machine Gun Company were listed as casualties.

At Pozieres, Frank suffered greatly. On the third day of the battle, a shell burst caused him severe concussion but, like many others, he bravely carried on. Days later, a more serious injury emerged. The inflicted trauma had shattered Frank's nerves. Medical officers noted a loss of memory, halting speech and, at times, his total inability to speak.[15] Incredibly, despite these symptoms, Frank was not removed from the battlefield. His fragile mental state was further challenged when he received tragic news that his brother, Corporal Fred Loud of the 7th Battalion, had died at Pozieres.[16]

Less than four weeks later, while Frank battled his grief and trauma, orders came for the troops to march back into the hell they had just left. The new objective was Mouquet Farm, a ruined farmhouse a short distance north. The gunners took a position just 1500 yards south of the farmhouse and Frank, already shell-shocked, entered another three days of intense fighting that was characterized again by heavy bombardment and constant shelling.

Mercifully, his Company was relieved from the front line on 23rd August. They then moved, with the rest of the Australian divisions, to the Ypres sector in Flanders, a quieter area where they could recover their strength. As the winter began, orders were received to return to the Somme. Frank and his Company were stationed in the Flers sector where they suffered severely. It was the coldest winter experienced in 25 years and, in the trenches, the bitter cold, the constant rain and mud made life unbearable. During this dismal time, on 1st January, Frank received promotion to Lance Corporal.

As the months passed, sickness in the trenches became rampant. Many soldiers suffered trench feet, frost-bite, rheumatism and respiratory diseases. Frank, with lungs already damaged after being twice gassed during the Battle of the Somme,[17] succumbed to pleurisy. In early March he was hospitalized at Rouen and shortly after evacuated to England. The diagnosis was severe bronchitis, but Frank was also mentally and physically exhausted. At the end of two months in hospital, he was discharged, but his health remained weak. As a consequence, instead of returning to the front, Frank was posted to the Machine Gun Training Camp at Hareham and later to Perham Downs.

Six months later, in December, 1917, he re-joined his 3rd Machine Gun Company in the front line trenches near Messines. Another bitter winter was beginning. For Frank, the wretched weather and mud filled trenches were horribly familiar. In January, the snow melted, causing the trenches to flood. Water and mud was recorded at 50 centimetres deep.[18] In the midst of this, the Germans targeted the gunners with frequent, extreme artillery fire. Frank resigned himself to an uncertain fate. Some respite finally came in February when his Machine Gun Company was removed from the front line for three weeks' training at Kent Camp in the Neuve Eglise area. For Frank, there was also a bonus of two weeks' leave. From 24th February to 5th March, he savoured the delights of Paris.

Regrettably, when the gunners returned to the front, the war had taken a menacing turn. On 21st March, a strengthened German army launched a new devastating offensive. Areas such as Pozieres, Mouquet Farm and Bapaume, that Frank and his mates had fought so hard for, were lost. In an effort to stem the enemy's advance, Frank's company was sent to harass enemy roads, aeroplanes, gun and mortar positions on the front line at Spoil Bank in the Hollebeke area of Belgium. Their special orders revealed the seriousness of the situation - *'If the section cannot remain here alive, it will remain here dead.... Should any man, through shell shock or other cause attempt to surrender, he will remain here dead.'*[19]

Also in March 1918, a new 1st Machine Gun Battalion was formed and with this new Battalion, Frank participated in some of the important final actions of the war, including the successful defence of the critical railhead at Hazebrouck. The machine-gun's influence on the battlefield increased markedly and, throughout the summer, the gunners provided effective support that helped the Allies eventually break the Hindenburg Line. By October, the Germans were in full retreat.

The course of the war was changing, and Frank reflected on the luck that had allowed him to survive more than three years on the battlefield. To his delight and surprise, more good fortune followed. As an original Anzac who volunteered in 1914, he was granted two months' long service leave in Australia. In October 1918, with 700 other 'original' Anzacs, Frank left the war forever.

During their long voyage home, peace was declared. When their ship docked in Melbourne on 2nd December, 1918, Australia was still celebrating. Newspapers reported, *'people turned out in thousands to welcome back the lads who thought that they were coming home for only a holiday but happily will not have to return.'*[20] The joyous fanfare that greeted them was overwhelming and infectious, but, for the veterans, the mood was temporary. *'Few of the Anzacs could be induced to speak of their experiences. Many wore upon their breasts ribbons denoting the possession of medals won at great risk, but they were silent as to their exploits.'*[21]

For the rest of his life, Frank also remained silent. He desperately wanted to forget. However, the legacy of war was difficult to extinguish. As well as damaged lungs, Frank returned home with a serious nervous condition. The medical board deemed he had a 50% disability and granted a part pension.

The First Ashore

After his discharge on 31st January, Frank moved back to the family home at Albert Park and attempted to re-establish his life. To the delight of his dying father, he joined his surviving brother in a partnership to manage the family's contracting business, "W. Loud & Sons". It was hoped a quick return to work would keep Frank's mind busy and help him suppress the memories of war, but the stress of business only aggravated his nervous condition. His constant headaches, stutter and sleeplessness did not abate. It quickly became apparent Frank's new temperament was not suited to business or city life. In 1921, desperate to distance himself from these pressures, Frank moved to Bairnsdale to manage the company's less demanding rural contracting jobs. Unfortunately, this was not enough. Two years later, on doctor's advice, he dissolved the partnership and forfeited his share in the family firm.[22]

It was a pivotal year. Frank also proposed marriage to Jean Bryan, a dental nurse from East St. Kilda. Family members described Jean as a generous-hearted woman with an indomitable pioneering spirit who was an ideal partner for a man like Frank.[23] Their large wedding in August 1923, at St Margaret's Presbyterian Church, East St Kilda, marked a new beginning. The couple planned to move to Queensland to re-start the life Frank had mapped out for himself before he enlisted. A road trip adventure in Frank's Dodge was organized that would take them across Australia and eventually settle them in Queensland.

However, at Bairnsdale, their grand plans ended unexpectedly. As the couple passed through town, previous work connections persuaded Frank to put in a bid to build the town's first concrete structure. It seemed a smart opportunity to make some extra money before continuing their road trip. Frank won the contract and successfully constructed an ornate concrete building that boasted an elaborate arched portal. Fondly referred to as 'The Big Garage,' it became renowned as the largest motor garage in Victoria and, even today, remains as a building of historical and architectural significance, registered as a National Trust site. Recognition of his work quickly followed with offers of more contracts. The next year, Frank developed the Glenadale to Lindenow Road and, in 1926, he began construction on the 100 foot high Bairnsdale water tower.

It seemed Bairnsdale was Frank and Jean's destiny. While constructing the garage, an undeveloped farm on West Clifton Road at Mt Taylor, outside Bairnsdale, caught their eye. Frank saw it as an opportunity to fulfil the dream that helped him survive the trenches – *'if ever I get back think I will take up a small block of ... land and take things easy.'* He purchased the property and, while continuing his heavy workload of contract jobs, he and Jean spent their weekends and spare time felling trees and pushing scrub. They began with only 10 acres of cleared land, but gradually they made their farm viable.[24]

The work schedule was exhausting, but Frank enjoyed farm life. During these first few years away from Melbourne, his health was generally good. There were recurring bouts of bronchitis and sleeplessness but, for a short time, his nerve condition seemed to improve. Consequentially, in February 1927, Frank cancelled his war pension.

As the farm became operational, family responsibilities grew. Frank became the proud father of three daughters – Marjorie, born in 1926, June in 1927 and Barbara in 1933. To provide for his growing family and the farm's continuing development, more contracting jobs were sought. Unfortunately, major projects, such as the construction of the first concrete footpaths in Bairnsdale,[25] produced a burden of stress. By 1928, Frank's nerves were bad again. His headaches and insomnia returned, and often he found it difficult to concentrate. There were frequent episodes of anxiety and his stammering also worsened. Jean recalled *'with physical exertion he would quite often collapse'.*[26] The Bairnsdale doctor advised nothing could be done except rest and freedom from worry.[27] Frank had no option but to retire from the contracting business and rely on the small income the farm produced.

Sadly, as his health continued to deteriorate, farm work also became difficult. In 1935, mounting financial pressures caused him to seek assistance from the Repatriation Board. Frank was confident, because of his extensive war service, his war pension would be quickly re-instated. However, the Repatriation Board ignore his historical medical records and insisted on new medical tests. The results showed Frank suffered neurasthenia ('shell-shock' or post-traumatic stress disorder) but, incredibly, the Board deemed this condition did not cause him any incapacity. Also, despite Frank being gassed at least twice during the war, his damaged lungs were not deemed due to war service. The Board's decision shocked and wounded Frank. He immediately appealed, but their re-consideration only allowed a meagre 15% pension.

The Second World War prevented any further appeal. Frank felt deeply betrayed by the Repatriation Board, but his sense of patriotic duty remained strong. In the war, he took an active role despite his age and poor health. Jean was left to manage the farm while Frank took a job with the Allied Works Council, a government organization formed to construct military infrastructure. Utilizing his construction skills, in 1941, he worked on the Inland Road Project between Charters Towers and Townsville and, the following year, on war-related projects such as the construction of an aerodrome at Sale.

By 1944, Jean was struggling to manage the farm alone and Frank's health was in significant decline. He applied for release from wartime duty and, in April, returned to Mt Taylor.[28] Regrettably, he now found farm work challenging. In 1945, friends and family encouraged Frank to make another application to the Repatriation Board for assistance. The Board's response was colder and blunter than before. His war service and wartime medical history were again callously disregarded. Cruel and unsubstantiated notes were recorded on his case file, '*This man is very introspective – has a circumstantial tale of woe. Not v. intelligent.*'[29] Another appeal was made but again refused.

Accepting the decision, Frank and Jean continued to struggle on their farm. Ten years later, a third application was made and also immediately denied. Four years later, when a condition of pulmonary fibrosis was diagnosed combined with unresolved pneumonia and deafness, Frank attempted again. The Board answered with another cruel rejection. At 68 years of age, he was defiant and responded immediately with another appeal, which was also disallowed.

Sadly, by 1960, his lung problems had become cancer. The right lung, the focus of his pulmonary disease during the war, was successfully removed, but Frank was now dying. Realizing his time was running out, he stepped up his battle with the Repatriation Board. He was no longer fighting for himself, but for Jean to receive a war pension as a widow. Over the next 12 months, four more desperate appeals were made. Sadly, each one was heartlessly disallowed. By then, Frank was a beaten man. He had no more energy to fight. Jean later wrote, 'Following the Tribunal Appeal, his strength deteriorated and such a lethargy overcame him.'[30] Frank passed away at Mt Taylor on 10th November, 1961, aged 70 years.

Despite the injustices inflicted by the repatriation system, in all other areas, Frank's life had been an inspirational triumph over adversity. His wartime sacrifices were immense. As an 'Original Anzac', with courage, resilience and some good fortune, he survived countless horrors at Gallipoli and on the Western Front. At home, although his wartime battles continued, Frank achieved much. At Bairnsdale, he proved his genius at building things and at Mt Taylor, he established a sheep farm and raised a much cherished family. His almost 30 year fight with the Repatriation Commission drove him to despair but, characteristically, Frank Loud refused to give up.

Lance Corporal Frank Thomas Loud was cremated at the Springvale Crematorium, Melbourne, on 13th November, 1961. His ashes were scattered.

Private James Dundee Bostock

No. 1009, A Company, 9th Battalion
(later Captain, Volunteer Defence Corps)

Believed by some to be the second ashore at Gallipoli, James (Jim) Dundee Bostock devoted his life to the Anzac tradition of mateship and service. He enlisted twice in World War 1 and, throughout his life, completed over seven years' wartime military service. Described as a quiet man with a proud dignity, Jim worked tirelessly to improve the lives of veterans and to ensure the memory of Gallipoli was not forgotten.

His dedicated connection to the military was deeply rooted in Bostock family history. His Grandfather, Major General James Bostock, served in England's 6th Regiment and his Great Grandfather was Captain William Dundee of the 62nd Wiltshire Regiment. A Great Uncle, Frank William Dundee, also was a Major of the 31st Regiment of Foot.[1] Family stories of these Empire men and their daring military adventures captured Jim's imagination as a young boy and had a profound influence on him.

Other important inspirations in Jim's early life were his parents and the Church. His father, Robert Dundee Bostock, was a prominent and successful Queensland public servant, draftsman and land agent who instilled in Jim an understanding of the virtues of hard work, respectability and entrepreneurship. His mother, Mary Wilson, daughter of Reverend Edward Wilson, ensured her children received a religious upbringing. The family were active members of the Congregational Church at North Ipswich and Rockhampton and, as a child, Jim regularly attended the Sunday School Bible Class.[2]

Born at Rockhampton in 1896, the second son of four children,

Jim's early childhood was spent in Rockhampton. When he was six years old, the family moved to Ipswich where his father took the position of Land Agent.[3] A happy home was established at 24 Brisbane Road but, sadly, two years later, tragedy struck. Jim's mother suddenly passed away.[4] Jim was only eight and his youngest sibling was just eight months old.

The grief was overwhelming but, mercifully, the following year, the family was given the opportunity to start a new life in Brisbane. Jim's father received an important promotion to head of the Inquiry Branch in Brisbane's Lands Office. A comfortable home was found at 3 Hamilton Place, Brookes Street, Bowen Hills, and Jim and his brother were enrolled at the nearby Fortitude Valley State Boys School. Jim enjoyed school life, and he proved to be a very capable student, attaining the top merit prize for his year group in 1908.[5]

As life for the Bostocks seemed to improve, another unforeseen tragedy struck. Jim's father contracted tuberculosis and, after a brief illness, he died on 18th April, 1913.[6] Jim was 16 and had just begun his first job at the Government Prickly Pear Experimental Station at Dulacca, 420 kilometres west of Brisbane. While his younger orphaned siblings went to live with their Aunt Minnie at Ipswich, he remained at Dulacca.

Distance from family made the loss more difficult to bear, but Jim's job kept his mind busy. At a young age, he had gained the position of research assistant to scientist, Dr Jean White, who was conducting important experiments into biological controls of the prickly pear menace spreading across Australia. Jim's inquiring mind and youthful enthusiasm made him well suited to the job. He found the work exciting, although, sometimes, difficult. Dulacca station was isolated and, with over 1335 experimental plots and a staff of just two, there was much to do.[7]

18-year-old Jim was dedicated to the work at Dulacca but, when war was declared in August, 1914, the prospect of an overseas adventure in Australia's new volunteer army held much allure. After weeks of deliberating, the difficult decision to leave Dulacca was made. On 2nd November, Jim travelled to Toowoomba's recruitment office and, from there, to Brisbane's Enoggera Camp where he was accepted into the 9th Battalion's 1st Reinforcements.

The First Ashore

Soon after, the Reinforcements departed for Melbourne and, from there, they sailed on the troopship, "Themistocles" to Albany, Western Australia. They joined Australia's second convoy of 17 ships with a cargo of 13,000 Anzacs and 123 nurses. Bristling with apprehension and excitement, Jim left Australia for war on New Year's Eve, 1914.

Their destination was Mena Camp, near Cairo, where the Reinforcements joined the rest of the 9th Battalion participating in a regime of intensive military training. For the next four weeks, Jim's daily routine involved rifle and bayonet practice, digging trenches, night manoeuvres and long route marches through desert sand in full kit. Although the schedule was exhausting, time was also found to experience exotic Cairo. The young lad from country Dulacca was not immune to the wayward behaviour that characterised many Anzacs on leave. During his month in Egypt, he managed to acquire tattoos of both the Pyramids and the Sphinx on each forearm.

Jim left the desert camp on 28th February, naively eager to fight the Germans. When the troops were disembarked, instead, on the Greek island of Lemnos, he and his mates felt bitterly disappointed. Five long weeks were spent on Lemnos and another two weeks on board a troopship moored in the harbour. Impatiently they waited as the rest of the invasion force slowly arrived.

About mid-day on April 24th, 1915, orders were finally received. Jim's A Company was sent aboard the battleship "HMS Queen", the lead boat of the flotilla that would transport the Anzacs to the Turkish coast. At about 2.30 a.m., the next morning, disembarkation began. 36 crowded rowboats, in groups of three, towed by steam pinnaces, took the first landing wave on an uneasy journey to the beach.

> *'I remember the whole affair just as if it had happened yesterday. Lieutenant Chapman was in the bow of the boat (which was No. 1 tow) and I was crouched alongside him, my position at that time being signaller attached to No.3 Platoon Commander, and as such my duty was to be in close contact with Lieutenant Chapman so that I could transmit or receive any messages.'*[8]

Jim clearly recalled landing ahead of the other boats and being on the beach when the first shot was fired.

> 'Glancing over the gunwale of the boat I could dimly discern the other pinnaces and their boat tows, always slightly behind and to the right of us. When the pinnace cast off we consequently had a slight lead and our No.1 boat naturally maintained an advantage over the others as soon as the rowers commenced their work. I can remember Lieutenant Chapman calling "All out!" and we immediately hopped over the side. I saw the Lieutenant's silhouette as he hopped overboard and I followed him, in water up to our waists, and we scrambled ashore... It was whilst taking off my sodden pack on the beach that the first shot was fired.'

He firmly believed Lieutenant Chapman was first ashore and also that he followed closely behind.

> 'I want to make a statement which I have always believed to be correct, and that is, that I consider that I was the second man to land. I fully realize that this statement will not go unchallenged and that I will never be able to prove my assertion but I feel confident in my own mind that such is the case.'[9]

For 18-year-old Jim, Gallipoli was a horrific ordeal. Persistent shelling, rifle and sniper fire created a constant threat of death. Brief entries in Jim's wartime diary reveal this unrelenting nature and awful cost of the Campaign. In the first week, he wrote,

26 APRIL MONDAY:	*Our lot scattered. Have been in several battalions in firing line … Several friends gone.*
27 APRIL TUESDAY:	*Entrenched on hill next beach, shrapnel all around us …. am feeling done up as are most of others.*
28 APRIL WEDNESDAY:	*Muster of 9th on hill; about 250 there, 52 in our compy.*
29 APRIL THURSDAY:	*Shrapnel fell around us all night. …. Went over with about 100 to our new camp in valley and dug in. Very cold night.*
30 APRIL FRIDAY:	*Several snipers at work … shots fired, also few shells but no damage. Village on our right in flames.*

1 MAY SATURDAY: *Aroused 4.30, all stood to arms as attack expected… About 10 o'clock shifted out …. and moved to valley on right where we entrenched. Shrapnel fell pretty close … Heavy firing in front all day. Nearly all our officers killed or wounded …… Can only muster 400 out of battalion.*[10]

During an engagement on 19th May, the killing escalated significantly. At about midnight, the Turks launched a fierce counter-attack that continued without pause until dawn.

19 MAY WEDNESDAY: *Just after midnight Turks attacked all along line furiously but were driven back, and again at 3.30 bringing machine guns into play.*

20 MAY THURSDAY: *Fighting went on all night enemy getting within 25 yds in places – right up to our barb-wire entanglements which had been smashed by shells. 19 of ours killed (9th) I believe – could see dead Turks lying around outside in numbers.*

Jim survived three continuous months on the Peninsula. He was evacuated as a casualty on 28th July after a Turkish hand grenade (a 'cricket ball') inflicted a serious shrapnel wound to his left thigh. On-board the overcrowded hospital ship "Sicilia", two operations were performed to remove the shrapnel.[11] Two weeks after his wounding, the hospital ship finally reached the island of Malta, where Jim was admitted to St Ignatius Hospital. Diary entries describe many sleepless nights and enormous pain. The wound would not heal and continually discharged blood and puss. As a consequence, almost a month later, medical officers recommended Jim's return to Australia. However, at the last minute, a new military directive prevented patients with open wounds from travelling. Jim was instead sent to England.

He was admitted to the County of London War Hospital on 10th September, where his wound healed slowly. At the end of six months of convalescence, unfortunately, Jim remained incapacitated and the medical board declared him unfit for further active service. On 17th March 1916, he reluctantly embarked on the troopship "HS Ascanius" for Australia. Leaving his mates, and the job he enlisted for, caused much despondency.

Australia greeted the disabled veterans on board the "Ascanius" with an extraordinary welcome home. After disembarking in Sydney, the Queensland contingent of 55 wounded soldiers and three nurses travelled by special train to Brisbane.[12] At every station on route there was a rousing and emotional reception. The brief stop at Ipswich station held special significance for Jim. Among the large passionate crowd on the platform were his brother, sister, aunt, uncle and other family and friends proudly celebrating his safe return.[13] An hour later, an even larger celebration was staged at Brisbane's Central Station. Jim was overjoyed to be home, but there were also feelings of unease. The fate of mates on the battlefield weighed heavily on his mind.

Adjusting to civilian life was also an enormous challenge. Return to his old life at Dulacca was not an option, as manual work was no longer possible. At the age of 20, he carried a serious disability. Jim left the army on the 31st May with a war pension of £3 per fortnight,[14] which was insufficient to live on. Fortunately, his aunt Minnie and her husband, Francis Whitehead, who ran an extremely successful photography business in Ipswich, were able to provide support by offering him light duties as a photographer.[15] The work supplemented his pension, but, more importantly, it kept Jim's mind active.

As the months passed, his leg gradually gained some strength. He followed the news of the war closely and, each day, grew more restless. Eager for a more active role in the war effort, he enlisted in the home service, but his gnawing frustration at being unable to serve overseas remained. In April 1918, another desperate attempt was made to re-enlist and, this time, to his surprise, he passed the medical examination. Accepted into the 6th Reinforcements, 9th Battalion (No.58200), because of his previous battle experience, he was sent immediately to the NCO School to be trained to be a Corporal.

Weeks later, the 6th Reinforcements prepared to leave for war. Before departure, with his pride restored, Jim was prompted to propose marriage to girlfriend, Gertrude (Truda) Chardon. Hurriedly a wedding was organized and, in a quiet ceremony at the Holy Cross Church, Wooloowin on 24th August, the couple wed.[16] Ten days later, Corporal Bostock left Sydney on "HMAT Bakara".

The First Ashore

Mercifully, an unusually long sea voyage caused the 6th Reinforcements to arrive in London on 14th November, three days after Germany's surrender. It seemed fortunate timing. However, the Reinforcements' sea journey had been almost as deadly as frontline service. The 'Spanish Flu', the epidemic that would kill over 20 million people worldwide, took hold on board the "Bakara". In the close confines of the ship, the sickness spread quickly with two-thirds of the troops succumbing. The small hospital on board could not cope. Sick and dying clogged the decks. A soldier's diary records, '*250 men now in bed on deck with the disease. Men lying everywhere with eyes on them like saucers.*'[17] Newspapers in Australia later revealed that between 30 and 40 soldiers died on the journey.[18]

Jim was fortunate to survive. He joined the 9th Battalion Reinforcements training at Fovant in the Salisbury Plain area and, six months later, returned to Brisbane on the troopship "Orantes". Upon discharge from the army on 17th July, 1919, he eagerly returned to married life. Work was found as a clerk and, by 1922, the Bostocks were able to purchase a house at Derby Street, Hendra. This much loved residence became the home of Jim, Truda and their three children for the next 55 years.

While grateful for the comfortable family life he was able to establish, Jim was also acutely aware of the problems other veterans were facing. Their plight weighed heavily on his mind. Over next decades, Jim worked passionately for the veteran cause. He became a vigorous advocate for the RSSILA (Returned Sailors and Soldiers Imperial League of Australia), today's RSL, believing the interests and welfare of ex-servicemen and their families were best promoted through its work. In a 1933 speech, he described the RSSILA as '*the mouthpiece of all returned soldiers.... not hindered by political and sectarian fetters.*'[19] In various capacities, Jim supported the organization's work. He became the District Secretary of the RSSILA's South-East District and, in 1938, he represented S.E. Queensland at the RSSILA Congress in Cairns[20] and was also elected delegate to the Federal Executive.[21] As publicity officer for the Toombul Returned Soldiers (1939),[22] he earnestly promoted projects supporting veterans. In 1934, he pushed for the formation of a tennis association for returned soldiers believing the fraternity of such clubs provided a crucial means of addressing the psychological problems faced by veterans.[23]

Among the many projects he worked on, Jim's proudest achievement was the role he played in establishing Brisbane's first residential home for unemployable and "burnt-out" diggers. As the secretary of the organizing committee, he contributed enormous energy and time to its fundraising activities.[24] In June 1938, success was finally achieved. "Kingshome", on two and a half hectares at Swan Road, Taringa, opened its doors to 63 distressed and struggling veterans. At the official opening, a crowd of 3000 people gathered to celebrate the achievement and, with proud satisfaction, Jim and his wife attended, with the Governor, Premier, President of the RSL and many other notable citizens, as part of the official party.[25]

Throughout his post-war life, Jim also constantly sought opportunities to ensure the memory and sacrifices of Gallipoli and World War One were not forgotten. He often addressed school children at Anzac Day commemorations, with vivid and inspiring accounts of the landing.[26] He was a key speaker at many community events and, in 1934, he appeared on a popular 4BK radio programme, 'Talks with a Digger.'[27] At Brisbane's Anzac Day commemorations, Jim also took a prominent role. He acted as orderly officer at city marches and, for the 20th Anniversary commemoration of the Landing at Gallipoli, he served on the Anzac Day Commemoration Committee.[28]

After "Kingshome" was established, Jim focused his energy on a campaign to ensure the preservation of Brisbane's Anzac Square. He feared the future of this focal point for commemorating 9th Battalion sacrifice was being endangered by the encroachment of commercial buildings and, from as early as 1935, he agitated for the Square's protection and extension. He campaigned loudly for the space to be expanded through to Queen Street and for the Council to resume buildings between Anzac Square and the Post Office. Frustrated by a lack of support from the RSL,[29] Jim did not live to see this dream come to fruition.

In December 1941, when the Second World War expanded to a war against Japan, Jim resigned his job as a sales representative for building materials company, G P Embleton and Co. At the age of 45, he joined the Volunteer Defence Corps. While most other volunteers completed part-time duty of about six hours per week, Jim took a full-time command position. His aptitude, military experience and high profile in the RSSILA meant he was quickly promoted to Lieutenant. Further officer training courses were completed and, after serving three years as a Lieutenant, in 1943, he attained the rank of Captain.

When the war ended, he returned to his old job with Embleton and Co. Regrettably, over the next decade, Jim's mobility suffered. His left leg, that carried the shrapnel wound from Gallipoli, became weaker. An incident in 1959 shook the 63-year-old veteran's confidence. When alighting from a tram in Brisbane, the weaker leg gave way, causing him to fall onto the street. A significant injury was sustained. As the years passed, his leg and persistent backache caused increasing discomfort and pain.

Realizing his working life was ending, Jim applied for a war pension but was shocked to find his application rejected. He appealed the Repatriation Board's decision in 1960 and again in 1961, but without success. Persistence was rewarded in 1967 when, at 70 years of age, his full war pension was finally granted.[30] The last years of his life were enjoyed at Hendra, surrounded by family. As always, the mateship and the fraternity of ex-serviceman also remained important.

On 15th August, 1982, aged 86, Jim passed away. His many friends remembered him as a true Anzac who used the awful experience of war to create a rich life path. As a tireless and effective activist in the early RSL movement and through projects such as Kingshome, he helped improve the lives of many veterans. Through his school visits, radio interviews, letters to the editor and his work on Anzac Day Commemoration Committees, Jim also persistently strove to ensure the Anzac tradition lived on and the sacrifices of World War 1 were not forgotten. In 1984, two years after his death, Post Office Square, the green space between Anzac Square and Queen Street that he envisaged and fought for, was finally created.

Captain James Dundee Bostock's ashes were interred at Brisbane's Albany Creek Memorial Gardens.

Private Eli Coles

No. 315, C Company, 9th Battalion
(later Sergeant Cook, 9th Battalion)

For Eli Coles, war came at a most inconvenient time. Already the proud father of two boys under three years, he was about to be a parent for the third time. Although deeply devoted to his young family, he believed it was his duty to help defend the Empire. Separation from them for four long years caused him much anguish but, with selfless courage, Eli fought gallantly and displayed a remarkable dedication to duty.

Leaving his children was difficult. Eli feared they would suffer the same hardships he experienced as a fatherless child. Born in Brisbane on the 10th April, 1882, he was the second illegitimate child of Harriet Coles. Eight years earlier, Harriet, a single mother, escaped a wretched life of poverty in England by migrating to Queensland. In Brisbane, she relied on her brother Jesse's goodwill. However, a year after Eli's birth, Jesse died unexpectedly. Harriet inherited his small struggling farm on the outskirts of North Brisbane at Downfall Creek, known today as Chermside,[1] but running the farm alone proved too difficult. In order to keep her children, her only option was to find a husband. In 1888, Harriet married German carpenter, Alois Engeler of Nundah. It was an unsuitable match. Less than five years later, Alois disappeared, leaving Harriet and her children destitute.[2] At 12 years of age, Eli left school to support the family. His job as a mill hand at a nearby saw-mill was difficult but provided a small income.

As an escape from the heavy responsibilities he bore as a teenager, Eli developed a fondness for outdoor life. Camping and shooting became favourite pastimes. Fortunately, the local citizen militia provided a means for him to freely pursue these interests. Four years before military training was made compulsory, Eli was an active and enthusiastic member of the Moreton Regiment. Almost all his weekends and spare time were devoted to military camps, field training exercises and militia parades.

As he grew older, Eli was enthused by the exciting work of the Submarine Miners who maintained the system of mines strung across the entrance of the Brisbane River. Its 153 members, the 'Miners', were stationed at Fort Lytton and were popularly regarded as the 'defenders of the city.'[3] Eli was eager to join their ranks and share their prestige. In 1911, he applied for transfer and was thrilled to be accepted. Two years later, when the volunteer defence forces were reorganized, in order to continue his work as a submarine miner, he moved to the Engineers Company.

By then, Eli was married with two children. He wed 25-year-old, Annie Mogridge from Lutwyche, on 21st July, 1909. Ernest, their first child, was born on 3rd October 1910 and another son, Alan, came in 1913. Life was happy, but also a struggle. Supporting his growing family on the small wages of a sawmill worker was difficult. Unable to afford a home of their own, they lived with Annie's parents at Bradshaw Street, Lutwyche.

Ever mindful of his responsibilities as a father, Eli searched earnestly for a better job. When Brisbane's tumultuous General Strike occurred in 1912, he astutely realized that the Queensland Tramways Company would not be re-employing many of its striking employees. He applied immediately and his quick action gained him the position of motorman.

This job became his passion. For over 20 years, Eli worked out of the Light Street Tram Depot, driving trams on the Ascot and West End tram lines.[4] He enjoyed the responsibility and revelled in the fraternity and mateship that the Company offered. The family's social life soon came to evolve around work. Eli was an enthusiastic member of the Tramway Rifle Club and, in 1913, he was elected onto the Club's committee.[5] Annie also became an active member of the Tramway's Branch of the Red Cross, a cause she worked tirelessly for during the war years.[6] The family's future looked bright. The regular income of a motorman provided a comfortable lifestyle and their dream of having a home of their own home was within reach.

Regrettably, the declaration of war on 4th August changed everything. Believing it would all be over by Christmas, Eli volunteered almost immediately. Four weeks later, he departed Brisbane for overseas service on the "SS Omrah." Saying goodbye to his family caused him much heartache. His boys were one and three years old, and Annie was only months away from having her third child. She feared the months ahead without the support of her husband.

Eli was eager to do his bit to bring the war to a speedy end and extremely disappointed when the 9th Battalion disembarked in Egypt instead of France. For almost four months, they remained in the hot desert camp near the Pyramids. Although the intense training that they undertook during this time was a crucial preparation for the inexperienced army of volunteers, for Eli, who already had almost 7 years' military experience with the citizen militia, it was a frustrating delay. His only consolation was that the exhausting routine helped take his mind off home.

Homesickness was a serious affliction. Eli missed his family very much and anxiously waited for news about their baby's birth. Regrettably, it could take up to two months to receive a letter from Australia. A daughter was born on the 14th January, 1915, six weeks after the Battalion's arrival in Egypt, but it is probable the news did not reach Eli before the Gallipoli landing.

As a member of Lieutenant Duncan Chapman's No. 3 Platoon, Eli was one of the first ashore at Gallipoli. He was also one of the first casualties. During the charge from the beach, he incurred a significant injury that necessitated his immediate evacuation to a hospital ship. Official records refer only to a sprained ankle, but his condition was much more serious. He spent the next two months convalescing in No.1 General Hospital in Cairo.

Eli re-joined his unit at Gallipoli on the 17th June. After such a long stay in hospital, he returned with some apprehension. However, he was not prepared for the situation he met. A strong smell of death pervaded the Peninsula's hot summer air. Water was being rationed. There was a plague of flies and, in the trenches, diarrhoea was prevalent. Day and night, soldier's nerves were tested by the constant threat from Turkish artillery and sniper fire. Eli felt overwhelmed and feared what lay ahead. Fortunately, two days after his return, his Battalion withdrew from the firing line and was placed in reserve for rest. This welcomed reprieve allowed him time to adjust but Eli soon found no place on the Peninsula was safe. On the first day in reserve, one of the Battalion was hit by shrapnel.

By September, he had endured two months on the Peninsula and, like many others, his health was suffering. On the 15th, Eli reported to the

3rd Field Ambulance, barely able to walk. He was immediately transferred to the hospital ship, "Nevassa" where an initial diagnosis of lumbago was made. However, four days later, at 1st Auxiliary Hospital in Cairo, a spinal abscess was detected. Eli remained in hospital for almost four months.

When he was discharged, the Gallipoli Campaign had already ended. He re-joined the 9th Battalion in Egypt as they began another period of great hardship. For five weeks, at their Gebel Habieta desert camp, near the Suez Canal, his unit performed the arduous task of fortifying Egypt's defences. Their work was painstaking. Due to frequent sandstorms, as fast as they built trenches, the sand collapsed them. Eli also was increasingly frustrated by what he saw as another delay to their fight against the Germans.

In March 1916, welcomed orders were finally received to move to France. Eli was relieved. He proudly believed Australia's move to the Western Front would bring the war to a speedy conclusion and bring him a step closer to reuniting with his family and his new daughter, already one-year-old.

His first major engagement with the enemy occurred at the end of July, 1916. The 9th Battalion's mission was to take the small ruined farm village of Pozieres in the Somme valley. Their battle became a living hell fought under a relentless German artillery bombardment. At times howitzer shells were landing at the rate of one every three seconds.[7] One survivor recounted, *'All day long the ground swayed and rocked, backwards and forwards ... men were driven stark staring mad .... Any amount of them could be seen crying and sobbing like children, their nerves completely gone ... We were nearly all in a state of silliness and half dazed.'*[8] It is believed more Australians lie in the ground at Pozieres than any other battlefield in the world. The 9th Battalion lost a third of its men, including Eli's commanding officer, Lieutenant Duncan Chapman. While Eli was fortunate to leave the battlefield physically unscathed, the experience of Pozieres remained with him forever.

Incredibly, weeks later, on 19th August, the exhausted survivors were ordered to return to the frontline to face another hellish encounter. A few kilometres from the ruins of Pozieres, at Mouquet Farm, they met the enemy again. For almost 48 hours, a heavy barrage of German fire rained upon them and, over the next three days, courageous attempts were made to take the ruined farmhouse. Eli left Mouquet Farm suffering from a severe lack of sleep and with nerves shaken to the core. 47 men from his Battalion were killed and 125 were wounded.

After some much needed rest, the 9th Battalion moved north to the front line at Flers in the Ypres area. They arrived at the beginning of an extremely bitter winter. Freezing temperatures and constant rain created deplorable conditions and, over the next months, many soldiers succumbed to frost-bite and trench feet. For Eli, the severe cold increased his lumbago and muscle pain. His bouts of rheumatic pain became frequent and much more intense.

Mercifully, in late December 1916, the 9th was removed from the front line for nearly two months. Training schools were set up and Eli was eager to participate. He was pleased to be selected to join the 3rd Army Cookery School but, after attending only two weeks of the course, he fell ill with what doctors at Rouen again diagnosed as rheumatism. After two weeks' hospital rest, the pain eased and, on 6th March, Eli re-joined the 9th Battalion on the Somme battlefields.

As the cold, wet weather continued, the Australian line was stretched dangerously thin. On 15th April, the Germans took advantage of their weakness and launched a massive attack forcing four Australian battalions, including the 9th, into a desperate retreat. Many lives were lost and the village of Lagnicourt was quickly overrun. Although outnumbered, the 9th Battalion refused to accept defeat. They joined a daring counter-attack that took the Germans by surprise. Their courage and speed enabled Lagincourt to be retaken. It was a great triumph that did much to boost the Battalion's flagging morale.

Weeks later, another major ordeal was faced. The 9th entered the brutal fighting of the 2nd Battle of Bullecourt. Against intense machine gunfire and attacks from dreaded German flame throwers, an almost worthless gain of about 600 metres of damaged trenches was made at a cost of 161 casualties. Eli was exhausted by the endless cycle of battles but his dedication to duty did not wane.

By mid-1917, after serving almost two years on the frontline, his skills as a soldier were recognized. In July, Eli was promoted to Lance Corporal and then Temporary Sergeant. In this new role, he led a platoon in the Battle of Menin Road Ridge and the successful capture of the western edge of Polygon Wood. The operation inflicted heavy losses. On 20th September, as they passed through Chateau Wood, a

German flare detected their position and, for 30 minutes, in the early morning darkness, a heavy barrage of artillery descended upon them. A second bombardment followed at 5 a.m. that included gas shells. Despite mounting casualties, Eli and his platoon continued their advance. Ground was slowly made and, with artillery support, the Battalion was successful.

A week later, Eli's role in the war changed significantly. He was sent back to the Army Corps Cookery School and returned with a promotion to Sergeant Cook. In this new rank he took responsibility for the provision of hot meals to front-line troops, a task that was crucial to maintaining soldier health and morale. *'Stew and tea were brought up to the front line in great metal containers about three feet high.... Strapped to men's backs; each vessel held sufficient for about 40 men.'*[9] The work was heavy and exhausting. There were also many challenges. Maintaining the field cooking ranges, the "cookers", and keeping their fires alight during the progress of a march was extremely difficult. As well, his unit faced frequent danger when transporting food through muddy trenches, often under the cover of darkness.

Despite this, Eli remained highly committed to his new role. Battalion historian, Norman Harvey noted, *'Sergeant Coles, promoted from "A" Company, made a very efficient sergeant cook'* and on almost all occasions, he was able to get hot meals up to the troops in the front lines.[10] His outstanding efforts were appreciated by the troops and, as Sergeant Cook, Eli became very popular within the Battalion.

As the war progressed, his dedication to the welfare of soldiers in the trenches became almost obsessive. When given the opportunity to return to Australia, incredibly, Eli refused. He was allocated Special 1914 Leave of two months in Australia but, purposefully, made himself unavailable by volunteering for another short cookery course. It was a clever ruse, but unfortunately, it did not work. On completion of the training, Special Leave was again granted and this time, his superiors accepted no excuses. Eli departed England on "HMT Gaika" shortly before the war ended.

The soldiers on the "Gaika" received a magnificent hero's welcome. After a huge reception in Sydney, the 211 Queensland soldiers journeyed by special train to Brisbane and, at every station stop, large crowds gathered to honour them. They arrived at Brisbane's Central Station on New Year's Day. Among hundreds of well-wishers on the crowded platform were Annie and the children, beaming with excitement and pride. Their hearts leapt with joy, when Eli stepped from the train. He appeared fit and gallant in his Sergeant's uniform and, compared to the other bandaged and limbless veterans, it seemed he was unscathed by war. Eli's scars were hidden.

Like most returned soldiers, for Eli, the transition to normal family life was not easy. After four years' absence, he returned almost as a stranger to his children. Ernest, his eldest son, was now a nine-year-old lad, and he was meeting Jean, his four-year-old daughter, for the first time. Although desperate to re-establish connections with his family, so much had changed. What he had been experienced in the last four years was impossible to share and, for a time, he felt like an outsider.

Fortunately, the generous support of his old employer, the Brisbane Tramway Company assisted his repatriation. The Company guaranteed the jobs of employees who served in the war and re-employed them on pay rates that took into account their overseas service. Annual leave was also allowed to accrue which gave Elli the opportunity to spend some extended time with his family. The fraternity and mateship of Tramways' workers, who were largely ex-servicemen, also had a positive benefit on Eli's mental well-being.

Gradually, his old life was re-built. Another child, Stanley, arrived and a bigger and better home, "Khandala" was purchased at 61 Wesley Street, Lutwyche. Eli continued to enjoy his job as a motorman, and his leisure time became busily filled with the activities of the Tramways Rifle Club. Other high priorities in Eli's life were various returned soldiers' associations and veteran reunions. Over the next two decades, the Coles' family became active and well known members of their local community.

Sadly, in 1937, unexpected tragedy struck. After a brief illness, at the age of 53, Annie suddenly passed away. Eli was heartbroken. They had been married for 28 years of marriage and he missed his Annie greatly. Eli remained at 61 Wesley Street with his son, Alan and Alan's new wife, Una, but felt lost and acutely lonely.

Fortunately, some happiness returned to Eli when, while working his Ascot tram route, he made the acquaintance of Bertha Anna Morrison, also recently widowed. They enjoyed each other's company and, after a short romance, married. At 56 years of age, it was a new beginning for Eli. He moved into Bertha's residence at 303 Lancaster Road, Ascot, and continued working as motorman on the nearby tram route.

Seven years later, the contented life they established was disrupted by the Second World War. Eli's two sons and Bertha's two sons enlisted, and were posted overseas. Throughout the war years, Eli and Bertha faced enormous anguish and heartache. Thankfully, Eli's boys survived, but Bertha was not so blessed. Her eldest son was killed fighting in New Guinea and the other died in an air battle over the Netherlands. The losses had a devastating impact on the rest of Bertha's and Eli's lives.

For Eli, solace was found in his firm belief in the Anzac spirit. He clung to the virtues of mateship and service, and, by so doing, was able to gain some acceptance of the tragedy of war. Remembrance was held dear and, for almost 40 years, Eli was a well-known and popular figure at Brisbane's Anzac Day parades. He believed it was his profound duty to honour and remember the lives of the fallen. At every Anzac Day parade, he would don the carefully kept uniform which he had worn during the First World War. As the years passed and the lines of Anzacs diminished, Eli, the tall, proud veteran wearing his original uniform, became a prominent feature of Anzac Day parades. In 1955, he gained almost celebrity status when a large photo of him wearing his 1917 issue uniform appeared in the Courier Mail. In his newspaper interview, he loudly and proudly proclaimed, *'I was in the first boat, you know!'*[11]

Eli's last Anzac Day parade was in 1954. Although 72 years old, he marched as tall and tenacious as ever in his immaculate uniform. When a reporter in the crowd asked about his thoughts during the march, he thoughtfully replied. *'As the march starts I think of our boat coming in. I can see us scuttling into the water, crossing the beach, and scrambling up the slopes. After that, it's all the boys who were killed.'*[12]

Two years later, on 13th September 1956, Sergeant Eli Coles quietly passed away. Family and friends mourned his death and reflected on the steely resilience that enabled him to survive the war and build a purposeful and happy post-war life. The wartime service of this proud 'Original' Anzac had been immense. Eli fought at Gallipoli, Pozieres, Mouquet Farm, Lagincourt, Bullecourt, Menin Road and Broodseinde Ridge and almost every major engagement that the 9th Battalion participated in. Throughout the war, his dedication to duty and to his mates was truly remarkable.

The grave of Sergeant Eli Coles is found in Brisbane's Lutwyche Cemetery.

Private William Arthur (Andy) Fisher

No. 362, C Company, 9th Battalion
(later A Company)

'Sunday, April 25th, a day that I will never forget as long as I live.'

One week after the Gallipoli landing, Private William Arthur Fisher, known as Andy, penned these words in a letter to his fiancé in Brisbane.[1] As he lay wounded on a hospital ship, he vividly recounted to her the horror, tragedy and excitement he had experienced. He was unware Gallipoli would shape the rest of his life and inspire a lifetime dedication to public service.

Born in Liverpool, England on 12 May 1886, Andy was the second son of Phoebe and William Fisher. His father was a successful timber merchant whose lucrative business afforded the family a large comfortable home at 75 South Road, Liverpool and the employ of three servants. It was a privileged lifestyle that, sadly, became marred by misfortune and tragedy. Andy's father was a heavy drinker[2] whose frivolous activities sometimes strained family finances. In 1898, while returning home intoxicated, he stumbled in front of a train.[3] Andy was just 12 years old and away at boarding school when he learnt of his father's death.

Financial ruin for the family soon followed. With seven children to provide for, savings evaporated. Their family home had to be sold and rooms were rented in another family's house.[4] For Andy and his brother, Cecil, boarding school was a luxury that could no longer be afforded. Andy obtained a position as a printer's assistant and later worked as a lowly paid Liverpool canal boatman.[5] In 1911, seeking adventure, he joined the crew of the cargo ship "Persic" as an engine room fireman.

The First Ashore

The work was hot and exhausting but it provided the opportunity for travel and eventually a voyage to Australia.

Andy arrived in Sydney in 1912, two years before the outbreak of war. Eager for change and a new start, he left his ship and travelled north to Brisbane where work was found as a clerk for the John Burke Shipping Line. He rented a comfortable room nearby at 51 Sutton Street, Kangaroo Point, near Custom Ferry and looked forward to a secure and rewarding future. With his strong views on sobriety and the virtues of hard work, lessons learnt from his family's misfortunes, his success seemed almost assured.

Yet, when war was declared, Andy's aspirations and plans were quickly given up. Motivated by a fierce loyalty to the Empire, he was among the first to volunteer. The Fisher family also had a rich tradition of military service, which Andy was keen to continue. His father served as a Lieutenant in the Kings Liverpool Regiment and later as a Captain in the 1st Volunteer Battalion. His Grandfather was Colonel J. McCallum and eight Great Uncles were officers in the Royal Horse Artillery.[6] With pride and enthusiasm, Andy joined Queensland's 9th Battalion and, a month later, embarked on the "HMAT Omrah" for overseas service.

He recorded his first experience of battle in a letter to his fiancé, Anna, written on 3rd May, 1915. Surrounded by wounded and dying men on the deck of a hospital ship, his writing was sometimes a jumble of mixed emotions, but vividly described the Gallipoli landing. Although the trauma was still raw, Andy's words convey no hint of self-pity or complaint. Instead, repeatedly, he reported his intense pride and boasted a new Queensland identity. *'Our boys were great.... There was no stopping them. Great Scot, they did fight.'.... 'I expect you will think I am conceited. Well dear I am and proud to know that I was one of the 'Queenslanders' and it is something to be proud of...'* Astutely, he also predicted to Anna the historical significance of what had occurred, *'and I expect by this time the work of the Australians on Sunday April 25th is being talked about all over the world.'*

Andy's letter is important as it provides the earliest recorded eyewitness evidence that Lieutenant Chapman's boat was first to touch shore. It references the same criteria that war historian Dr Charles Bean used, decades later, to determine the first ashore. Andy wrote, *'I might say now dear, that the Queenslanders had the honour to be the first* to land and my company was the first to get there......... we hit the beach about 4.30, just about daybreak. Half of our chaps got out of the boat without anything happening.'

According to Andy, preparations for the landing began very early that Sunday morning. His Company left the battleship, "HMS Queen" at about 2 a.m. in rowboats towed by steam pinnaces. When near shore, the boats were released into the darkness and, quickly and stealthily, Andy and the other rowers in the rowboats manned their oars. With each stroke of the oar, he waited and wondered if the landing would be a surprise. Duty and the objectives of the day weighed heavily on his mind. *'You see, we the landing party, or I should say the covering party, had to drive the Turks back and hold them while the others landed. Our orders were that we were to 'take that hill at all costs,' and that 'the success of the landing depended on us'. 'We had a letter from Lord Kitchener telling us that the position we were about to take was almost impregnable, and could only be taken with great sacrifice and he said lots of other things, I can't remember.'*

Andy's boat hit the beach just as daylight was breaking. *'half of our chaps* (were) *out of the boat without anything happening,'* when a single shot suddenly sounded from the hills above. *'We were just beginning to think that the Turks were not there when one shot was fired. Then the shots came in all directions.'* The rowers, including Andy, were the last to scramble from Chapman's boat. The gunfire had already become intense. A shot hit Andy's cap, throwing him backwards into the water. Quickly regaining his senses, he clambered to shore. *'My Anna, the bullets were flying around'.* Fortunately, all from Lieutenant Chapman's boat safely made the dash across the beach. Taking refuge at the base of a sandy hill, they paused for breath, and for the next few minutes, watched helplessly. *'We could see several chaps hit from the other boats' ... 'We lay at the foot of the hill for about 10 minutes, and the bullets did fly around.'*

As more and more men landed, companies and platoons became mixed on the narrow beach and soldiers quickly lost contact with their commanding officers. Bayonets were fixed. Then, *'There was one huge cry of "Come on, Queenslanders! Come on, the 9th!" and we went up that hill. It was great. Queensland ought to be proud of her boys.'* In the face of heavy fire, they scaled the vertical slopes. *'Of course we were not the only ones, but we were the first.'*

Plugges Plateau was quickly reached, but all formation was lost. Because of the rugged terrain, soldiers became scattered into small groups. According to Andy, *'It was about 7.30 when we reached the top of the hill.' 'I was feeling alright at this time, just a bit leg weary and of course wet through... It was terrible country to travel over, all hills and bushes.'* Moving forward, they fiercely stormed the Turkish trenches, *'we very soon got the Turks on the run, we chased them over the hills for about 3 miles, killing and wounding a good many. We lost very few going up the hill, although one of my pals was killed very early.' 'I expected to feel nervous when I got under fire for the first time, but I didn't get time to feel anything. I was too busy dodging them.'*

Early in the day, Andy's group penetrated far inland. He estimated he covered approximately 3 miles, almost 5 kilometres, and reached a position somewhere on the left flank, *'we moved over to the left and then the fun started.'* It is possible he joined Major Robertson who, Battalion history records, at about 9 a.m., gathered about 95 men of the 9th Battalion and went far to the left in the vicinity of Baby 700.[7] Times and actions mentioned by Andy also correspond closely to those described by Scout Sergeant Coe (aka Kemp), another member of the first boat ashore, whose small group fought on the left flank around the strategically important high ground of Baby 700 and Battleship Hill.[8]

As the morning progressed, Andy found himself in the midst of an intense battle as the Turks staged a major counter-attack. *'.. the order came along that the Turks were advancing on the left in large numbers... It simply rained bullets and shrapnel all day... Our chaps were dropping all over the place. Anna, it was hot!'* Despite this, defiantly, they held on. The position they were holding suddenly became crucial. If they lost the left flank, the Turks would easily enfilade the centre and right flanks.

There were many close calls. Early in the day, a piece of shrapnel hit Andy in the head. Although dazed for a few minutes, he carried on. Later, *'half of one of my tunic pockets (got) blown away. I then stopped another with my entrenching tool.'* For three hours, Andy and his pals lay with their heads close to the ground as the Turkish fire intensified. About 2 o'clock, *'two chaps, one on each side of me were wounded.' 'I lay there expecting to get one every second and never expecting to ever get out of it.... It was awful lying there and not being able to move.'* It was about 2.30 p.m. when six Turkish battalions bore down upon them. Valiantly they attempted to hold the slopes, but by 4 o'clock the high ground was lost. The order to retreat was welcomed, but any movement under such heavy fire proved almost impossible. *'We got up and ran. I managed to fall over and get left. I got up and made for a gully and had just reached it when a lump of shrapnel got me in the arm. It turned me round, and I found the bottom sooner than expected. I lay there for some time; I hurt my back a little and could hardly move. I couldn't see any of our chaps and didn't know which way to go.'*

Incredibly, despite his dire predicament, with courage and some good luck, Andy survived. Exhausted, traumatized and suffering the severe pain of a shattered arm and damaged back, he crawled in what he hoped was the right direction. In the darkness, he met an Indian Battery and a few 9th Battalion men who pointed him in the right direction and, after more than two hours, he reached the safety of the beach. *'What a sight there was there! Hundreds of our chaps lying there wounded. I was feeling pretty bad and my arm was quite numb.'*

Late that evening, Andy left the beach's chaos for the overcrowded hospital ship, "Clan McGillivray". On-board, the huge and overwhelming number of casualties meant nurses could only provide basic care. When loaded with its bloody cargo, the "Clan McGillivray" left for Alexandria, 1050 kilometres away but, by the time it reached Egypt, all hospitals were overflowing. The ship was turned away and another seven days passed before Andy was finally admitted to a hospital on Malta. It was on this voyage that he penned his letter to Anna.

After three weeks' recuperation on Malta, Andy was sent back to Gallipoli. With Fred Thomas, another wounded mate from the first boat ashore, he re-joined the 9th Battalion in the trenches on the forward slope of Bolton's Ridge on 23rd May. The situation he met was grim. The campaign had turned into stationary trench-warfare and the men were suffering greatly. As well as the heat, flies, poor sanitation, scarcity of water and sickness, there was the constant threat of Turkish artillery and sniper fire.

By August, sickness was spreading rapidly. 30% of the Battalion, including Andy, were evacuated that month. Because of poor sanitation and contaminated water, he contracted a severe case of enteric typhoid fever. Two months were spent in Cairo's hospital and then he was transferred to 'a concentration camp for convalescent enteric cases'[9] at Port Said. A month later, with his health showing no signs of improvement, orders came for Andy to return for three months of convalescence in

Australia. He left the war on 13th December, 1915 on the transport "Wandilla" with 314 other wounded and sick Gallipoli veterans.

The Queensland contingent on-board reached Brisbane's Central Railway Station on the 18th January, 1916. Anna Kruse, the young dressmaker from Kangaroo Point, stood among the large, cheering crowd of enthusiastic well-wishers, eager to be re-united with her sweetheart. After an emotional reunion, because of his acute typhoid fever, Andy was taken immediately to the Military Hospital at Kangaroo Point. Fortunately, Anna lived only a couple of streets away. She became a regular and much cherished visitor who greatly helped his recovery. At the end of his three months convalescence period, there were obvious improvements to his health. However, to Andy's dismay, medical officers decided he remained unfit for further active duty. On 21st March 1916, he was reluctantly discharged from the army.

Transition to civilian life was relatively trouble-free. His old room at Sutton Street was available to rent, and he quickly found a job as a bookkeeper. More importantly, Anna accepted his proposal of marriage. They wed on 26th May, just two months after his discharge, in a small low key ceremony, without guests, at St Pauls Presbyterian Church in Leichardt Street, Spring Hill.[10] Unable to afford a home of their own, they lived with Anna's family at 58 Holman Street, Kangaroo Point. Within a year, their first son, Alexander, was born.

Compared to most veterans, Andy's post-war life seemed fortunate. However, Gallipoli had forged in him an overpowering commitment to mateship and duty. He was bitterly disappointed and frustrated by his discharge from the army and, as if to compensate, his patriotism and commitment to the war effort increased tenfold. War and duty dominated his thoughts. Determined to carry on the fight at home, he became an extreme advocate, rigid and almost fanatical in his beliefs.

With boundless energy, he also worked constantly to improve the welfare of returned and serving soldiers by taking many leadership roles. When the Queensland Returned Soldiers Association was formed in early 1916, he was one of its first members and, with an ambitious zeal, worked to promote its objectives. At the first Federal Congress of the state organizations held in Brisbane in September, 1916, Andy attended as one of Queensland's delegates (accompanied by another member from 'the first boat ashore', Claude Henderson). When the

Australia-wide Returned Sailors and Soldiers Imperial League, the RSSILA, the forerunner of today's RSL, was formed, Andy was elected as a committee member and Honorary Treasurer of the Queensland Branch.[11] He also was a diligent worker on the RSSILA's many sub-committees and Honorary Treasurer of the new Residential Club for Ex-serviceman.[12] Eager to do more, in February 1917, he applied for the position of State Secretary but was unsuccessful. Undaunted, his ambitious passion continued and, in November 1917, Andy's dedication and abilities were recognized. For the next five years, he held the powerful position of State Secretary of the RSSILA.[13]

The workload was heavy, but Andy relished the job. He did not confine his duties to administrative tasks but, instead, spent much time lobbying politicians, unions and employers for a better deal for veterans. In particular, he devoted much energy to a campaign to achieve preferential employment of returned soldiers.[14]

The first years of his tenure as Secretary were tumultuous. As Australia became war-weary, the number of volunteers plummeted (from 165,942 enlistments in 1915 to 45,101 in 1917)[15] and, in response, the government sought to introduce conscription. In the fierce referendum debate that followed, Andy, as Secretary of the RSSILA, was able to exert much power and influence. He became a vocal leader and controversial activist for conscription, engaging in many public meetings, debates and lectures.

In Queensland, the debate grew dangerously volatile, with ultra-loyalists like Andy unremorsefully fuelling the rising tension. Using his position as RSSILA Secretary, Andy encouraged open hostility towards all anti-war demonstrations and workers' organizations such as the IWW (International Workers of the World). On the pretence of maintaining 'law and order', he advocated the use of RSSILA members as a vigilante movement to combat anti-conscription sentiment.

When Queensland's Labour government, led by Premier T. J. Ryan, publicly opposed Prime Minister Billy Hughes' campaign for conscription, Andy's involvement in vigilantism and undercover surveillance increased markedly. He shared the Prime Minister's concern about perceived disloyal activities in the 'rogue state' of Queensland and supported his decision to create a Commonwealth Police Force that could report on the subversive activities of those opposed to the war or the Commonwealth government. Ignoring the RSSILA's commitment to political neutrality, Andy formed a close association with this new Police Force. It consisted initially of 50 plain clothes officers, almost all of whom it stationed in Queensland. Leading Queensland historian, Raymond Evans noted 'Most of the constables initially appointed were returned soldiers, many of whom were directly recommended for the positions by W.A. Fisher, State Organiser of the Returned Sailors and Soldiers Imperial League of Australia (RSSILA).'[16]

As tensions continued to escalate, Andy's activism led him into trouble. On 29th July, 1918, with two other returned soldiers, he was arrested after almost instigating a riot in Brisbane's Domain Park. That Sunday afternoon, opposing organizations, the Returned Soldiers Association and the Industrial Council, held large rallies. When the soldiers' meeting ended, Andy and six other ex-servicemen moved menacingly toward the nearby Industrial Council meeting. They arrived as returned soldier and anti-war campaigner, 'Gunner' Taylor was addressing the crowd of approximately 1500 citizens, and immediately began some vigorous heckling. The speaker was knocked from his platform and later physically assaulted by Andy and his mates. With tempers flaring, a riot seemed inevitable. Fortunately, the anti-war radicals were committed to peaceful demonstration and responded only with song, loudly singing their anthem, "The Red Flag." The soldiers met this challenge with equally loud voices singing "Rule Britannia" and "Australia Will Be There".[17] Within minutes, an extremely dangerous situation dissipated into a light-hearted and somewhat comical duelling rendition of songs. The police quickly arrested Andy and two others. However, although regarded as instigators, they charged them with only the minor infringement of creating a public disturbance.

Over the next two years, anti-radical hysteria and xenophobia continued to escalate in Australia. In Brisbane, sentiments often reached fever pitch with targeted attacks made on socialists and other elements of society considered dis-loyal. In almost all these incidents, the attackers were ex-servicemen and Andy was a chief protagonist and often the leader.

On the night of 24th March 1919, Brisbane witnessed one of its most disturbing events, the Red Flag Riots. The previous day, minor scuffles had broken out in the Domain when 1000 people gathered to hear unionists and leftists speak on rights, revolution and militarism.

That evening, the volatility escalated when a large crowd of loyalist ex-servicemen alarmingly approached the headquarters of the Russian Workers' Association in Merivale Street, South Brisbane. The members inside felt so threatened, they fired warning shots above the oncoming crowd. The pack dispersed but, in response, the next night, between 7000 to 8000 men, chiefly ex-servicemen, assembled at North Quay calling for blood and talking of arson. Many carried revolvers while others were armed with home-made 'jam-tin' bombs. Under the banner of a large Australian flag, they marched across Victoria Bridge, singing 'Australia will be There" with interspersed chants of "Burn them out! Hang them!"[18] Waiting anxiously at Merivale Street were two lines of police with bayonets fixed. The fighting that followed lasted over two hours. 'Gunshots rang out, as rocks, bricks and bottles flew through the air.' Over 100 men received bayonet wounds, between 14 and 19 police were injured and ambulance evacuated 19 ex-servicemen. When peace was finally restored, the Russian Hall was almost completely destroyed. When a deputation of ex-servicemen responsible for the damage, were invited by the police to tour the wrecked building to rouse out any unionists or leftists still hiding inside, Andy's prominent role in the riot became clear. The leader of the deputation was Andy.[19]

Involvement in vigilante activities continued throughout 1919 and, often, it seemed, Andy had police approval. On 21st October, trouble arose again. While Prime Minister Billy Hughes was giving an election campaign speech in Brisbane's Albert Square, a blackboard with the slogan "Vote Labour" and "Next Prime Minister T. J. Ryan" was displayed from the office window of the Australian Building Industry Employees Union in the nearby Kent's Building. The sign caused outrage and, in response, several returned soldiers, including Andy Fisher, quickly left the Prime Minister's side and stormed the office displaying the offending propaganda. After battering down the door, a clerk and a female worker were assaulted. Office furniture and records were cast into the street. Chairs and tables were damaged, and they took £7 and 10 shillings from the cash box. Multiple witnesses identified Andy as the leader. '*Two men rushed up ahead of the others. A tall man with a grey suit put his shoulder up against the door. The crowd closed round and the door burst open. Mr Fisher was the man in the grey suit.*'[20] The arrest of Andy and two other soldiers followed, but they received only a minor charge of wilfully and unlawfully damaging a Yale lock and door frame. Incredibly, at their trial, eyewitness testimonies were disregarded, and the jury found them 'not guilty'. It was argued the ex-servicemen had a right to enter and remove offensive material.[21]

Although Andy's vigilante actions often gained public support within the RSSILA, there was a growing concern that the official policy of political neutrality was being flouted and the organization's image was being damaged. Andy was reluctant to give up his position, but realized it was time to move on. As a paid employee of the RSSILA, he could not hold any official political or union positions. By resigning, he could enter politics.

In 1921, a new phase was heralded in Andy's life when he won a seat on the South Brisbane City Council as alderman for Ward No 4, South Brisbane.[22] His workload was heavy again, but Andy found the job satisfying and he made many important achievements. Substantial road improvements such as the concreting of Grey Street in South Brisbane were initiated and, in 1922, he successfully campaigned for the Council's acquisition of the Brisbane Cricket Ground. Later, Andy worked to promote its further development as the venue for Brisbane's first test matches[23] and, thus, played an important role in establishing the iconic sports stadium known today as the 'Gabba.' As always, his major focus was on the welfare of returned soldiers. In 1923, his hard-fought campaign for the remission of council rates for incapacitated returned soldiers and sailors was finally won.[24]

Despite his many duties as an alderman, Andy also remained active in various other areas of public service. He was a founding member of the Queensland Liquor Reform League, and in April, 1923, was made Secretary of the Queensland Football Association.[25] He was also a founder of the Returned Soldiers Soccer Club. As well, his devotion to the RSSILA's work did not diminish. Soon after becoming Alderman, Andy accepted the position of Honorary Secretary of Moreton District branch of the RSSILA.[26]

However, by 1924, after almost 10 years of intense community service and political activism, Andy was weary. Two weeks before the South Brisbane election, he withdrew from the contest.[27] He left the public arena of politics to take a less stressful job with the Brisbane City Council as a clerk and reader of electric light meters.[28] This change and its slower pace allowed Andy for the first time in many years to enjoy family life. However, his interest in and involvement in community affairs did not diminish. He remained a committee member and office holder for a wide range of organisations, including the 9th Battalion Association,[29] Queensland Cricket Association[30] and the South Brisbane State School Committee.[31]

When World War 2 broke out, with pride and much anxiety, Andy watched his three sons enlist. In 1940, when the threat from Japan intensified, his own sense of duty compelled him at the age of 54 to also join the army. Andy became Pay Sergeant in the District Accounts Office and remained in service for over five years, enjoying the comradery of military life.

After retiring in February 1948, he enjoyed his last years at the family home, "Oban" in School Road, Yeronga. Andy remained extremely active, with sport occupying much of his time. Lawn bowls became a popular pastime, and he closely followed his beloved soccer and cricket teams. Among his many pursuits, his most valued involved re-unions with ex-servicemen and meeting up with old army mates. As he grew older, their comradeship continued to hold great significance.

He regarded Anzac Day as the most sacred day of the year. The march was his means of commemorating war's loss and sorrow while also celebrating the mateship it forged. At the 1936 March, a newspaper journalist asked him about the meaning of Anzac Day. Andy thoughtfully replied,

'A day full of sadness, pride and joy. At the dawn service.... The most sacred of all, beautiful in its stillness, I live again through that eventful day of April 25, 1915. My mind wanders back to that long tow to the shore. I see again the outline of the hills, that mad rush up the steep slopes. I see again poor little Ginger C—fall by my side, the first man I saw killed. I live through it all again, and feel the sorrow and joy ....There is a more joyful side to Anzac Day... when old comrades of all ranks meet once a year... for amongst the men who faced the horrors of war together there is a comradeship which time will never sever.'[32]

Andy's death was sudden and unexpected. At the Anzac Day parade in Brisbane in 1958, while warming up for the march with his old mates from the 9th Battalion, the 72-year-old veteran collapsed and died. It seemed a fitting end to a life defined by war and mateship.

Private William Arthur Fisher's ashes were interred at Mt Thompson Memorial Gardens, Holland Park, Brisbane.

Private Frederick Young Fox

No. 389, C Company, 9th Battalion
(later Captain, 49th Battalion)

In 1914, Fred Young Fox Junior was the embodiment of the Australian bush legend. He was 20 years old, physically strong, a skilled scrub rider and bushman who loved outback life and relished its mateship and egalitarianism. When war was declared, these traits made him a natural and popular leader. He rose rapidly through the ranks from Private to Lieutenant and became Captain at the young age of 23 years. Sadly, the experience of war stole much from his life.

Fred was born in 1894 into one of central Queensland's pioneering pastoral families. From his father, he inherited his love of the land. Frederick Young Fox Senior had purchased an unimproved isolated block on the Isaacs River, halfway between Mackay and Clermont and, through hard work and further acquisitions, he turned it into the historic "Bombandy Station." It was the Fox family's home for 40 years and, throughout Queensland, gained a reputation for breeding cattle and fine racehorses.[1]

The early years on Bombandy were challenging, but Fred regarded growing up on the remote station as a wonderful adventure. Ponies and horse riding were favourite pastimes. With his two older brothers, Sydney and Norman, and sister Madge, there was always much to explore, and the large Aboriginal camp nearby meant playmates were plentiful. As the station developed, a substantial settlement grew with stockmen, casual workers and travellers coming and going. For a young boy, the bustle of station life was fascinating. Fred especially enjoyed the regular visits of the Clermont stagecoaches. He would sit and wait eagerly to hear the sound of the coachman's bullock horn blown from miles away to signal their approach.[2]

By 1901, Bombandy had become a fine homestead sitting proudly on the picturesque banks of the Isaacs River. It was renowned for its hospitality with many of the district's social events hosted there. The region's first picnic races held at Bombandy in 1903 were something nine-year-old Fred would never forget. Drays, buckboards, buggies, packhorses and prancing steeds brought visitors from afar, and a mass of snowy white tents suddenly appeared around Fred's home. Over the next two days, he was captivated by the horse races, the fancy ball, sports day, and dance that was held.[3] Such events inspired Fred's lifelong love of country life.

With no schools nearby, Fred was educated in Rockhampton. He boarded with family friends and attended Central Boys State School and, then, Rockhampton Boys Grammar School.[4] When his high school years finished in 1910, the 17-year-old rushed back to Bombandy. He looked forward to his future as a grazier, running the station with his brothers and enjoying life on the land. Throughout Central Queensland, the Fox boys became known as expert scrub riders and skilled stockmen.

Regrettably, Fred's future was not as he envisaged. Fred Fox Senior realized Bombandy Station could not support his three sons and their future families. In 1912, he, therefore, attempted to expand his holdings by purchasing the neighbouring property, 'Carfax'. This well- intentioned plan, unfortunately, created unsustainable financial stress and led to heartbreak. One year later, the banks forced the sale of Bombandy.[5] The Fox boys were devastated. Syd and Norman moved onto 'Carfax' while young Fred left home to work as a stockman on Yaccamunda Station near Charters Towers.

When war was declared, it took more than a week for the news to reach him. Fred was jackarooing on the Belyando River, far to the north of Clermont. His reaction was immediate. With great haste, he left Yaccamunda with his horses and headed directly to Carfax, a ride of more than 300 kilometres. There, he persuaded his brother, Norman to join him and, together, they rode a further 300 kilometres to the recruitment office in Rockhampton.

When the brothers arrived, the war was already four weeks old. The skilled horsemen were eager to join the Light Horse Brigade, but Rockhampton's enlistment quota was already filled. With no other option, Fred and Norman reluctantly left their horses and, on 4th

The First Ashore

September, enlisted as infantry soldiers. From Rockhampton, they travelled by train to the bustling new training camp at Enoggera and joined the 9th Infantry Battalion's C Company.

Just two weeks later, with little military training, the brothers boarded the troopship, "SS Omrah", the first to leave Queensland for war. Events were moving at a reckless speed, but Fred and Norman were undaunted. Bursting with patriotism, they believed they were embarking on a great overseas adventure. In Egypt, their optimism and high spirits continued. They explored the Pyramids, swam in the Suez Canal and revelled in Cairo's sights and exotic delights.

However, by the end of their third month, Egypt's desert was losing its appeal. Eager to join the battle against the Germans, they and their mates clung to rumours that the 9th would soon be sent to France. Unexpected orders to move to the Greek island of Lemnos, instead, brought enormous frustration. For five long weeks on the island, the 9th carried out fatigue work, guard duty and long pointless marches. Two more restless weeks followed on board a troopship moored in the bay as they waited for the rest of the Australian division to arrive.

Finally, on Saturday 24th April, battle orders were received. At about 11 a.m., Fred's A Company (amalgamated from the original A and C Companies) was transferred to the battleship "HMS Queen". His excitement was hard to suppress. Later that day, the "Queen" led the armada of warships, destroyers and transports out of Lemnos harbour towards the Turkish coast.

After a sleepless night, at about 2 a.m., orders came for the troops to fall in on deck. With well-rehearsed precision, disembarkation began. Fred and the rest of his section silently scaled down the rope ladders and positioned themselves in their allocated boat. Each landing boat, carrying two and a half sections or about 30 men,[6] was fastened to two others and then attached to a steam tow. Fred felt some reassurance as he sat beside his good mate and fellow jackeroo from central Queensland, Peter Stuart, a rower in one of the boats in No. 1 Tow. Quietly and nervously, they waited for cast off but, at the last moment, unexpected orders were shouted from above. Some soldiers, including Fred, were to move to another boat.[7] With speed, he reluctantly left Peter's side and clambered into the leading life-boat of No. 1 Tow, commanded by Lieutenant Duncan Chapman.

On their five kilometre journey towards shore, Fred anxiously searched the darkness for a sign of the enemy. Dawn would soon reveal their approach. About 50 yards out, the lifeboats were unhitched, and the order given, 'Down oars'. Nervously, the rowers pushed the boats the last few metres. Fred waited for the bang of gunfire. A ladder was put down from the bow of his boat and men scrambled ashore. Still, the morning remained silent. Fred clearly recalled moving up the beach and dumping his pack before the Turks fired one shot.[8]

As boat upon boat landed on the small crowded beach, the situation became chaotic and confused. Fred's mate, Peter Stuart, who landed from the second or third boat of No. 1 Tow, recorded he lost contact with Fred almost immediately. When Peter left the beach, he moved inland to the right with a group of about 40 soldiers, but he recalled he did not see or hear of Fred or Norman on the right flank at all that day.[9] It is possible the Fox brothers, upon leaving the beach, took a route towards the left flank. Fred recalled he progressed far inland early in the day and reached a position where he could see the narrow straits of the Dardanelles. Other members of the first boat ashore, who fought on the left flank, Scout Sergeant Fred Coe and Private Archie Reynolds made similar claims. Like them, Fred also recalled that late in the day, there was a massive Turkish counter-attack, moving southwards, which forced their retreat.[10]

Fred and Norman were fortunate to survive the first day. Many mates were not so lucky. In a letter to his parents, Fred later wrote,

Just a line to let you know that Norman and I are still both well. We all had a rough time in landing. In fact, the only way I can describe things is that hell seemed to be let loose. Poor old Peter (Stuart) was seen hit over the eye the first day.... Since then he has not been heard of........ Norman and I have had marvellous luck in not being put out of action, and I fancy the hardest is over. Allan Radcliffe is missing, and Bert Hamilton is wounded through the thigh.'[11]

For almost four months, the Fox brothers endured constant dangers on Gallipoli. Every day, their resilience and courage were tested. In a letter home, three weeks after the landing, Fred described one near miss, *'Jack, Norman and I were at work with the rest of the company when a shrapnel burst over our heads, a piece of which went through Jack's arm above the elbow and came out the opposite side.'*[12] Week after week, unsuccessful bids were made to break the Turkish lines. Fred's last significant engagement occurred on the 29th June. The Battalion was ordered to create a diversion that would prevent the Turks sending reinforcements south. To meet the objective, the men had to be highly visible and to advance at all costs until the Turks were fully engaged. Their sacrifice was unavoidable. At 1 p.m. the attack began, and the Turks responded immediately. Over 100 men were lost in half an hour.[13] The enemy's heavy shrapnel and shellfire continued all afternoon and into the evening but, fortunately, the day before, Fred, Norman and Peter Stuart had built a sheltered dugout for themselves. In his diary Peter wrote, *'(we) had dug a pretty good posie for ourselves.'* He described, *'Shells bursting about all roads – wounded coming in galore....'* and the next day, he lamented, *'It is pitiful to see the line of dead laid out over there. Alas, this war is awful. Fred's great mate Edward Williams was killed yesterday.'*[14]

As the months progressed, the Campaign's constant stress strained the nerves and health of every soldier. Fred had to be hospitalized on the 16th August and Norman two weeks later. While Norman succumbed to 'diarrhoea', a sickness prevalent in the trenches because of poor diet and a lack of sanitation, Fred's diagnosis was 'debility.' This was an ambiguous term used to describe a wide range of conditions. His mate, Peter, made a more apt assessment. In his diary, on 16th August, he simply stated Fred was *'played out.'* Four months of continuous service had damaged him physically and mentally. By August, the morale and mental health of the whole Battalion was in serious decline. Peter wrote, *'16/8/15. Fred Fox, with a lot more that are sick, – played out - are leaving today – going away for a spell – about time. 16 weeks was in the trenches. Ought to send the whole 9th away. They are all done.'*[15] Fred was evacuated to Cairo and sent to the Convalescent Camp at Helouan for seven weeks, while Norman was hospitalized at Ghezireh. For the first time since leaving Rockhampton, the brothers were separated.

However, as their good health gradually returned, fortune favoured them. Instead of returning to Gallipoli, Fred and Norman received postings to Zeitoun, a training base just north of Cairo. Fred was sent for two months officer training commencing on the 13th October and, weeks later, Norman arrived to take a position as assistant instructor at Zeitoun's Imperial School of Instruction. Fred completed his course diligently, and he left Zeitoun, comforted by the knowledge that his brother remained stationed at the School, far from the dangers of battle.

He re-joined his Battalion as it moved to Egypt to begin the laborious and almost impossible task of constructing trenches in the desert sand at Gebel Habeita, near the Suez Canal. Four weeks later, unexpectedly, war dealt a most tragic blow. News came from Zeitoun that while his brother was instructing troops on the use of trench mortar, a grenade accidentally exploded. Norman was critically injured.[16] Desperate to be at his brother's side and with no time to seek leave, Fred went AWOL. He rode alone through the night across a dangerous and inhospitable desert to reach Zeitoun, 120 kilometres away, the next day, but, sadly, his determined effort was in vain. Norman's abdominal injuries were severe. He died shortly after being admitted to hospital on the 18th February.[17] Fred was devastated. He returned to Habeita, numb and overwhelmed with grief. There was an expectation there would be serious disciplinary action to face, but his dangerous desert trek earned much admiration, and superior officers were obliged to turn 'a blind eye' to his absence.

For Fred, more anguish followed a week later. Too soon after losing his brother, an unexpected transfer to the newly formed 49th Battalion removed from the crucial support of his 9th Battalion mates. His consolation was that his good mate Peter Stuart, who had been at Zeitoun at the time of Norman's death, was also transferred. For both men, the move also brought important promotions. On the 17th March, Fred and Peter became 2nd Lieutenants. The new role was another challenging burden, but it provided Fred with a much needed distraction from the grief that was consuming him.

On the 5th June, 1916, the 49th Battalion left on the transport ship, "Arcadian" for France. Fred's eagerness to join the battle that he and his brother enlisted for was now enhanced by a reckless determination to avenge the loss of Norman's life. His first major encounter with the enemy was at Mouquet Farm, north of Pozieres. A series of desperate and unsuccessful attempts to capture the shattered farmhouse on the hill had been carried out over the preceding weeks. On the 3rd September, the 49th joined the 51st and 52nd Battalions in a last attempt. At 5.10 am, Fred's Battalion led an attack on the extreme right and, in successive waves, they made good progress. Casualties were heavy, but important trenches were taken and, momentarily, the farm was captured. When, at 8 a.m., the Germans unleashed a heavy artillery barrage that forced the Australians to retreat, Fred's 49th Battalion refused to fall back. Lieutenants F. Kay, R. Gore, R. Colvin and 2nd Lieutenant Fred Fox tenaciously held on and managed to retain important trenches. For their actions, these officers were later recommended for honours.[18] Fred also received congratulations from Sir Douglas Haig. As well, Major-General Sir H.V. Cox, the commander of the 4th Australian Division, sent a personally written message commending his gallant conduct.[19]

The honour and respect that the 49th Battalion gained at Mouquet Farm came at a heavy cost. They incurred 406 casualties in three days of fighting. Seven officers were killed, and another seven wounded.[20] Fred was the only officer to leave the battleground unscathed.[21] Mentally, however, he was exhausted and in great despair. One of the officers fatally shot was Lieutenant Peter Stuart.[22] Since leaving Rockhampton, Fred and Peter had been almost inseparable. Besides his brother, he was his greatest friend and support. Suddenly, Fred faced the war alone. Breaking military protocol, he made it his immediate responsibility to personally notify Peter's parents in Rockhampton via cable.[23]

While adjusting to the tragedies of 1916, late that year, Fred was fortunate to be relieved from battle. He was seconded for three months to the 13th Training Battalion at Codford in England. In this new role, with full promotion to Lieutenant, Fred helped re-train wounded and invalided soldiers for return to the trenches. His empathy and experience of war equipped him well.

From Codford, he returned on the 2nd February, 1917 to the 49th Battalion in France. Although the worst of the harsh winter of 1916-17 was over, Fred prepared himself for a long and difficult stint in the trenches. Four arduous months later, there was some reprieve. After a transfer to the new 69th Battalion, Fred was sent in June to the Clapham Bombing School to train as a bombing instructor. Each day became an aching reminder of Norman's death and Fred began to look forward to the day he could return to the misery of the trenches.

He was pleased when manpower shortages on the front caused the 69th Battalion to be dismantled, enabling him to re-join his 49th Battalion. Two weeks later, in October 1917, Fred's skills and dedication to duty were again recognized. The 23-year-old boy from the bush was promoted to Captain and placed in charge of his own Company. Accountable for the lives of 200 men, Captain Fox remained in the bitterly cold frontline trenches throughout the winter, leading various defensive actions.

As the winter ended, in February 1918, Fred was grateful to receive three weeks' leave in England. As on his previous trips, he was a frequent visitor to the London home of Mrs Annie Wheeler, an old family friend from Dingo in central Queensland[24] who had become known as the "Mother of Anzacs". When war was declared, Mrs Wheeler was visiting London with her daughter, Portia. Rather than return home, the pair stayed to provide care for central Queensland's soldiers. She corresponded with them, forwarded their mail, advanced funds, supervised hospital stays and sent Queensland's newspapers updates about their progress. Her efforts were appreciated and admired and, today, she is regarded as one of Queensland's finest World War 1 heroes.[25]

Although Fred keenly supported Mrs Wheeler's work, the real motivation for his frequent visits was Mrs Wheeler's 21-year-old daughter, who had captured his heart. Usually when on leave, the young couple would enjoy sightseeing, the theatre and even some wining and dining at the Savoy. However, during Fred's February leave, Portia had little time for romance. Because her mother had recently suffered a breakdown. Portia had taken over her huge workload. With over 1500 soldiers on her books, van loads of parcels and hundreds of letters arriving each week for distribution,[26] there was little time for Fred.

When Fred re-joined his unit in France on the 2nd March, the Germans' major Spring Offensive had begun and the war was quickly turning against the Allies. The old Somme battlefields that had been paid for with the blood of thousands of soldiers in 1916 were lost. In this dire situation, Fred's battalion took up a position around Dernancourt. Outflanked by a massive German force, they fought gallantly in a battle that culminated on the 5th April with a 2½ hour barrage of high explosives and gas shells. The Australians suffered greatly but courageously they held their ground.

Weeks later, Fred took part in one of the most important battles of the war. The Germans, supported by tanks and flame-throwers, had quickly captured the village of Villers-Bretonneux and, at 10 p.m., on the eve of the 3rd anniversary of Anzac Day, the Australians responded with a daring and courageous counter-attack. After much hand to hand fighting, they eventually dislodged the enemy. It was during this ferocious assault that Fred's luck finally ran out. In the early hours of Anzac Day morning, a piece of shrapnel entered his leg above the left knee. It slid up the bone to his thigh, causing his leg to be badly mutilated. Fred left the battlefield in enormous pain.

Over two months were spent convalescing in England. As his leg gradually healed, his energy and strength slowly returned. He received orders to return to the front on 30th July 1918. Another major offensive had been launched. As Fred's Company engaged in the initial fighting around Bray, Fred braced himself for another cycle of battles and horrendous ordeals. However, to his delight, as they joined an attack against the dreaded Hindenburg Line's outposts, on the 18th September, an unexpected order came. Fred was selected as one of the first recipients of a new entitlement, "Special 1914 Leave", that gave 'original' Anzacs, like himself, two months' furlough in Australia.

Greatly relieved, he left the war on the 26th October, 1918,[27] hoping to be home before Christmas. His anticipation increased tenfold when, in waters off Africa, news reached their ship that the war had ended. However, instead of a joyous arrival in Australia, there was only disappointment. Because of the world-wide influenza pandemic, their ship was placed in immediate quarantine at Freemantle. Weeks later, when they reached Melbourne, another long quarantine period was endured. Fred and many other troops were extremely disgruntled and refused to travel further by ship. Using their own money, they bought rail tickets to Sydney and Brisbane.[28]

Fred finally reached Brisbane a few days after Christmas. Waiting anxiously to greet him was his sister, Gypsie, who had journeyed from Rockhampton. Their reunion was emotional and joyous, but the absence of Norman and Peter was painfully apparent. The guilt that Fred felt for returning home alone was difficult to hide.

Days later, Fred left his parents' home in Rockhampton with his father for Carfax Station.[29] He was eager to return. The hope of one day working again with his family on Carfax had sustained him throughout the war. Fred also remained determined to honour the lives of Norman and Peter by fulfilling their dream of returning to the bush. However, there were obstacles. His father and his brother, Sydney, doubted the ability of Carfax to support another person and instead persuaded Fred to take the position of manager at Iffley Station, an untamed isolated property 60 miles from Clermont, upstream on the Isaacs River.[30]

He took the disappointment in his stride, but discontent and frustration were to be common stumbling blocks in Fred's post-war life. Separation from Portia made repatriation more difficult. Almost a year after announcing their engagement,[31] Portia and her mother remained in London without the funds to return to Australia. Fortunately, as more soldiers returned home, word spread about the "Mother of Queenslanders" and slowly Mrs Wheeler's wartime work received public recognition. Eventually, public pressure was placed on the Commonwealth Government to pay for their return.

Fred met their ship in Sydney in 1919 and travelled with Mrs Wheeler and Portia, via Brisbane, to Rockhampton.[32] By then, they were well-known celebrities, welcomed everywhere as war heroes. In Central Queensland, the reception was overwhelmingly magnificent. At Rockhampton, over 5000 people waited to greet their train. Fred's pride was hard to contain. Dressed smartly dressed in his Captain's uniform, he was designated as Mrs Wheeler's official companion and given the challenging task of guiding her safely through the throngs of well-wishers. From the railway station, grateful soldiers slowly towed her car through crowded streets as thousands of cheering citizens followed behind. Upon reaching Leichardt Hotel, there was a large public reception[33] at which, to her great surprise, Mrs Wheeler was presented with keys to a new home at Emu Park, gifted by the citizens of Central Queensland.[34]

Although Fred and Portia were eager to be married, public commitments allowed no time for a wedding. During the first two months of 1920, Fred guided the Wheelers on a hectic tour of receptions held to honour them in almost every central Queensland town. He delighted in their public recognition but also impatiently looked forward to the day when life would return to normal. They eventually organized a wedding in March 1920 at Emu Park. After a short honeymoon was enjoyed at nearby Yeppoon, the couple travelled to Iffley Station.

For Fred and Portia, transition to their new post-war life was challenging. Iffley Station's isolation and rough living conditions starkly contrasted with the life Portia had led in London. She found the loneliness difficult. Also, the scars of war left Fred, like many veterans, unsettled and prone to stress. In the decades after the war, as he moved through eight different occupations, the young couple's home life often became chaotic. Fred also found consolation and comfort often in the company of his many wartime friends and, sometimes, this involved spending time and money at hotels. In the 1930s, a friend described him as 'a casualty of the first war.'[35]

Concerned about his wife's happiness, Fred left the loneliness of Iffley and returned to Carfax. Rather than live on the station, they rented a home in Clermont where Portia could enjoy the community and social life that Clermont offered. Fred owned a third share of Carfax, but his move to the station proved troublesome. His brother, Sydney, had managed Carfax independently for more than seven years and the property now strained to adequately support two families. When livestock prices fell, to keep Carfax viable, the brothers purchased a butcher shop in Clermont. Their aim was to generate an income by killing Carfax cattle and selling them through the shop. Portia invested £800 of her savings to finance the ill-fated venture.[36] As the price slump continued, Carfax Station's debts continued to rise and the butcher shop eventually had to be sold. Sadly, this was not enough. The sale of Carfax Station became inevitable. Fred and Portia lost everything.

Yet Fred's resilience and determination remained. He mounted one last bid to stay on the land. Fred's wartime friend, the famous 'Gallipoli sniper', Billy Sing, had recently walked off "Pernois", a sheep grazing property, 26 kilometres from Clermont. Billy selected this soldier settlement block in 1919 and, for five years, he bravely attempted to make a living.[37] However, like many soldiers who joined the soldier settlement scheme, he did not succeed. Fred optimistically overlooked this reality. A deal was made with Billy, and Fred moved his family onto "Pernois" in about 1925.[38]

The property was in heart break country and Fred's timing was unfortunate. The following year, the district suffered a severe drought. Son, Norman recalled his father's despair as he struggled to keep his flock alive. Despite desperate hand feeding, most of the sheep died. Then, *'when the drought broke, he lost the remainder of his flock, bogged after a heavy storm.'*[39] Disillusioned, Fred walked off Pernois in 1927.

He was a broken man and, in March that year, he declared himself bankrupt.[40] The experience delivered an enormous blow and, according to his son, it depressed and worried Fred for years afterwards.[41]

Portia and the children returned to live with her mother at Emu Park while Fred left for Brisbane in search of work. A temporary job was found as a stores clerk and, later, a better job was obtained with General Motors. When Fred was able to rent a small flat at Windsor, the family reunited.

At General Motors, Fred's dedication and diligence were quickly recognized. He received a promotion to the position of sales supervisor for north-western Queensland and, two years after losing "Pernois", the family happily returned to live in the country. His new job was well paid but, according to his son, Fred *'never seemed to save much – too many grazier and war time friends about and while he was travelling he lived in hotels.'*[42] Their first home was in Charters Towers but, in 1932, Fred was transferred to General Motors' larger Rockhampton office. Pleased to be back in Rockhampton, near old friends and family, he and Portia established a comfortable home at 193 Caroline Street.

It seemed their life was improving when, six months later, the Great Depression hit. General Motors was forced to close its Queensland operation and, suddenly, Fred was unemployed again. In an attempt to keep their house in Rockhampton, he found a job at the Mount Morgan mines but, it soon became obvious strenuous physical work was no longer an option for the war veteran. Like many soldiers who endured gas attacks during the war, Fred had developed lung problems. Once again, Portia was obliged to move back to her mother's house at Emu Park while Fred went to Brisbane to find work. In their dire situation, financial help was sought from the Repatriation Board and, in 1935, a small pension was granted.

Ever resilient, in Brisbane, Fred found work as a car salesman. A wide circle of friends and his affable nature ensured his success. By 1938, with commissions steadily growing, the family's fortunes again improved. A home was purchased at Ardoyne Road, Corinda and, soon after, they were able to buy their first motor car. However, Fred remained unsettled. His heart was in the country and he longed to return to the bush. When a job was offered with the well-known wool brokers and stock agents, Winchcombe Carsons at Charleville, he could not resist. Portia and the children remained at Corinda while Fred moved to Charleville.

The Second World War brought more change. Fred did not hesitate. On the same day that the Prime Minister declared war, he phoned Portia from Charleville to say he was on his way to Brisbane to join up.[43] He was commissioned immediately as Major and placed in charge of the Garrison Battalion at Cowan. A later transfer to the command of the army depots on the Darling Downs saw the family re-locate to Toowoomba. A new home was established on a small acreage, named "Sunning," in West Street.

Fred enjoyed his return to the familiarity of army life but, as the war progressed, his health declined significantly. An ulcer caused anxiety and his bronchial asthma and emphysema worsened. Ever resilient and dedicated to duty, he refused to accept the severity of his condition. However, by 1944, medical discharge from the army became inevitable.

Fred was only 50 when he reluctantly left the army. He was determined to remain active, and focused all his energy on one last project, the establishment of a poultry farm at "Sunning". Success was achieved but his health continued to worsen. Admissions to hospital became frequent.[44] Regrettably, in 1951, the poultry farm had to be sold.

Health problems plagued the last years of Fred's life. There was a new diagnosis of pulmonary fibrosis, a condition common to World War 1 veterans who had been exposed to mustard and chlorine gas. He was admitted to St Vincent's Hospital, Toowoomba for the last time on the 4th July, 1964. Two days later, Fred passed away, aged 70 years. The popular and gallant Anzac was deeply mourned by a loving family and a wide circle of friends.

Captain Frederick Young Fox was cremated at the Brisbane Crematorium on the 8th July, 1964.

Private Harold Reginald Roy Hansen

No. 70, A Company, 9th Battalion
(later Sergeant, A Company, 9th Battalion)

The distinguished war service of Harold Hansen surprised many of his friends and family. Prior to the war, the 18-year-old held a strong contempt for military life. Yet, when war was declared, he was one of the first volunteers. After landing with Lieutenant Chapman's first boat ashore, he served five gruelling months on Gallipoli and then fought gallantly on the Western Front, where he was promoted to Sergeant. On the battlefield, Harold, also known as Roy, was a true Anzac.

His attitudes before the war were incongruent with the soldier he later became. As a young lad with a headstrong dislike for authority, Roy resisted the tide of militarism spreading through Australia. When compulsory military training was introduced in 1911, he defiantly refused to take part. As a consequence, throughout 1912 and 1913, there were frequent court appearances. On the three occasions he was charged with disobeying the Defence Act and found guilty but boldly chose to ignore the court's directions.

Roy had grown up surrounded by conflicting views about the approaching war. His family's background and religion influenced his patriotic values and loyalty to the Empire. Roy's father, Peter Hansen, was a Danish born immigrant and his mother, Ann Clark, came from proud Irish Catholic stock. Her family, like many other Irish Catholic families of the time, held strong anti-English sentiments, which made them reluctant to join the citizen militia. When war was declared, very few Roman Catholics were among the first volunteers. (Protestants made up 86% of the 1st AIF.[1])

Roy, the first child of Peter and Ann Hansen, was the first born on

13th May 1895 in the working-class suburb of Woolloongabba. Two years later, another son, Peter, arrived. For the Hansen boys, life began happily and secure. In their neighbourhood, a large and loving extended family surrounded them. Their grandparents lived nearby and, a short walk away, in Amelia Street, was Uncle Hans, with his family of cousins and young playmates.

Sadly, the joy of childhood was short-lived. In 1901, when Roy was six years old, his father contracted pneumonia and died nine days later.[2] Roy's mother, devastated by the loss, struggled to raise her two sons alone but, less than 12 months later, she contracted tuberculosis and, on 14 November, 1903, also passed away.[3] Eight-year-old Roy and six-year-old Peter were orphaned.

Grieving and confused, the boys were taken from their Woolloongabba home to live with their grandmother, Mrs Mary Clark, a widow, who ran a busy lodging house at 437 Upper Edward Street in the City. Mrs Clark loved her grandchildren, but managing her business allowed her little time for the needs of two orphaned boys. Newspaper advertisements for her establishment proudly boasted *'no children allowed'*.[4] Six months after moving to the Edward Street house, Roy was the victim of an appalling crime. In a railway tunnel near Gloucester Street, the emotionally fragile young boy was cruelly assaulted. A fruit vendor from South Brisbane was later sentenced to three years' imprisonment.[5]

Fortunately, at 12 years of age, Roy was able to escape Brisbane and its painful memories. His grandmother sent him to Toowoomba to work and live with Mrs O'Brien, the well-respected head of an influential Irish Catholic family. Recently widowed, Mrs O'Brien owned and managed one of Toowoomba's largest grocery stores and the city's very successful flour mill, Defiance Flour. As an orphaned child herself, she felt much empathy for Roy. She provided a home and employed him as an apprentice yardman. For the next five years, Roy worked diligently and learnt his trade.[6] He held Mrs O'Brien in high regard and was forever grateful to her.

After gaining his qualification as a tradesman, in 1912 Roy, keen to seek new surroundings, travelled north to find work in Rockhampton. The next two years were turbulent. The influence of the O'Brien family's staunch Catholic, pro-Irish views, plus Roy's youthful, rebellious nature, brought him into constant conflict with the authorities.

New compulsory military training laws required all 14 to 18-year-olds to enrol in the senior cadets, and 18 to 26-year-olds to register and complete 16 days' military training every year with the home defence militia. Roy defiantly chose to repeatedly disobey these laws. In a 12-month period between 1912 and 1913, he appeared three times in Rockhampton Police Court on charges of breaching the Defence Act. His first charge was for refusing to complete Senior Cadets training with the local No.3 Battalion as a 17-year-old. By December 1912, he had also failed to attend 44 hours of military drills. On this occasion, after pleading guilty, the court imposed a hefty fine of £10 plus costs.[7] In October the next year, there was another prosecution for failing to render 64 hours of military service. Again Roy pleaded guilty and this time his punishment was confinement in custody for 20 days.[8] Yet he refused to comply. Two months later, he was in court again for failing to attend a two week military training camp. Again, he pleaded guilty and received another 20 days in custody.[9]

By 1913, Roy had enough of the troubles Rockhampton brought him. In June that year, after returning to Brisbane for his Grandmother's funeral, he chose to stay on. His mother's sister, Aunt Mary, offered him a room in her home at Jane Street, Fortitude Valley where his brother, a dairy hand, also boarded. Roy enjoyed being surrounded by the comfort of family. He found work nearby as a barman in Queen Street's Royal Hotel and, eager to avoid a repetition of recent troubles, he immediately joined the 7th Infantry (Moreton Regiment). Surprisingly, the Regiment's comradery and activities were more amiable than expected.

It seemed Roy's life was finally on track, but the declaration of war suddenly changed everything. When the recruiting office opened its doors in Brisbane on 18th August, Roy was among the first in line. With the regiment number, 70, he was assigned to the new 9th Battalion's A Company. His impulsiveness and rush to enlist puzzled old friends, but Roy saw enlistment as a doorway to overseas travel and adventure. Like many young men, he feared if he did not act quickly, he would miss out. Also, the unbridled, patriotic enthusiasm that swept the city and his workplace was infectious. From the bar of the Royal Hotel, he witnessed mass euphoria on a scale never before seen. The night after war was declared, an estimated 5000 people marched up and down Queen Street, jubilantly waving flags and singing anthems.

The First Ashore

The atmosphere outside the Royal was infectious, as celebrations and parades continued until almost midnight.[10] Another important factor influencing Roy's eagerness was the stark division that existed between Protestants and Catholics in Australian society. Enlistment allowed Roy to rid himself of the exclusion and prejudice Irish Catholics often faced. By showing his willingness to share the sacrifice of war, he gained immediate acceptance from his peers. As a soldier, he was an equal untainted by sectarianism.

Weighing just 63 kilograms, with blue eyes and locks of reddish hair, the skinny 20-year-old departed for war in high spirits. Buoyed by the mateship and the fraternity of the 9th Battalion, he had little idea of what lay ahead. After arriving at Mena camp in Egypt, for four months, there was a gruelling relentless regime of route marches, drills, mock battles and intensive military training. For the barman from the city, it was an extremely challenging time. However, Mena transformed Roy into a tough, physically fit soldier. His growth, self-assurance and confidence are evident in a photo taken by the Pyramids, shortly before the Battalion left for Gallipoli. Roy stands tenaciously proud as a member of No. 1 Section, No. 1 Platoon of the 9th Battalion's A Company.[11]

Despite this strong connection to No.1 Platoon, at the Gallipoli landing, Roy did not come ashore with these mates. Instead, for an unknown reason, he landed with Lieutenant Duncan Chapman's No. 3 Platoon in the lead boat of No. 1 Tow.[12] Roy survived the high casualty rates that the Battalion experienced at the landing and, for the next four months, without injury, he bravely endured Gallipoli's ordeals. Although small, he was physically and mentally tough. While many older and more experienced soldiers cracked under the pressure, he held on. Nevertheless, in August, sicknesses like diarrhoea were spreading rapidly through the trenches. Almost 30% of the 3rd Brigade had to be evacuated that month and Roy was one of these. After being admitted to the Casualty Clearing Station at Anzac Cove on 22nd August, he moved the next day to the tented hospital on Lemnos Island where five weeks were spent recuperating. The stay provided much needed respite from the mental stress of battle.

When he returned on 28th September, Roy was disappointed to find conditions on Gallipoli had not improved. Frequent rain storms were often flooding the trenches, and the stress of constant sniper and artillery fire had not abated. As the weeks passed, Roy and his unit made use of parachute rockets, dummy figures and dummy machine-guns in frequent efforts to draw enemy fire, but the stalemate persisted.

Casualties continued to mount and the battalion's strength grew considerably weaker. By the end of October, Roy was one of only 536 men left out of the 9th Battalion's original 1337 who had landed at Gallipoli. Exhausted, they waited impatiently for their turn for rest on the island of Lemnos. Finally, on the 16th November, it was granted. The 9th left the battlefield, but Lemnos was not kind to them. The weather was extremely cold with blizzard like winds. Yet, despite the discomfort, Roy was pleased to be out of the trenches and, on 4th December, a promotion to Corporal lifted his spirits.

Weeks later, the Gallipoli Campaign ended. Instead of moving to the war in France, the 9th Battalion returned to the Egyptian desert where, from January to the end of March, 1916, they constructed trenches along the Suez Canal. It was strenuous work. Sand storms and an intense desert heat sapped morale. Also, a re-organization of the infantry further weakened spirits, with almost half of the 9th Battalion reluctantly drafted to a new battalion. Roy was relieved not to be chosen. He remained with the 9th and was pleased to receive a further promotion to Temporary Sergeant.

In this new role, he moved onto the battlefields of France and Belgium. Full promotion to Sergeant came on 17th April, 1916 and the next day, the 9th marched to the firing line at Rue Du Bois. C and D Companies went into reserve, but B Company and Roy's A Company were selected to take up position on the front line. He was eager to finally face the Germans and prove his abilities. He soon discovered the Germans were a formidable enemy with a powerfully destructive artillery.

Over the next 17 months, Roy participated in a series of tragic battles. The first, at Pozieres in the Somme Valley, was a fiery bloodbath. The Battalion lost 57 lives, with another 271 wounded and 65 men missing in action during its effort to take the village. Roy was a fortunate survivor, but the fierce fighting and heavy enemy artillery bombardment left a lasting legacy of stress and trauma. War historian Charles Bean described 'the Pozieres ridge as more densely sown with Australian sacrifice than any other place on earth.'

Weeks later, the 9th was sent to join the battle to capture Mouquet

Farm, a ruined farmhouse, about 1800 metres north-west of Pozieres. Although Roy's A Company was given a support position behind the frontline, for three days and nights they suffered another ferocious and relentless German artillery barrage. Trenches collapsed, burying men alive and the nerves of Roy and his men were again shattered. The battle for Mouquet Farm cost another 27 Queensland lives, with 125 wounded and 12 missing.

After a short rest period, the Battalion received orders to move back to the Ypres area in Flanders. They arrived as one of Europe's coldest winters was beginning. Positioned in the front-line trenches at Flers, Roy and his platoon suffered from constant exposure to freezing temperatures in trenches that were often deep in mud. As well as frostbite, trench-feet and gangrene, the proximity of so many dead bodies caused diseases like typhoid and typhus to spread. At Flers, Roy sometimes felt the threat of German fire was only a secondary danger.

As the winter thawed, preparation for the advance on the Hindenburg Line began. In the spring of 1917, the 9th engaged in successful battles at The Maze and at Lagincourt. After all the horrors of 1916, these two encounters boosted Roy's confidence as a sergeant and the morale of his men. Heavy fighting occurred again on 3rd May at the 2nd Battle of Bullecourt. Once more the 9th prevailed but, alas, the cost was high. 26 of the Battalion were killed and 135 wounded for the capture of 800 metres of trench.

Mercifully, after Bullecourt, the Battalion left the frontline for almost four months. It was their longest and most complete rest period since the war began, although much of their time was spent preparing for the upcoming battle of the Menin Road. Upon returning to the firing line, the 9th was sent to engage the enemy in the Polygon Wood sector, near Menin Road. On the 19th September, under the cover of artillery fire, Roy led his platoon gallantly forward and helped capture the western edge of the Wood. As usual, the casualties were high. 35 were killed, 149 wounded and 56 men were missing.

Mercifully, a month later, Roy's long and rigorous frontline service finally ended. His last battle was the Battle of Broodseinde. On 4th October, as heavy rain set in, the Australians made a successful assault on the high ground around Broodseinde village. Like so many times before, Roy and his platoon were positioned in one of the muddy support trenches. For two days and nights, from 6th October, the Germans shelled their location relentlessly. On the second day, a high explosive shell tore their trench apart. Roy's shoulder and back were severely wounded. Described in medical reports as a widespread puncture to the back and a severe shrapnel wound to the upper arm, he was lucky to survive.

After spending 24 hours at the Casualty Clearing Station, Roy was admitted to the 2nd Casualty General Hospital at Etaples and, a fortnight later, evacuated to England. At the end of two months in the Queen Mary Military Hospital at Whalley Lanes, a medical report noted his condition remained severe, *'Marked wasting of muscles and loss of bone... Cannot use hand and arm has no power in it. The fingers have lost sensation. The fingers can be moved slightly.'*[13] Deemed unfit for further active service, on the 15th February, 1918, Roy returned to Australia.

His troopship, "Llanstephan Castle" docked in Sydney and, from there, the Queenslanders travelled by special train to Brisbane. At Central Station's very crowded Platform 5, a magnificent hero's welcome greeted them.[14] Surrounded by family and friends, the emotional homecoming filled Roy with joy and much optimism. He was admitted to the Kangaroo Point Military Hospital for a brief stay and then moved to the Rosemount Orthopaedic Hospital at Windsor, his home for the next six months.

Roy eagerly discharged from the army on 18th May, 1918, but settling back into civilian life was a difficult task. He left the army with a half disability pension, a meagre amount that was impossible to survive on. Even while residing at Rosemount, Roy was forced to rely on sustenance payments from the Repatriation Board. When finally discharged from hospital, he applied to the Board for a grant of £35 to establish a home and purchase some furniture.[15]

His arm injury limited his employability and the influx of so many returning soldiers meant jobs were scarce. Roy realized he no longer could carry out the heavy duties of a yardman but, optimistically, hoped he could return to his pre-war job as a barman. He searched widely but was unsuccessful. It was not until 1919 that his circumstances improved. Many 9th Battalion mates had found jobs with the Brisbane Tramways Company and, with their help, he gained a position as a tram conductor. It was a job Roy came to enjoy immensely and, for almost all his remaining work life, he worked on the Clayfield to the City tram line.

Attaining secure employment gave him confidence to propose marriage to his long-time girlfriend, 24-year-old Gertrude Sarah Cross of New Farm. The couple married in a quiet ceremony in February 1919 and moved into Gertrude's modest family home at New Farm at 166 Merthyr Road, on the corner of Hawthorne Street and Merthyr Road. This became the Hanson family's address for over 30 years and home to Roy and Gertrude's three children, Clara, Harold and Mavis.

Despite his gruelling war service and the inflicted trauma and disability, Roy built a fortunate post-war life. Always dependable, his solid character carried him through 39 years of marriage and more than 32 years as a tram conductor. However, by 1951, his life followed the path of most other veterans. Roy's health began to decline. Hypertension, headaches, sleeplessness and heart pain became common ailments. As a consequence, at 56 years of age, he was persuaded to take early retirement. It was a decision that he soon regretted. Roy missed the purpose that work gave his life and also the comradery of his workmates. Months after retiring, he took another job with the rapidly expanding Queensland Can Company. Unfortunately, health problems persisted. Four years later, Roy again was forced to resign. Determined to remain active, in 1954, he took part-time work as a car washer for Coleman Car Sales and then, between 1955 and 1958, he worked as a part-time messenger in the Department of Health and Home Affairs.[16]

Sadly, during these years, Roy's ill health worsened significantly. Heart pain and cardiovascular problems became severe and, by 1957, he was frequently visiting the doctor. His life ended suddenly in April 1958. At the age of 64, the 'original' Anzac suffered a massive heart attack.

Sergeant Harold Roy Hansen was buried at Mt Thompson Memorial Gardens, Holland Park, Brisbane.

Lieutenant Duncan Chapman (Infantry), photographed in the Queenslander Pictorial supplement to the Queenslander, 1914 (SLQ).

Sergeant Walter Edward Latimer (SLQ)

Lance Corporal James Claude Henderson (SLQ)

Lance Corporal Frank Loud (Gunson)

Private James Dundee Bostock (Bostock family album)

Private Eli Coles (SLQ)

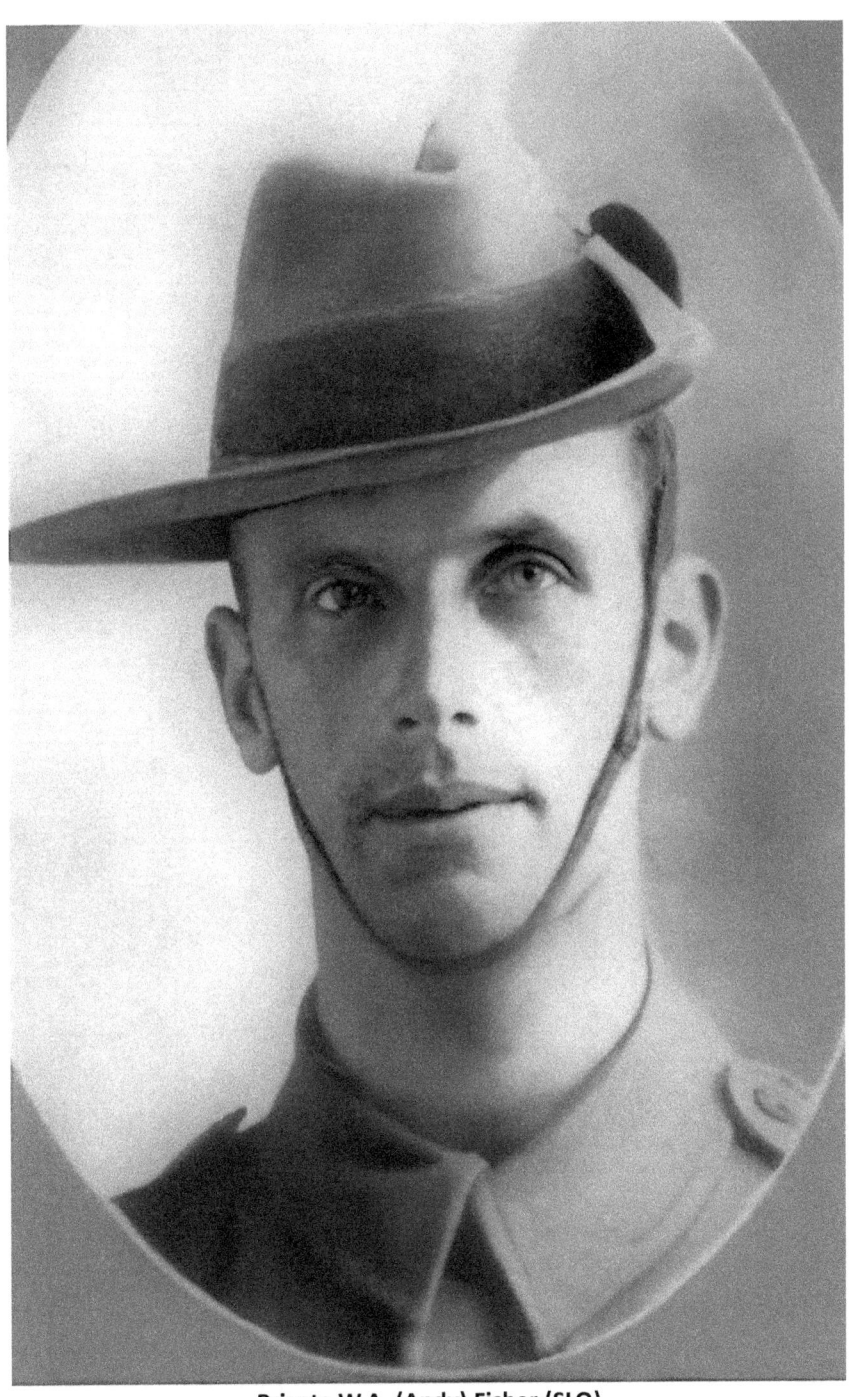

Private W.A. (Andy) Fisher (SLQ)

Private Fred Young Fox (SLQ)

Four of 'The Bearded 9th.' L.H.S. Wilson, J.W. Short, C. Holdway, B.H. Kendrick (Wrench)

Private Cecil Holdway (SLQ)

Private William Jarrett (SLQ)

Private Ben Hugh Kendrick (Mrs L G Holdway)

Private David Kendrick (SLQ)

Private Cecil Kelynack Holdway

No. 295, C Company (later A Company),
9th Battalion
(later Sergeant, 11th Field Artillery Brigade)

Cecil Holdway endured four years and 22 days of overseas war service. After landing with the first boat ashore, he served six continuous months at Gallipoli and, on the Western Front, he fought in the bloody battles of the Somme and at Passchendaele. With strength, persistence, courage and some good luck, Cecil survived and returned home in 1918 as a proud 'original' Anzac. War created a deep commitment to the Anzac tradition of mateship and service, and scars that were slow to heal.

Cecil was a second generation Australian, born in 1892 to George and Georgina Holdway. His father was a policeman in Rockhampton but later transferred to Gladstone, where Cecil and his brother Charles commenced school. Two years later, Cecil's childhood changed dramatically when his father took a job in Capetown, South Africa.[1] For an eight-year-old boy, the experiences and adventures of Africa were unforgettable.

The Holdways returned to Brisbane in 1904. Cecil's father re-joined the police force, and the family established a comfortable home at Pioneer Street, Toowong. Cecil and Charles, now teenagers, continued their schooling at Toowong State School. They enjoyed much of their leisure time along the nearby banks of the Brisbane River. Toowong's floating baths were a popular haunt and, when the Toowong Swimming Club opened in 1909, both boys became active members and competitive swimmers.[2] Upon completing high school, Cecil obtained an apprenticeship with Mr McDonald's plumbing business across the river at nearby West End.[3] He applied himself diligently, and his future looked secure.

The First Ashore

During these years, Cecil also developed a strong interest in military matters. Like many young Queenslanders of the time, his heroes were the noble and bold soldiers serving throughout the Empire. With much enthusiasm, he joined the local volunteer citizen militia before military training was made compulsory in 1911. As a member of the 9th Moreton Regiment, serving in H Company under Captain Maddock,[4] military parades, camps, rifle practice, competitions and drills became important aspects of his young life.

When war was declared, unsurprisingly, Cecil's response was immediate. He and his good mate, Lionel Wilson, an office clerk, also from Toowong, were among the first in the queue at Brisbane's recruiting office when it opened its doors on the 18th August. After passing their physical examination, the young men, dressed in civilian clothing, eagerly joined other first recruits pitching tents in Bell's Paddock, Enoggera.

Three weeks later, with only very rudimentary training, Cecil and Lionel left for war on the troopship "Omrah" as members of the 9th Battalion. They held a naïve belief that this was the beginning of a grand adventure and eagerly anticipated the fight against the Germans. Fortunately, more than five months would pass before the new Australian army would see any action. After arriving in Egypt, they entered the large military camp set up at Mena beside the Pyramids and commenced months of rigorous training.

From Egypt, the troops moved, on 1st March, to the peaceful Greek island of Lemnos. It was an agreeable change from the hot Egyptian desert, but, like most other soldiers, Cecil regarded the move as another annoying delay to his desire to get on with the war. During four weeks on the island, the 9th engaged in a dreary routine of route marches, landing supplies and equipment, and also the construction of a jetty.

Finally, on 8th April, the troops transferred to a transport ship, the "Malda", anchored in the harbour. Over the next two weeks, Cecil watched in awe as ships of various sizes and classes from all over the world gathered. By the 23rd April, one of the largest invasion flotillas in history had been formed.

Cecil's anticipation steadily rose. The next morning, his Company was transferred to the battleship "Queen" where, later, they received from General Hamilton a message revealing details of an *'adventure unprecedented in modern war'*. The General's written statement advised they would be part of a covering force and that *'the whole world will be watching your progress.'*[5] In the afternoon, the men were gathered on deck. From every vantage point, they listened intently as Brigade-Major Brand explained that their Battalion, plus the 10th and 11th, had been selected to form the landing party. He bluntly warned the mission would require great sacrifice. After the men viewed and studied the plan of attack, respective duties were given and they were dismissed. For the rest of the afternoon, despite the Major's ominous warning, the sounds of their laughter, card games and general joviality filled the crowded decks.

However, as the hours passed, the atmosphere changed. By midnight, the battleships and destroyers were within seven miles of the coast. When the moon set, the men began their disembarkation. In anxious silence, Cecil took his position in the first rowing boat of No.1 Tow. Fearfully, he focused on the approaching land and the task ahead. The Company's instructions rang loudly in his mind. The Turks had to be driven back and held in order for the others to land safely. The landing depended on their success.

Cecil's boat grounded on an eerily quiet beach. For a few brief moments, there was a sense of disbelief that the enemy was not there. Half the men from Lieutenant Chapman's boat were on shore when suddenly Turkish gunfire shattered the morning. After running for the shelter of the steep hill, Cecil watched helplessly as troops from other boats came ashore under a rain of bullets. Quickly the cry came, 'Come on Queenslanders,' 'Come on the 9th', and with bayonet fixed, he joined the rapid charge up the slopes.

In the confusion, like so many others, Cecil became separated from the rest of his platoon. He joined a small band of Victorians from the 8th Battalion[6] and fought with them for most of the day. As they advanced, close to Turkish lines, some important Turkish officers were encountered and Cecil proudly recalled, *'I was the man responsible for firing at the 2 high-ranking officers of the Turkish Army on the right of our line and missing unfortunately, though very close.'*[7]

On Tuesday afternoon, three days later, orders were received for the 9th to re-assemble on the beach. Cecil was exhausted. He had not slept since the landing and welcomed the opportunity to return to the beach's shelter. At the roll call on Wednesday, 28th April, the catastrophe suffered by 9th Battalion was revealed. 1000 Queenslanders landed, but only four officers and 251 other ranks mustered that morning.[8] Although overwhelmed by the loss of so many, Cecil was relieved to reunite with his good mate, Lionel Wilson, from Toowong. They would spend the next six months on Gallipoli looking out for each other.

On 4th May, 1915, Cecil penned a short message to his family to re-assure them he had survived the landing. Paper was extremely scarce, so he cleverly improvised by using a small piece of cardboard taken from a cigarette box. His carefully worded postcard revealed no hint of the horror or loss endured. (Today it survives as a proud exhibit at the Australian War Memorial.)

> *'My Dear Mother and Father,*
> *Just a few lines to let you know I am in the best of health at present hoping this will find all at home in the best of health. We are having a church parade behind the trenches today. Lionel and I are still together.*
> *I am your loving son, Cecil.'*[9]

As the weeks passed, the campaign quickly turned to trench warfare and conditions worsened. As well as the constant threat of sniper fire and shrapnel, soldiers suffered diarrhoea, dysentery and enteric fever. Because of poor sanitation, diet and lack of clean water, thousands succumbed, and many had to be evacuated. Cecil suffered recurring fever,[10] but he was never hospitalized and he never left the battlefield. He became one of the very few members of the 9th Battalion who survived Gallipoli without injury or evacuation.

For these steely survivors, it became a test to see who could stick it the longest. From the ranks of the 'original' 1000 men who landed on 25th April, and the 500 reinforcements who arrived soon after, only 63 could boast they had remained on the Peninsula for the entire campaign.[11] Cecil was one of these proud men. Their incredible feat of endurance was recognized by an unofficial medalet, known as the Kilcoy or Butler Medal. Prompted by the Battalion's Medical Officer, Colonel Butler, the residents of the doctor's small hometown of Kilcoy raised funds and organized an award for Battalion soldiers who endured service of six or more continuous months. Designed and struck by

Hardy Bros of Brisbane, it bore the battalion colours with each soldier's number and name inscribed on the back. Cecil was a very proud and worthy recipient.[12]

When the 9th Battalion finally withdrew for rest on Lemnos on 16th November, Cecil left Gallipoli for the first time. He eagerly welcomed this reprieve from battle, although it was not what he hoped for. On the island, food was inadequate, the weather was bitterly cold and a diphtheria outbreak placed the battalion in quarantine throughout most of December. Also, for the first time, Cecil succumbed to diarrhoea, the sickness that had devastated the Peninsula.

A celebrated photo survives that records Cecil's time on Lemnos. It chronicles a bemusing incident. Because Lieutenant Colonel Robertson believed his men would soon return to a bitterly cold Gallipoli winter, he gave the unusual order for all ranks to cease shaving. Within a short time, 9th Battalion men took on an unkempt, hairy appearance which gained them the nickname, the 'Bearded 9th' or 'Hairy 9th'. To record the incident, four friends - Cecil Holdway, Lionel Wilson, John Short and Ben Kendrick - posed for a photograph. Although their image reveals battle worn soldiers with bearded faces in ragged uniforms, a spirit of larrikinism remains. Despite the ordeal of Gallipoli, there is a defiant strength in their pose.

After the evacuation at Gallipoli, disappointedly the 9th Battalion returned to Egypt. Weeks later, their morale took another blow when half of the Battalion, including Cecil, received a transfer to a new 49th Battalion. For these men, losing their proud 'Original' 9th identity was devastating. Particularly challenging for Cecil was separation from Lionel Wilson and Ben Kendrick, with whom he had enlisted and stayed beside throughout the entire Gallipoli Campaign. Five days after his transfer, he fell ill. The diagnosis was 'debility', a broad term associated with mental and physical exhaustion.

After a brief stay in hospital, Cecil decided he had enough of the infantry. The newly formed 4th and 5th Divisions were hurriedly selecting experienced soldiers for a heavy artillery section of 3000 men. Cecil volunteered and immediately moved to the 44th Field Artillery Battery, 11th Brigade, to train as a gunner.

His new role required a new set of skills. Cecil needed to learn how to operate powerful guns that could fire large 8.4 kg shells from a distance of six kilometres. As a team of six horses moved each heavy gun, veterinary courses also were completed. He enjoyed the new training and his aptitude was quickly recognized. At the end of the first month, Cecil was promoted to Acting Bombardier and, on 12th September, was made Bombardier.

After three months' training, the 4th Division Artillery moved to France. Cecil's 11th Brigade joined the Battle of the Somme, taking part first in the bloodbath at Pozieres and, shortly after, in the fight at Mouquet Farm. Fortunately, the gunners fared far better than the infantrymen in both these horrific encounters. Almost all the 7000 men lost at Pozieres were infantry soldiers. Also, as the dreadful winter of 1916 approached, Cecil found himself in a more favourable position. While the infantry froze in muddy trenches, gunners took positions further from the frontline where they were largely out of the mud.

Regrettably, the good fortune of Cecil's unit did not continue into the spring. His Artillery Brigade took part in the hastily planned and disastrous First Battle of Bullecourt and, on the fourth day of the battle, on 15th April, the gunners suffered severely. Positioned near the village of Langatte, south of Bullecourt, at about 30 minutes before dawn, the Germans caught them unprepared. A heavy enemy barrage ignited several ammunition pits and three guns were destroyed, with half their crews killed or wounded.

Bullecourt was a significant blow to soldier morale. However, there was little time for reflection. The gunners moved quickly to Belgium, where preparation was underway for another big attack, the Battle of Messines Ridge. Cecil's Brigade joined the massive artillery effort of 2,266 guns placed along the front. Day and night, for over a week, they engaged in a continuous bombardment of the German lines. The heavy shelling and creeping barrage of the artillery aided significantly the battle's eventual success.

The victory at Messines Ridge lifted spirits, but like most Anzacs who had been on active service since 1915, Cecil was battle fatigued. Fortunately, 10 days of leave in England did much to restore his energy. Although it was a brief respite, Cecil was determined to make the most of every moment. He travelled to see his family's ancestral home, Kelynack, a quaint village in Cornwall, near Land's End, after which he took his middle name. It was a long but fortuitous journey. While staying in accommodation at nearby Penzance, he met 19-year-old Violet Kevern. Their friendship would comfort and sustain Cecil through the hard months ahead.

From July until November 1917, Cecil participated in a series of bloody battles known as the Passchendaele Offensive (the 3rd Battle of Ypres) that aimed to drive the Germans from the high ground around Passchendaele. His Division was sent to Ypres-Comines Canal, south of the village of Zillebeke, where they hastily joined a brutal battle, more dangerous than anything experienced. German shells, supported by the enemy's air-force, reached positions miles behind the front line. For the first time, artillery soldiers, whether in their bivouacs, battery positions or on the road, suffered more than infantry troops. Their situation was made more perilous because the battlefield had become a muddy quagmire. Movement of heavy 18-pounder gun carriages was almost impossible. With teams of gasping horses, the gunners faced a real danger of being sucked into the thick mud.

Cecil endured these horrific conditions for almost four months as his unit worked to support the infantry at Ypres. War correspondent Captain C.E.W. Bean reported, *'The work of the artillery was beyond praise ... battery positions were heavily shelled both by day and by night, and the casualties were severe... Rest at night was usually impossible owing to hostile gas shelling.'*[13] He concluded the Battle of Ypres had been a battle of artillery and paid great tribute to the work of gunners like Cecil, *'The great physical strength of our gunners and drivers stood them in splendid stead in dragging themselves and their guns, horses and ammunition through these mud valleys, but the strength of their great hearts was still more splendid.'*[14]

During the Offensive, German gas attacks also tested the strength of the gunners. Throughout July and August, hundreds of thousands of mustard gas shells fell on the lines near Ypres. The 4th Division's Artillery units were shelled repeatedly and lost over 120 men in the first three weeks. Each attack was a horrific ordeal. Within an hour or two of exposure, soldiers suffered sore eyes, headaches and vomiting. As the vapour soaked into their woollen uniforms, painful skin blisters occurred. The gas also inflicted permanent lung damage as it attacked bronchial tubes and stripped mucous membranes. Although artillery soldiers were repeatedly exposed, only the worse cases could be evacuated. Cecil, gassed at least twice[15], was neither hospitalized nor evacuated.

By the end of 1917, Cecil had survived the Battle of Menin Road, Polygon Wood and the final push for Passchendaele. The war had weakened him physically and mentally. However, despite this, his extensive battle experience made him an obvious choice for promotion. In October, he proudly accepted the new role of sergeant.

On 22nd January 1918, more good fortune favoured Cecil. He left the dangers of the frontline for a six month posting as an artillery instructor to Heytesbury camp, Weymouth, England. Vi Kevern, the girl from Cornwall with whom he had been corresponding since early 1917, welcomed the news wholeheartedly,

> *My Darling Boy,*
> *.... Stay in England as long as you possibly can sweetheart for my sake. I am sure what you have to do can't be so bad as it is in France. I am simply longing to see you. I wish the days would pass quicker.*
> *Yours only,*
> *Vi.*[16]

Removal from frontline duty improved Cecil's mental wellbeing but, regrettably, his physical health continued to worsen. While in England, he grew thinner and his cough became more constant. At the end of his six months at Weymouth, the medical board examined his suitability for return to the front and reported, '*He felt fairly fit till the beginning of 1918 when he began to lose weight and appetite. ... He was gassed in August 1917 and since then has had an almost constant cough. Six months ago he was 12 stone 9lbs now he is 11 stone.... He complains of lassitude and anorexia.*'[17] The diagnosis was 'gas poisoning effort syndrome' and doctors recommended his immediate return to Australia.

Cecil left the war reluctantly. He felt the job he enlisted for was not complete and that he was deserting his mates. Also, the prospect of a long and distant separation from Vi was agonizing. Disgruntled, he arrived in Brisbane hoping a joyous family reunion would lift his spirits. Instead, unexpected sadness greeted him. His grieving mother and sister broke the news that, weeks before, his father had died. He was only 51.

The bereavement and the shock added to Cecil's burdens. Four years and sixteen days of overseas war service left many scars. War dreams constantly disturbed his sleep. He suffered shortness of breath, giddiness and rapid heartbeat deemed to be the result of gassing. Doctors also described him as sometimes 'uncommunicative.'[18] They recommended his immediate discharge from the army with a 75% incapacity pension granted for 6 months.

Returning to his old life proved difficult. He resumed work as a plumber at West End, but it was quickly obvious that the job he once enjoyed was now too difficult. Within two months, he quit. Unemployed, in poor health and missing Violet greatly, Cecil feared his life was spiralling downwards. He desperately wanted to re-establish himself, but felt increasingly disconnected and alienated.

In August 1919, in an effort to turn his situation around, Cecil decided to return to England and to seek out Violet. The couple had not seen each other for almost a year but, within three months, they married. Their union brought much happiness and, at first, it seemed Cecil's health was improving. They established a home in Penzance, but finding work proved difficult. With Cecil's war pension reduced to 50%, the young couple struggled to make ends meet. Local doctors reported Cecil was getting tired very easily, carried a worried expression, displayed a forcible character, and had trouble sleeping. The diagnosis was neurasthenia (shell-shock).[19]

After 10 tough months of struggling at Penzance, Cecil and Vi concluded Australia would offer a better future. They returned to Brisbane where Cecil obtained a job as a motorman with Brisbane Tramways, a company offering preferential employment for returned soldiers. On the 5th October, 1920,[20] he began a rewarding 20 year career driving trams on Brisbane's Paddington line. He especially enjoyed the interaction with passengers and the comradeship of other ex-diggers who were also re-establishing their lives in the Tramways.

With secure employment and a steady income, Cecil and Vi purchased a home at 62 Lewin Street, Bardon, and began to plan a family. In 1922, their first child Roy was born and another, Leslie came in 1925. Soon the Holdways were respected and well-known members in the Bardon community.

At work, Cecil, believing in the solidarity and fraternity of workers, took leadership roles in the Tramway Union. He was union Vice-President between 1926 and 1935,[21] and became an advocate on important issues relating to tram safety, such as the dangers of one-man cars. He believed working conditions could only be improved by stronger unions and, in 1922, campaigned loudly for the Tramways Union to join 46 other affiliated unions on the newly formed Queensland Trade and Labour Council.[22]

Comradeship was an ideal that Cecil valued above all. He was forever grateful for the mateship of diggers. Their shared experience of horrific ordeals had forged bonds and an understanding that helped Cecil through his difficult times. Veteran organizations, reunions and associated events dominated his post-war life. He became a proud and active member of the Omrah Association, the Gallipoli Legion of Anzacs, the RSSAILA (RSL) plus various associated committees. Much time and support was also given to veteran projects such as the construction of a RSSAILA Memorial Hall at Bardon.

Even at 70, Cecil's enthusiastic work for veterans continued. Despite failing health, he was an energetic fundraiser for a Gallipoli Fountain of Honour that would commemorate Gallipoli's 50 year anniversary. In the heated controversy over where to locate the fountain, Cecil threw himself into the public brawl. He wrote letters to newspapers and appeared in articles ardently supporting the original Botanic Gardens site.[23] Disappointingly, Cecil did not live to see the Fountain completed. It was finally switched on in 1978 at Roma Street, three years after Cecil's death.

During the last decades of Cecil's life, the effects of war and gas poisoning increasingly impacted his health. In June, 1940, short windedness, heart pain and a racing heartbeat forced him to take 10 weeks' leave. Soon after, as his health steadily declined, at the age of 48, he reluctantly gave up his job at the Tramways.

When Cecil left his job, he believed his long war service made him eligible for a war disability pension. He was shocked and disillusioned when the Repatriation Board argued that because he had not claimed assistance or medical treatment in the previous 20 years, his present medical problems were not because of the war. His application was totally rejected. Without financial assistance, Cecil had no option but to return to work. He took a job with lighter duties as a store cleaner but, by 1952, at the age of 59, his health problems became too severe. A doctor's report noted he had no energy, was not sleeping well, and was breathless and nervy. Again, he was forced to give up work.

Cecil appealed to the Repatriation Board to re-consider their 1940 decision and a meagre 20% war service pension was allowed.[24] Believing he was being denied his right, over the next 15 years, Cecil fought the Board's decision. In 1962, doctors described the 'original' Anzac as 'depressed and uncommunicative'. He was hospitalized at the Greenslopes Repat Hospital for nervous disorders but tenaciously continued to mount appeals against the Board's decision. Finally, in 1966, his persistence was rewarded. After a struggle that involved more than seven appeals, the Repatriation Board granted a 100% war service pension.[25]

Cecil's last years were spent in the Mechain Nursing Home at Ashgrove with his wife, Vi. Later he moved to the Nimbin Nursing Home in New Farm where, sadly, he passed away in 1975, aged 83. His fighting spirit and determination stayed with him to the end. Cecil Holdway lived as a proud Anzac who valued, above all things, the Anzac spirit of mateship. The self-sacrifice and devotion to duty he displayed in war continued throughout his long life as he dedicated himself to serving the RSSAILA, the Gallipoli Legion of Anzacs, unionism, Brisbane Tramways and the Bardon community.

Sergeant Cecil Holdway was cremated at Mt Thompson Crematorium on 15th October, 1975.

Private William Jarrett
No. 311, C Company (later A Company), 9th Battalion

27-year-old William Jarrett entered the war as an enthusiastic patriot, thirsty for adventure and eager to defend the Empire. He served five months on the Peninsula and fought courageously in the Battle of the Somme. Gassed and wounded twice, when Private William Jarrett returned to Australia, in December 1917, he was sick and broken.

William's loyalty to Empire was rooted in his family's strong connection to England. The Jarretts proudly traced their history over many centuries to a small, picturesque corner of Gloucestershire. William was born on 8th July, 1887 in Kingswood, St George, in the same village that his father and grandfather spent their childhoods. When he was four years old, the family migrated to Queensland, but they always kept their close bond with Gloucestershire.

In Brisbane, the Jarrett family prospered. William's enterprising father began a business in Doggett Street, Fortitude Valley that sold recycled bottles to breweries such as Kops in nearby Chester Street. Its success afforded the family a large comfortable home, a few blocks away in Anne Street, described on electoral rolls as *'the 2nd house from Chester Street, 5th house from the gasometer, across the road from the Waterloo Hotel.'*[1] Although they enjoyed the life they established in Brisbane, the Jarrett family's fondness for the home country did not diminish. In 1895, they returned to Gloucestershire. For William's elder brother and father, it was a brief visit, but his mother and the rest of the family stayed on for almost two years, returning to Brisbane when William was 10 years old. The experience enriched William's childhood which was otherwise marred by much sadness. Four years after returning to Brisbane, his older brother, Samuel, was killed in a shooting accident and, three months later, his mother died unexpectedly.

As he came to terms with these tragedies, William took comfort in the comradery offered by the military. Before the government made military training compulsory, he eagerly joined Brisbane's part-time volunteer, citizen soldier movement. Like many young men of the time, he wished to emulate the noble and heroic Imperial soldiers protecting the Empire. He first enlisted in the Queensland Volunteers and, later, in 1907, the Queensland Rifles Regiment[2] and the Oxley Regiment. Most of his leisure time was devoted to attending drills and rifle practice. Cricket matches with the Queensland Rifles Cricket Club were also enjoyed, as well as weekend militia camps at Ormiston[3] and to improve his physique, there were the militia's weekly gymnastic class.

When war was declared, unsurprisingly, William was one of the first volunteers. He took his oath of allegiance before Lieutenant Duncan Chapman on 28th August, 1914. Ten days after being assigned to the 9th Battalion's C Company (later A Company), he embarked on the steamer, "HMAT Omrah", the first troopship to leave Queensland for war.

William was excited by what lay ahead. He was pleased to escape his tiresome job as a labourer in Brisbane and believed he was beginning a great overseas adventure. The first disappointment came in Egypt. Four months in a desert camp at Mena was not what he expected. Nor did he enjoy the relentless regime of training carried out every day under a hot desert sun. There were long marches through sand, repetitive drills, tiresome exercises, lectures and difficult mock battles. William and his mates were desperate to join the real war in France. Their disappointment and frustration mounted when, after leaving Egypt, they endured another delay of seven weeks on the Greek island of Lemnos. When orders finally came on 24th April, 1915, William was well prepared and eager for action.

His experience at the Gallipoli landing has fortunately survived. From hospital, eight days after the landing, William wrote two letters to his sister Minnie in Brisbane. Although the original documents were lost, excerpts were printed in Brisbane's Courier Mail on 11th June 1915.

> *'We landed at 4.10 a.m. on April 25. We jumped into water up to our necks and when we got near the shore, the Turks opened fire. We fixed bayonets and charged up a mountain in the face of shrapnel. I was in the firing line for ten hours. The boys fought*

> like heroes, but we lost many men wounded and killed, and a number of the navy men were also lost during the landing.... It was a great sight to see our fellows going up the mountain. The Turks waited for us to get close before they fired but when they saw us coming with our bayonets fixed they ran.... The troops were cut up with the machine guns but when we charged the Turks fled for their lives. I was in three bayonet charges, and during the last one fell down a trench about 18 feet in depth and was hurt, but I don't think I am hurt much.'[4]

William recounted he was out of the boat, but still in the water, 'near the shore', when the Turks' rifle fire began. This is similar to recounts by other soldiers from the first boat such as rower, Private Fisher, *we reached the beach about 4.30, and half of our chaps got out of the boat without anything happening.*'[5] The only inconsistent detail is the ascribed landing time. Stress and chaos, understandably, confused estimates of time.

Although William bravely assured his sister that *'I don't think I am hurt much'*, an almost five metre fall down a Turkish trench resulted in serious injury. In severe pain, he struggled back to the beach, where he joined hundreds of wounded men waiting for medical attention and evacuation to a hospital ship. Four days later, he was admitted to No. 1 Australian General Hospital in Cairo with an inguinal hernia. Surrounded by so many maimed and brutally wounded men, William regarded himself fortunate. After sixteen days in hospital, followed by three weeks in the Convalescent Depot at Helouan, his hernia pain did not abate. Strenuous exertion was impossible, and, therefore, William was discharged to Zeitoun, a training base north of Cairo and posted to light duties.

He returned to his unit on the 10th July, almost three months after the Gallipoli landing. After such a long absence, adjustment to the horrible conditions of the Peninsula was not easy. The deadly threat of Turkish artillery and sniper-fire was unrelenting. Poor sanitation, an inadequate diet and the lack of clean water caused rampant illness. In particular, diarrhoea and typhoid were prevalent. In three months, no worthwhile gains had been made and, as noted by Bean, men were being 'sacrificed needlessly by conflicting orders and poor management by the officers.'[6] Soldier morale was extremely low.

Soon after his return, William was encouraged by a successful operation that momentarily lifted the Battalion's spirits. A new trench, later called Leane's, was captured during an effective raid on the night of 31st July. A week later, however, at Lone Pine, morale was devastatingly crushed. The 9th Battalion's role in the operation was to lay heavy fire on the opposing Turkish trenches before a large-scale attack on 6th August was made by New South Wales Battalions. They completed their job gallantly and, when finished, sat on the parapet to witness the carnage unfold. As the bodies of fellow Anzacs piled four and five deep, they could do nothing to help. It was an image that haunted William forever.

The Campaign's attempt in August to move forward failed and, for almost another four months, the Anzacs tenaciously held on. Throughout the stalemate conditions, casualties and evacuations remained high, but because of good luck and his tough resilience, William endured.

When the Gallipoli Campaign finally ended, William was exhausted and eager for rest. After a brief rest on Lemnos, the Battalion moved back to Egypt where they were assigned an almost impossible project. For six long weeks, battling sandstorms and intense heat, they worked to construct a series of trenches that would fortify the Suez Canal from Turkish attack. During these hardships, a promotion to Lance Corporal on 29th February brought William some satisfaction. When orders came to leave Egypt in late March for France, every soldier applauded the news. William, like others, was pleased, at last, to be involved in the real war against the Germans.

His first major engagement on the Western Front was at Pozieres. The objective was to capture the strategic high ground surrounding this small village. Proudly, the 9th Battalion led Australia's 1st Division into the area on the 19th July. After marching through the night at 2 a.m., they reached their position approximately four kilometres southwest of Pozieres. The hour was late, but rest was impossible as the Germans greeted their arrival with a heavy rain of gas shells.

Three days later, the operation began. After a preliminary bombardment of the German line, in the early hours on 23rd July, William's A Company, with B Company, left the trenches and moved into no-man's-land. They charged heroically and quickly captured the Pozieres Trench. Fierce hand to hand combat followed and, by midday, the village was taken. However, the Germans launched ferocious counter-attacks and the bloody battle continued for four days and nights. Pozieres became a kind of hell. Day and night, without pause, a German artillery bombardment tore up the ground, collapsed trenches and blew men to bits. Adding to the soldiers' terror were deadly gas shells. Chlorine attacked the lungs and mustard gas, in contact with skin, caused excruciating pain. The wounded and dying were everywhere. The 9th Battalion entered Pozieres with 1016 men and left the battle with only 623. William remained on the battlefield until the 9th was finally relieved on 26th July. As the survivors marched from Pozieres, an observer noted, *'They looked like men who had been in Hell. Almost without exception, each man looked drawn and haggard, and so dazed that they appeared to be walking in a dream.'*[7]

With courage, endurance and good luck, William had survived Pozieres, but he did not leave the battle unscathed. Exposure to gas inflicted permanent lung damage. Also, his nerves were shattered and his once confident spirit gone. William doubted his ability to carry on and took the unusual step of requesting a demotion. On 3rd August, at his own bid, he reverted to Private.

Three weeks later, despite being a third under strength, the 9th Battalion was sent back into the firing line. The Germans had re-captured Pozieres Heights and were pushing the Allied line back towards Mouquet Farm, 2 kilometres north-west of Pozieres. On the 19th August, the soldiers of the 9th were sent forward, with the 1st Division, to relieve exhausted battalions attempting to take the large ruined farmhouse. As they took their position, an intense bombardment rained down on them that continued relentlessly for three days. William's A Company, stationed behind the Pozieres cemetery, less than a kilometre from the Farmhouse, was in the firing line. Shells burst above their trenches, burying men alive and, again, many soldiers became badly shell-shocked. The heavy shelling in front of their trenches made their advance impossible. 47 of the Battalion were killed and 125 wounded. During the terror, on the 21st August, William received a bullet wound to his left leg. The injury was serious but, fortunately, it removed him from the horror of the Somme.

Three days later, he was admitted to the 26th General Hospital at the port city of Etaples. A long period of convalescence followed at the notoriously strict Etaples Base Depot. As his leg gradually strengthened, other problems emerged. The effects of being gassed caused a persistent cough and worsening chest problems. He was returned to the Etaples General Hospital on the 25th February, 1917.[8] Unfortunately, his condition continued to deteriorate and a week later, he was sent to England.

With a diagnosis of severe bronchitis and asthma, William remained in hospital for the next three months. After a week at Edmonton Military Hospital, he was pleased to be transferred to the less disciplined and more homely VAD Hospital at Broxburn in Scotland. However, despite treatment, his health showed no signs of improvement. A medical report, dated May 1917, noted a *'poor bodily condition'*. *'His voice is still husky. Heart enlarged. Breaths through the mouth. Easily becomes breathless.'*[9] Doctors deemed further hospitalization to be of no benefit. Therefore, on 7th June, William was discharged with orders to report for duty to the Australian Command Depot at Weymouth. Excited to be free from hospital, he first enjoyed two weeks' of furlough in London.

Sadly, only one week was served at Weymouth. William was returned to hospital with a shameful and embarrassing new diagnosis. Like many other soldiers whose lives were surrounded by death and uncertain futures, William became ambivalent to the morality of sexual recklessness. He had contracted syphilis, the secret silent disease that 60,000 Australian soldiers caught during World War 1.[10] His blurred sense of morality led to a foolish dalliance in London that resulted in a serious disease and dishonour.

Soldiers with venereal disease were hidden away in a specially designated hospital at Bulford, a small village in Wiltshire. As the war progressed, its wards overflowed. During the first six months of 1917, its doctors treated 6368 soldiers and, in July 1917, the average daily number of patients was 1065.[11] After William was admitted on the 3rd July, his name was immediately placed on the Syphilis Register. He then began a painful and dangerous course of treatment. Penicillin did not exist and instead, daily injections of toxic heavy metals were used. William spent 18 days at Bulford and received seven injections of the arsenic based drug, Salvarsan 606, and seven injections of mercury.[12] Each had serious long-term side effects.

He left Bulford cured, but his lung problems persisted and his overall health remained weak. The Medical Board re-examined his case and concluded bronchitis and general debility made him unfit for active service. They therefore recommended his return to Australia. William was immensely thankful. He hoped to be home with his family before Christmas.

His troopship, "Port Lyttleton" arrived in Melbourne on 15th December. From there, the Queenslanders travelled by train to Brisbane, where they were greeted with great fanfare. Among the huge, cheering crowd at Central Station were William's siblings, Minnie, Esther, Mary, Thomas and Henry, plus numerous nephews and nieces. The platform overflowed with joyful family reunions, but for the Jarretts, there was sadness. William was greeted with the devastating news that five weeks earlier, his father, George Jarrett, had died. Shocked and overcome by grief, he had not anticipated re-starting his shattered life without his father's strength and support.

Suffering chronic bronchitis and a general debility, William desperately wanted to put the war behind him. To his great relief, in late February, he was permanently discharged from the army with a temporary pension of £1/10/- per fortnight. It was meagre compensation, but he was content. Fortunately, the Jarretts, a close knit family, were eager to provide care and support for their youngest brother. Without the means to live independently, he moved back to the family home in lower Ann Street, Fortitude Valley. Around the corner, his brother Henry and his family lived in Proe Street, and nearby were his sister, Mary Anne and her husband.

The comfort of the family was a healing tonic, but the damage from war was severe. As well as lung problems, doctors described his condition as 'nervous and tremulous.'[13] He suffered night sweats and communicated less. The youthful energy and physical strength he once possessed were gone.

Yet William was desperate to re-establish his life. He had optimistic plans. While in hospital in England, he met Edith Gertrude Arnold, a kitchen-maid who worked for the family of a London doctor.[14] Since his return from war, they had been corresponding regularly and, after more than 12 months of letter writing, in 1919, a nervous proposal of marriage was made. To William's delight, Edith accepted.

With marriage on the horizon, the need to find work suddenly became more crucial. Unfortunately, William's poor health limited his employability and jobs were scarce. After months of unsuccessful searching, he decided his only option was to create his own job. Aided by his family and some of the entrepreneurial skills he inherited from his father, William became a 'fuel merchant,' selling firewood from the family's Ann Street home. In Brisbane newspapers, in 1920, he placed a series of advertisements,

'W. Jarret, Anzac. Ann Street opp. Waterloo Hotel. Wood 10/- per load. Orders promptly attended. Phone 6991.'[15]

His small venture had ample time to establish itself as the war bride scheme worked frustratingly slowly and Edith's arrival was delayed. Although her application for a free sea passage under was approved in mid-1919, she did not depart England until almost six months later. With 600 other anxious brides, she arrived in Sydney on the bride-ship, "Megantic" as 'Private William Jarrett's fiancé', reaching Brisbane on 28th February 1920.[16] For the 25-year-old bride, it was a courageous move. She left friends, family and the comfort of home to travel to the other side of the world to marry a man she had not seen for over two years. Their wedding, less than a month after her arrival, on 27th March, marked the beginning of a happy union that lasted 20 years.

They established a home in a new housing estate, named College Hill (today Boondall) on Brisbane's northern outskirts. Doctors had concurred William was unfit for manual labour, but he chose to disregard their advice. In the rapidly growing suburb, there was an enormous demand for firewood for household wood stoves. Therefore, William determinedly continued his work as a 'fuel merchant', chopping and selling firewood to neighbouring homes.

He and Edith enjoyed their life in the suburbs and quickly became involved in the growing local community. As always, family remained important. His brother, Thomas, lived with them for some time and, on the same street, Kingston Avenue, his sister Minnie lived with her husband and children. Although William and Edith remained childless, they became active members of the newly established Boondall State School committee working on various projects to raise funds for the school.[17] They were also proud gardeners who exhibited flowers at many local shows. The Jarretts won four awards at Boondall's first flower show in 1927.[18]

Sadly, at Boondall, William's health continued to deteriorate. By 1924, he was making fortnightly visits to Rosemount Hospital. Doctors noted he was losing weight, suffering shortness of breath and tired easily. The radiologist also reported well-marked fibrosis on both sides of his chest and that he was probably in the early stages of tuberculosis. Strong advice was given to cease work and, in September 1924, on his behalf, the hospital applied for his pension to be re-instated with a further application made by his doctor in December.[19]

With defiant determination, William refused to submit to illness. Even in the final years of his life, he stubbornly continued his firewood business. However, with each year that passed, the quality of his life diminished. By 1939, aged 51 years, he was in the final stages of tuberculosis. His condition became critical and, in January 1940, doctors recommended his urgent admission to Rosemount Hospital. As usual, William refused their advice. Eventually, on 26th February 1940, an ambulance had to be called. He was rushed to Rosemount but died that day.[20] His death, at the age of 52, was officially recorded as a consequence of war. William Jarrett became one of the thousands of sometimes forgotten Anzacs who died prematurely after the war.

Private William Jarrett was buried in the Monumental Section of Lutwyche Cemetery (Grave 54).

Private David Kendrick

No. 386, C Company, 9th Battalion
(later Corporal, A Company, 9th Battalion)

Private David Kendrick endured much during World War 1. After landing with the first boat ashore at Gallipoli, he served three continuous months on the Peninsula and, later, on the Western Front, he fought gallantly at the Battle for Mouquet Farm, Hazebrouck, Meteren and at Froissy Beacon (Chuignes). Having survived injuries, trauma and illness, he returned from war with a new identity and a powerful determination to build a better life.

David had lived in Australia for only 12 months when war was declared. He still regarded himself as a proud Englishman. Born in 1887 in Wednesbury, Staffordshire, much of his early life was spent in the nearby coal mining town of West Bromwich, where his family had a terraced house on busy Bull Street.[1] The Kendricks were a well-known and well-respected family. David's grandfather had been the Mayor of the nearby city of Wolverhampton, while his father, Richard Pearson Kendrick, for many years was the furnace manager at Willingsworth Colliery in Wednesbury.[2] The family's connection to the district was strong. David's ten siblings married locally and raised families in the West Bromwich district. Only he chose to leave.

After completing school at 13, he gained an apprenticeship as a glasscutter. The trade suited David well and, throughout his life, it would provide him with reliable work and a comfortable income. When David was 21 years old, he proposed marriage to Annie Amelia Mills, the daughter of a local blacksmith who lived in nearby Tenscore Street.[3] After their wedding at West Bromwich's Parish Church, the young couple moved to Coventry, where David found work as a glasscutter. Family responsibilities quickly followed. Three children, Marjorie, Albert and Richard Arthur, were born during the first four years of the marriage.

Regrettably, three months after the birth of their third child, the young family separated. David left England on 14th March, 1913 on the immigrant ship "Orsova" to start a new life in Australia.[4] In Brisbane, he took a room at "Warrane", a comfortable boarding house at 413 Wickham Terrace,[5] and easily found work as a glasscutter. Although he missed his young family, his new life progressed well. He planned to quickly establish himself, hoping his wife and children would follow later. Regrettably, war dictated a different agenda.

David gave up his job immediately. When war was declared, without hesitating, he volunteered to join the newly formed Australian Infantry Force. Like so many others, he believed it was his patriotic duty to defend England and the Empire. Also, the opportunity to receive a free trip home to his family was too good to resist. David's children were now 5, 3 and 2 years old and he missed them dearly. Desperate not to jeopardize his acceptance as a recruit, he falsely declared to the recruitment officer that he was a widower. More curiously, when asked for details of his next of kin, David did not list his own parents or siblings but gave his father-in-law's name, Joseph Mills and the Mills' family address in West Bromwich.[6]

Three weeks after entering the new military camp at Enoggera, on the 19th September, with little preparation, David left with the 9th Battalion, for war on the troopship "Omrah." He embarked with an eagerness to re-unite with his family and a naïve belief that a glorious adventure lay ahead. The first of many disappointments followed. His return to England and his children failed to eventuate. The huge armada of Australian and New Zealand troopships did not reach Europe. Instead, the troops reluctantly disembarked in Egypt. Although this was seen as a frustrating delay, during the following four months, a grueling regime of intensive military training transformed David and his mates into fit and competent soldiers, well prepared for the awful trials ahead.

At the Gallipoli landing, he was one of the first Anzacs to come ashore.[7] David was a member of Lieutenant Duncan Chapman's No.3 Platoon[8] positioned in the lead boat of No. 1 Tow. On that first day, his Battalion suffered enormous casualties but David fortunately survived unscathed. He served in Gallipoli's trenches for almost four months without sustaining serious physical injury. However, the constant threat from Turkish shrapnel and sniper fire caused enormous mental strain and weakened him considerably. In August, almost one third of the 9th Battalion had to be evacuated. A soldier in David's company observed, '*16 weeks ... in the trenches. Ought to send the whole 9th away. They are all done.*'[9]

By the 6th August, David was '*done*'. Official records state he was evacuated suffering diarrhoea, but his condition was far worse. David left Gallipoli a broken man. Diarrhoea was just one symptom of his overall physical and mental collapse. After spending 15 days in hospital on Lemnos, he was evacuated to England. Another five weeks of convalescence followed at London's Lewisham Military Hospital, but David remained unfit for active service. Instead of returning to the front, on the 15th October, he was transferred to the Australian Command Depot at Weymouth on England's south coast. This overcrowded Depot was not a pleasant place. It housed the seriously sick and maimed casualties from Gallipoli who were not expected to be fit for active duty for at least six months. David remained here for eight months, overwhelmed by the suffering that surrounded him.

When he finally re-joined the 9th Battalion on the Somme battlefield on 29th July, 1916, what he met was beyond his imaginings. The fiery bloodbath at Pozieres had occurred three days before. Almost 400 from his Battalion were among Australia's 17,000 casualties and the survivors looked like they had been through hell. David's anxiety grew as he anticipated what lay ahead.

Three weeks later, his fears were realized. The 9th was ordered back into the line with orders to capture German trenches on a hill near the shattered farmhouse at Mouquet Farm. They took their position on 19th August and were immediately lashed with heavy shellfire that continued throughout most of the day and night. The deadly intensity quickly shattered the nerves of many men but, with great courage, on the 21st, the 9th Battalion mounted their attack. For two days, they clawed their way up the slopes towards the farm. Losses were heavy. 27 men were killed, 12 went missing and 125 were wounded. Fortunately, David again survived without injury. A week later, he received promotion to Corporal.

New perils and more wretched conditions soon followed. As the worst winter in living memory was beginning, in November, the Battalion moved north to the front line at Flers in the Ypres area of Flanders. Weeks of rain had already created a deadly sea of mud, which in many trenches was up to 30 centimetres deep. The severe cold and wet conditions caused ailments such as trench foot and gangrene to be common. Also, because of the proximity of dead bodies and a lack of sanitation, parasites and infections such as scabies and typhus spread.

In these deplorable conditions, David's health quickly deteriorated. Shortly after arriving, he contracted bronchitis and, on 18th November, was hospitalized. However, because of hospital overcrowding and manpower shortages on the front, patients were quickly discharged. Four days after being admitted, although unwell, David was sent back to the trenches. Within two weeks, his condition was critical. The new diagnosis was 'debility', an army term used to describe physical and mental breakdown. At the General Hospital at Camiers, despite ten weeks' treatment, his health failed to improve and again doctors declared him unfit for frontline duty and evacuated to England.

He reluctantly returned to the convalescent depot at Weymouth, where he had previously spent eight months. As his mental health was slowly restored, he was placed on permanent base duties. However, five months later, the medical board deemed David was still unsuitable for frontline duty. On 20th June, he transferred to the Training Depot at Weymouth and then to the Overseas Training Brigade at Tidworth, where he remained for another four months.

Finally, after more than a year's absence from the frontline, orders came for David to re-join his Battalion. With much trepidation, in March 1918, he took his place in the trenches near Ypres as the war took a dangerous turn. The Germans had just mounted a spectacular offensive and, within a week, all territory in the Somme, captured in the previous 12 months, was lost. In response, the 9th Battalion, on 6th April, moved south, but as they arrived, news came that the enemy had broken through in the north. Suddenly, it seemed the Germans were unstoppable. The Battalion was quickly ordered back to Flanders to help defend Hazebrouck, a junction on a vital rail line. During this operation, from the 16th to the 19th April, the Germans targeted them with extremely heavy artillery fire. Six men died but courageously David's Battalion held on.

After the defence of Hazebrouck, David marched uneasily with his Battalion, 12 kilometres east, to join an ambitious attempt to capture the village of Meteren. Taken by the Germans ten days before, the village was now heavily defended by a ring of German machine guns. For two days, an attempt was mounted but, without artillery support, the operation was doomed. 12 men from the 9th lost their lives and 32 were wounded. The experience of Meteren and Hazebrouck left David, and the whole Battalion, weakened and exhausted.

Welcome relief came on 29th April when, for five days, the 9th was removed for rest in comfortable billets at Borre. Regrettably, by the 5th May, David's unit was back on the frontline, about a mile southwest of Meteren, with dangerous and unusual orders. Stray cows had been sighted and, for the next several nights, his A Company was ordered into No-man's-land to round them up. Enemy shells often caused animals to stampede, which frustrated the success of each perilous mission. Men also complained about stumbling over dead beasts in the darkness.[10] On the 8th May, while on one of these missions, David sprained his ankle. He spent the next three months in hospital at Le Havre in France.[11] This long period of convalescence suggests a more serious ailment and a probable return of his previous debility. While in hospital, war dealt him another devastating blow. News arrived that his brother, Private Frank Kendrick of the Gloucestershire Regiment, had been killed in battle on the 5th June.

David, hesitantly, re-joined his battle-hardened mates on the battlefield once more on 13th August, 1918. He was one of 31 reinforcements, sent to replace 178 casualties suffered the previous day at the Battle of Crepy Wood. With little time to adjust to his new situation, at dusk, he anxiously re-entered the line. Throughout the night, the fighting was intense as they advanced their position by 200 yards. Mercifully, when relieved the next day, five days' rest was granted.

A week later, the 9th Battalion moved to join Haig's great offensive south of the Somme, the final stage of the war. Their first objective was to take the high ground at Froissey Beacon. Stealthily, they moved through Luc Wood along the Somme slope, but were met by a heavy bombardment that included gas shells. Casualties were high. Yet, at 2 p.m., protected only by a smoke barrage, the Battalion bravely attacked. Many more fell, but they pushed on and continued to advance through the following day, capturing important territory. It was a significant victory that did much to boost David's lagging morale.

The depleted and fatigued ranks of the 9th were relieved at 2.30 a.m. on 27th August. David relished the rest they were granted outside Cerisy village but despaired when, eleven days later, the Battalion marched to Tincourt to begin preparations for a dreaded attack on the feared Hindenburg Line. He desperately looked forward to the day when all these recurring ordeals would end.

On the 14th September, his prayers were answered. Prime Minister Billy Hughes had pressured the War Office to grant two months' special furlough for 'original Anzacs', the 7000 survivors of the first contingent who volunteered in 1914. David could not believe his luck. He was chosen as one of the first fortunate recipients of this coveted leave. With a jubilant stride, he marched out of Tincourt and out of the war. With 800 other veterans, David embarked on the troopship, "Kaiser-a-Hind" for Australia.

Although war had given David a strong new identity as a proud Australian soldier, his return to Australia was tinged with sorrow and regret. He was mentally exhausted and yearned for the emotional support of his family and friends in England. In West Bromwich, his parents and siblings were still mourning his brother's death, and he needed to be with them. As well, he desperately longed to see his children.

The despondency, that he felt, only eased on the evening of 11th November. As the "Kaiser-a-Hind" voyaged across the Indian Ocean, the ship's wireless received a two-word message, *'Unconditional surrender'*. Instantly, every deck erupted into boisterous celebrations. With dinner gongs, bugles and cornets, jam tins and anything that could make a noise, the soldiers paraded the decks, serenading their officers with patriotic songs and loudly singing "God Save the King".[12]

Australia was still celebrating when their troopship arrived four days later. At every port, enormous fanfare greeted them. From Sydney, the Queenslanders on-board headed north by special train and, along the journey, emotional receptions met them at every train-stop. In Brisbane, their welcome was extraordinary. The city had hosted many welcome home parades before, but few were as big as this. The Brisbane Courier reported, *'Thousands of persons gathered in the precincts of the Central Railway Station, and gave cheer after cheer for the band of gallant men who have helped to secure freedom and national life. From the station the heroes were conveyed ... along Edward, Ann, Wharf, Queen, George, and Ann streets, to Albert-square, where they were given a public reception..... Men and boys cheered, and many women and girls wept for very joy at the worthy representatives of Australia's famous army passed by.'*[13] David was overwhelmed and inspired with optimism. The Englishman returned from war as an 'Original' Queensland Anzac, strongly connected to his 9th Battalion mates and dedicated to an Anzac spirit.

After his discharge on 24th January, 1919, David worked doggedly to re-establish his life. He carried significant scars but was determined the sacrifices of war were not made in vain. He took a room at the grandly ornate, three storey Empire Hotel on the corner of Ann and Brunswick Street and returned to his trade as a city glasscutter.[14] By the end of 1920, thriftiness and earnest savings provided him with sufficient funds to return to England. He applied for his passport[15] but, at the last moment, inexplicably changed his plans. Instead, he invested his savings in a small tobacconist shop at 354 Brunswick Street, across the road from his room at the Empire Hotel.

For the next five years, his business was successful, and he created a rewarding life. However, as Australia moved towards Depression, profits tumbled. David was forced to sell his tobacco shop and return to glass-cutting. He also vacated his rented room at the Empire Hotel and moved to a smaller boarding house called "Waverley" in nearby Wharf Street.[16]

It was a major setback, but David's ambitious optimism remained strong. Astutely, he explored new business opportunities. In 1933, as real estate prices fell, a grocery shop and general store at 311 Gympie Road, Kedron became affordable.[17] The prominence of this grand building, with its large glass frontage and a wide shaded awning on Gympie Road, plus David's many army mates, ensured the business had a large customer base. His inexperience as a grocer was compensated by his strong work ethic.

While at Kedron, David's solitary life also ended. He managed his Gympie Road Store with the help of Alice, known to customers and friends as Mrs Kendrick.[18] For more than a decade, David and Alice formed a happy partnership. Her companionship and support helped David keep the demons of war at bay.

As the years passed, financial success was achieved. David was proud of his post-war achievements. His only regret was the distance between himself and his children in England. This remorse became painfully acute when, in 1942, the tragic news arrived that David's second son, David Albert Kendrick had been killed while serving on the British Navy ship, *"Empire Comet."*[19] However when floral tributes and messages of sympathy from customers and friends flooded his store, David felt grateful for the life and friendships he had created in Australia. On 16th November, he placed a notice in the Telegraph newspaper thanking the community for their condolences.[20]

Regrettably, soon after his son's death, David's relationship with Alice ended. The couple sold the Gympie Road store and, in 1946, David moved alone to a new home at Ida Street in Kedron. At 60 years of age, he found it impossible to remain idle. Another general store was soon purchased at 216 Days Road on the busy intersection with Grange Road.[21] It was a less demanding, smaller shop, but the long work hours took a toll on David's health. By 1950, stress-related health problems forced an early retirement at the age of 63.[22]

After selling his Days Road business, a comfortable inner-city home was purchased at 3 Taylor Street, Buranda. It was David's plan to continue to work part-time as a glazier[23] but, in 1954, he suffered a devastating stroke that left him with a disability. The quality of his life was diminished significantly, but he stubbornly maintained his independence, living alone in his Buranda home. Two years later, on 16th January, while working in his yard, David collapsed. He died in the ambulance on route to the South Brisbane Hospital.[24] He was 68 years of age.

Corporal David Kendrick was cremated at the Mt Thompson Crematorium on 18th January, 1957.

Private Benjamin Hugh Turner Kendrick

No. 319, C Company, 9th Battalion
(later Sergeant, A Company, 9th Battalion)

When Benjamin Kendrick entered the war, he was a smart, enterprising, ambitious young man with a promising future. On the first day of the Gallipoli Campaign, with bullet wounds to his thigh, arm and ear, he courageously willed himself to survive. More trials were faced on the Western Front, at Pozieres, Bullecourt and Polygon Wood. After being wounded on two more occasions, Ben returned home to face a life of ill health, economic hardship and depression.

Ben's early identity and character were forged in western Queensland. He was born on the 9th June, 1885 in the small outback community of Muttaburra, 100 kilometres north of Longreach, where his father, Robert Kendrick, worked as the Police Magistrate. The family later transferred to the more remote district of Thargomindah and then to Charters Towers, where Ben completed his schooling. From his childhood in western Queensland, Ben gained a love of the Australian bush. The challenges and isolation of the outback taught him the importance of resourcefulness and the loyalty of good mates. At Charters Towers, he trained to be a saddler while aspiring to attain the skills of an Australian bushman.

When Ben was in his late teens, the family moved to Brisbane. His parents purchased a large home named "Braemar" on Enoggera Terrace at Red Hill. Leaving the bush was difficult, but Ben, an enterprising young man, was determined to prosper in the city. Unable to find work as a saddler, he used his entrepreneurial skills to establish a small business selling timber and firewood to the residents of the surrounding suburbs. In the 1913 Post Office Directory, he proudly appeared as

'Benjamin Hugh Kendrick, Fuel Merchant.' With boundless energy, as his firewood business grew, Ben also sought secure employment with the Queensland Railways. He obtained a permanent position with the maintenance branch as a bridge carpenter.[1]

Leisure time was limited, but Ben filled it with a wide variety of interests. A favoured sport was competitive target shooting. Ben was a skilled rifleman and successful competitor at many local competitions.[2] Dog breeding was another passion. In partnership with his mother, he established breeding kennels at 'Braemar' for Airedale and Bull terrier dogs. At the Exhibition and other Brisbane dog shows, their dogs became well-known competitors.[3] A favourite was a pedigree bull terrier named 'General Buller', which became Ben's constant and much loved companion.

A keen interest in military matters was also maintained. Ben sought opportunities to follow in the steps of the popular heroes of the day, the noble soldiers of the Imperial regiments protecting the Empire. In 1906, when a volunteer company of the Australian Corps of Signallers was formed in Brisbane, he was one of its first recruits. With enthusiasm, Ben embraced military life. He attended parades three nights a week at Blackall Street, Petrie Terrace and on two Saturday afternoons each month.[4] Also, he enjoyed weekend camps and completed study courses on topics such as Morse code, the use of heliographs and transmitting messages by mirrors. Life was hectic, but Ben relished the adventure and comradery of the Signallers' No. 5 Company militia.

He did not hesitate when Australia entered the war. On the 18th August, Ben was one of the first volunteers to take the oath of allegiance at Petrie Terrace and, the next day, dressed in civilian clothing, he joined the first recruits pitching tents at the new military camp in Bell's Paddock at Enoggera. Accompanying him into camp was his treasured bulldog, 'General Buller,' which he expected he would soon have to farewell. However, to Ben's great relief, his dog quickly won the hearts of the other soldiers. It was decided Buller should remain in camp as the official mascot for C Company. To identify their mascot, the soldiers deemed Buller needed a uniform and the princely sum of 15 guineas (more than $1500 in today's value) was raised to cover the cost.[5] The result was an extravagant coat fashioned in the Battalion colours, with the Australian flag, a kangaroo and the words, 'General Buller, C Coy' intricately embroidered on either side. As any dog would, Buller relished the attention.

Five days before embarking for overseas service, Brisbane officially farewelled the 9th Battalion. It was a day Ben would never forget. As the regiment's mascot, General Buller led the infantry in a parade of some 2000 men. The route of several miles, from Enoggera to the City, on sun-baked roads was arduous, but, with Buller by his side, Ben marched with a formidable stride. Along the way, small groups gathered to greet them but, in the city, the Battalion's reception was extraordinary. From every window, veranda, and crowded pavement, spectators cheered their departing heroes. Queen Street was a blaze with flags and streamers. At the head of the Infantry, Colonel Lee rode on horseback and immediately behind him were 'General Buller' and Ben. The Telegraph reported, *'Buller was in the glory of a brightly coloured tunic and looked fully conscious of his honours.'*[6] Ben's pride was immeasurable.

In Egypt and throughout much of the Gallipoli campaign, Buller remained by Ben's side. While Ben was engaged in long hours of rigorous training at the desert camp at Mena, Buller kept busy ridding the camp of pariah dogs. He was also helpful in 'discouraging' itinerant Egyptian hawkers who were constantly harassing the troops. In a letter home, Ben boasted, Buller is 'quite a soldier' now, and he knows all the bugle calls as well as we do.'[7]

At the Gallipoli landing, silence was essential. Therefore, Buller could not land with Ben. He remained on the battleship, 'Queen,' but was brought onshore later that day. In the evening, it is said Buller was a conspicuous figure on the beach.[8] For almost two months, he remained by Ben's side in the trenches at Gallipoli. They were only separated when Buller received a gunshot wound to the ear and was evacuated, with other casualties, to the Auxiliary Hospital in Cairo, where he stayed for some time providing important comfort to convalescing soldiers.[9] Later, although not always with Ben, Buller served gallantly in France and was wounded four times. The troops held him in the highest regard, honouring him as an 'Original' Anzac. On the battlefield, he provided a comfort and was a treasured reminder of home. Sadly, at war's end, he could not return home with Ben. The much loved veteran of C Company died in a military dogs' home near London in 1932, aged 19 years.[10]

For Ben, the first day on Gallipoli Campaign was a torturous baptism of fire. His experience survives in a letter written to his mother, six weeks after the landing.[11] It reveals, by early morning, with a small group, Ben reached a position more than a mile ahead of the main body. He crossed 400 Plateau and moved beyond the 2nd Ridge into Legge Valley, where he joined one of the scattered isolated bands of soldiers heroically holding on against great odds. Their advanced position was made extremely perilous when, at about 10 am, Colonel MacLagan, commander of the 3rd Brigade, gave up all notion of capturing the 3rd Ridge and ordered arriving troops to dig in on the 2nd Ridge. This left scattered advance groups like Ben's, suddenly isolated without reinforcements.

Their situation worsened when, shortly after midday, the Turks launched a major counter-attack. Heavy guns pounded the Lone Pine area as the enemy moved forward across Legge Valley. Against this onslaught, Ben's group obstinately held on but, by the late afternoon, they had no option but to retreat. With a hail of Turkish bullets raining upon them, Ben made a desperate bid for safety.

'You will think it a wonder I am alive when I tell you I collected four bullets from my clothing besides those that really hit me. One went through my cap and down the side of my face and knocked a bit off my left ear.... That was when I was hit in the thigh.'

Bleeding, in pain and unable to walk or stand, and with the Turks advancing rapidly, Ben was in a dire predicament. According to the recollections of Lieutenant Fortescue, 9th Battalion, *'There were as many wounded men as whole ones, so to attempt to get these back would make a certainty of our being all wiped out.'*[12] They had no choice. The wounded had to be left behind.

'They had to leave me there. I said, 'You go on; I will get back somehow?'

The Turkish commander, Sefik, later reported, during his advance onto the Second Ridge, *'virtually all sides were covered in corpses – some wounded men were still lying in a state of agony, some in their death throes.'*[13]

As Ben lay there, believing he was about to face his death, he readied his rifle and fixed his bayonet. The Turks were very near. He was determined to make a stand rather than be taken prisoner.

'I could see them at times, and I intended not to be taken prisoner, and to sell my life dearly if it came to the pinch.'

Fortunately, Ben's instinct for survival was strong. He hid himself as best as he could and waited for the cover of darkness. Then, in excruciating pain, he crawled slowly on his hands and knees through the prickly bushes towards the Australian line. It took many hours to cover the almost two kilometres.

'You should have seen by hands and knees when I had gone about a mile. It was very rough country, and the bushes are very prickly, so when I came to a bit of a donga I tried another way - sitting down, and going backwards. It was a slight relief....... After about another half a mile or so, I came upon the boys digging themselves in.'

He arrived late in the evening and was advised to go immediately to the casualty dressing station on the beach, but, by then, adrenalin was blurring his pain and judgement. Incredibly, he ignored this instruction. The Turks were hitting the Anzac line hard, and, as Ben could still fire a rifle, he selflessly chose to stay to help.

'I wanted to give the beggars a bit back for what they had done to me.'

At about 4 a.m., his condition alarmed a medical officer who ordered him to immediately leave the frontline. *'I thought it was dashed bad luck to have to go in the thick of it, and leave the boys up to their eyes in trouble.'*

The overcrowded hospital ship, "Ionian", transported Ben to Cairo, where he spent the next 11 weeks recuperating.

When he re-joined his unit at Gallipoli on the 10th July, the situation on the Peninsula was deplorable. After almost three months, they had made no worthwhile gains. Swarms of flies and the stench of death were everywhere. His mates were in a terrible state. The constant threat of snipers and artillery had frayed the nerves of even the strongest men. Sickness was spreading and morale was very low. The horrors shocked Ben but, fortunately, during his first few weeks on the Peninsula, he was removed from the trenches. A good mate, Frank Loud, another member of the first boat ashore, saw that Ben's wound still caused him pain. As a favour, he relinquished to him his position as water guard at a spring behind the frontline. Frank wrote,

'About 12th July, one of my old mates arrived back from hospital. He had been hit the day we landed. The bullet passing through his thigh bone without breaking it and after a couple of days spent in the trenches the bone began to ache so I suggested he should take my place and take things quietly.'[14]

After this temporary respite ended, Ben returned to the trenches where he endured more than four arduous and dangerous months, taking part in numerous raids, counter-attacks, demonstrations and engagements. He fortunately survived unscathed and finally left the

Peninsula on the 16th November when the Battalion was granted an overdue period of rest on Lemnos. In a rare photograph taken while on the island, he and mates Cecil Holdway, Lionel Wilson and John Short, appeared exhausted and battle worn. The uniforms they had worn for more than six months were ragged but their pose remained defiant. Gallipoli had not destroyed their strength and spirit.

After leaving Gallipoli, Ben's first major encounter with the German enemy began on 23rd July, 1916, at Pozieres on the Western Front. For four horrific days and nights, shells and shrapnel rained on the 9th as they attempted to take this small village in the Somme River valley. The cost was enormous. The Battalion went into action 1016 strong but came out with only 623 men. Many of those who survived left the battlefield severely shell-shocked. After the loss of so many, the Battalion had to re-organize. On 1st August, Ben's abilities as a soldier were recognized with a promotion to Temporary Sergeant of A Company's No 2 Platoon.

On the 19th August, the 9th Battalion faced the enemy again. In his new role as Sergeant, Ben bravely led his platoon into the battle for Mouquet Farm, a ruined farm house on high ground near Pozieres. For three days, they fought desperately and were again subjected to a relentless German artillery bombardment. 27 Queenslanders lost their lives and 125 of the Battalion were wounded.[15] Like Pozieres, many suffered shell-shock. Ben was fortunate to survive. His full promotion to Sergeant came on the 26th September.

After the horrific ordeals at Pozieres and Mouquet Farm, the Battalion moved north to the Ypres area of Flanders to join the front line trenches at Flers. One of Europe's coldest winters was beginning and conditions were deplorable. Mud in some trenches was 30 centimetres deep and the pollution from dead bodies was causing widespread disease. In the unsanitary conditions, Ben contracted scabies, a dreaded ailment that caused intense itching and, if left untreated, infected sores that led to trench fever and typhus. On 8th November, Ben left the battlefield for two weeks' treatment at the 4th Stationary Hospital at Arques in northern France.

When he re-joined his unit, life in the trenches had become even more unbearable. The severe winter weather worsened. The only relief soldiers could hope for was when the mud froze. Like many other, Ben's physical and mental health declined significantly. He later recalled that it was during this time he experienced his first attack of heart trouble.[16]

After surviving the bitter winter, in the Spring of 1917, luck ran out. At dusk on the 6th May, the 9th was sent into the line to take over the left flank at Bullecourt. Ben led his platoon forward in the darkness through a communication trench choked with dead bodies. Upon reaching the enemy trenches in the early hours of the morning, they were immediately engaged in a fiercely fought battle along narrow passages. Pineapple bombs and the enemy's dreaded flame throwers caused heavy losses. Ben received a gunshot wound to his left hand. He was one of the 161 casualties that the 9th Battalion suffered for the capture of just 650 yards of German trenches. Amid the frightful action, Ben left the battlefield, fearing for the fate of his platoon. The next day, while waiting to be evacuated to England, tragic news arrived. His men had fought gallantly and survived the battle at Bullecourt, but as they left the trenches, a German shell burst upon them. There were many casualties. Four mates were killed.[17]

In England, exhausted and dispirited, Ben was admitted to London's Wandsworth hospital. Fortunately, the gunshot had not severed the tendons in his hand and the wound healed quickly. A month later, he was discharged and granted well deserved leave. For two weeks, Ben enjoyed London as a tourist and attempted to forget the horror of war.

On the 6th August, 1917, orders came for his return to the front. He re-joined his Battalion at Vieux-Berguin in France as they were about to enter the second stage of the great offensive known as the 3rd Battle of Ypres. During this operation, for the third time, Ben became a casualty of war. As they marched through Chateau Wood on the 19th September, a deadly enemy barrage fell upon them. It lasted 20 minutes but seemed like an hour. Another bombardment, including gas shells, followed twenty minutes later. The 9th lost all its company commanders and half its junior officers, but bravely pushed forward. The next day, at 5.40 a.m., in the morning mist, they continued their advance. It was then that Ben received another wound to his hand.

He spent three weeks recuperating at the Base Camp at Havre before returning once more to the front on the 29th October, 1917. Another horrific ordeal was about to occur in the trenches at Passchendaele Ridge. Five days after Ben's arrival, the 9th made a daring frontal advance at Tyne Cot against a stubbornly held trench. It was an ambitious operation that failed miserably and placed Ben's Company in great peril. He and his platoon became hopelessly trapped in No-man's-land and were forced to shelter in shell holes. All seemed lost. Death was imminent until B and C Companies mounted a clever response. Their swift counter-attack briefly distracted the enemy, allowing the trapped soldiers the opportunity to reach safety.

Ben began 1918 with an impressive battle record. He had survived Pozieres, Mouquet Farm, Bullecourt, Menin Road and Tyne Cot as well as Gallipoli, but each had taken a toll on his physical and mental wellbeing. Mercifully, a much needed reprieve came early in the year with a transfer on attachment to England to the 1st Training Battalion at Sutton Veny in rural Wiltshire. Two months in England allowed him to regain his strength.

Ben returned to the horrors in France in May. As he marched towards another uncertain battle, the overwhelming feeling of dread and foreboding was far too familiar. When his platoon was almost at their new position near Sercus, another devastating enemy shelling hit them hard. The barrage shattered Ben's nerves, but he survived and, days later, his good fortune continued. He received orders on 1st June to take up permanent duty with the 1st Training Battalion in England. It was with an enormous sense of relief that Ben returned to the Sutton Veny camp, where he remained for the last five months of the war.

On 28th October, after four years of overseas service, Ben became a lucky recipient of 'Special 1914 Leave'. As a soldier who volunteered in 1914, he was granted two months in Australia. However, as he earnestly made plans to leave the war, two weeks later, the Armistice was declared. Suddenly, thousands of troops also needed to be repatriated home. His name was added to the long waiting lists, but the prospect of a long delay was too much for Ben to bear. Desperate to return home, he arranged his own passage via a long and costly route through America. He left England on the 19th January, 1919 for New York[18] and then, after travelling for three days across the United States, on the 4th February, at San Francisco, he boarded the "Ventura" for Australia.[19]

Ben's discharge from the army came in June 1919. Like so many others, he re-entered civilian life, restless and haunted by trauma. He was uncertain about what to do with the rest of his life. Facing few job prospects in Brisbane, he looked to New Guinea for opportunities. Australia had received the mandate to govern the former German colony and appropriated more than 200 German plantations that needed overseers. Some of Ben's mates from the 9th Battalion, disillusioned by the soldier settlement scheme in Australia, had already taken jobs there. Ben also had useful and important family contacts in New Guinea. During the war, his two older brothers had established successful careers in New Guinea. Percy Kendrick managed Rorona Plantations and Robert Kendrick was Treasurer of Papua.

Ben aimed to replicate his brothers' successes and, for a short time, his prospects looked promising. He left for New Guinea immediately after his discharge and took a position as plantation overseer at Orona Plantation in the remote Eastern Highlands. It was a challenging job, especially for a shell-shocked veteran of war, but Ben was determined. Despite the isolation, he even found romance and, in 1921, married Brisbane girl, Florence Louisa Osmond at Port Moresby.

Less than 12 months after the wedding, their life in New Guinea fell into disarray. Ben's recurring shortness of breath, exhaustion and chest pains, which began during the war, became severe. After being hospitalized in Port Moresby for two weeks for a suspected heart attack, work as an overseer was no longer possible. In Brisbane, doctors diagnosed 'cardiac neurosis', also known as effort syndrome, 'irritable heart' or 'soldier's heart'. It was an ailment frequently diagnosed after the war to describe stress disorders found in soldiers who, after suffering prolonged mental stress, developed an inability to adapt to new environments.[20] In simple terms, Ben was suffering shell-shock or PTSD.

On his return to Brisbane, with the help of his family, a new future began. Another brother, William, who managed a large motor factory, the Canada Cycle Motor Body Works in Water Street, The Valley, provided Ben with a job as a motor trimmer. Assembling panels, upholstery and canopies on new motor vehicles was not physically demanding work and Ben was pleased to be part of an exciting new industry. With secure employment, he and Florence moved to a new home at Hilda Street, Alderley, named "Fernlea", and began preparing for a family.

Regrettably, unexpected tragedies and extraordinary sadness followed. In March 1922, Ben's mother suddenly died and three months later, his elderly father passed away. A third tragic bereavement occurred in February

The First Ashore

when Ben's brother, William, drowned while on a fishing trip.[21] However, for Ben and Florence, the cruellest and most severe blows followed in 1925 and 1928. Their first child, two-year-old Ivan, died suddenly, and three years later, their only other child, Ross, also passed away.

As they attempted to cope with these devastating blows, the Great Depression added more pain. Ben lost his job in 1929 and, like so many others, he and Florence were forced to rely on sustenance payments and food rations. Over the next four years, he joined Brisbane City Council's relief programme for the unemployed, labouring as a council road-worker. However, the work was irregular and, often, his health prevented him from working. Medical records indicate his unfitness for manual work. Ben continued to suffer severe shortness of breath, giddiness and occasional pains in the chest and shoulders. Also, there were serious bouts of depression. In September 1932, he was hospitalized for suspected heart trouble but doctors found no evidence of cardiac disease and, once again, concluded his symptoms were because of neurosis.

In 1933, a more suitable job with lighter duties was obtained as a cleaner in the Union Bank Chambers in the City. To be closer to his work, he and Florence left their home at Alderley and rented a house at 12 Wilson Street, Paddington. Sadly, despite the lighter workload, Ben's health problems continued. He spent four weeks in hospital in 1936 and another two weeks in 1938. In his own words, he was *'just hanging on to the job.'*[22] At the end of 1937, he gave up work altogether.

At 52 years of age, an old aged pension was not available to Ben. Instead, optimistically he applied for a war pension. To his great shock, the application was abruptly denied. The Repatriation Commission disregarded his extensive war service and callously deemed his medical condition was not because of the war. Disillusioned, Ben re-applied but was again rejected. Refusing to accept the decision, a desperate further appeal was made, but it was also rejected.[23]

Although Ben's disappointment and sense of betrayal was enormous, he maintained a strong belief in the spirit of Anzac. The fraternity of ex-soldiers provided him with great comfort and throughout his post-war life, Ben worked tirelessly to promote and preserve the Anzac tradition of mateship and service. He took leadership roles in various war veteran organizations. He was a long time Committee member of the 9th Battalion Reunion Association and also served as its President during 1926 and 1927.²⁴ As well, he was a very active member of the Omrah Association, an organisation founded in the 1930s to preserve the comradeship of the men who sailed to war on the first troopship, "Omrah". Even when his health was failing in his last years, Ben continued his work as an event organizer for the Association. He was a key facilitator for the 1937 farewell given to Gallipoli veteran, Matron Paten, on her retirement from Rosemount Repatriation Hospital.²⁵

Sadly, in August 1942, suffering severe chest pains, Ben was admitted to the hospital for the last time. The incredible toughness of this proud original Anzac could no longer be sustained. He died at the Diamantina Hospital on the 21st August, aged 57 years.²⁶ Although the ordeals of Gallipoli and the numerous battles on the Western Front were survived, war left him broken. Over the years, neuroses and depression gnawed at his health. The official cause of death was recorded as congestive heart failure, but, more accurately, this brave Anzac was a casualty of war.

Sergeant Benjamin Kendrick was cremated at the Mt Thompson Crematorium.

Private Samuel Aubrey McKenzie

No. 292, C Company, 9th Battalion
(later Lieutenant, A Company)

Private Robert McNeil Crawford McKenzie

No. 289, C Company, 9th Battalion
(later Lieutenant, A Company)

The McKenzie brothers arrived in Australia in 1913. Less than twelve months later, when war was declared, they were among Queensland's first volunteers. They landed with the first boat and fought gallantly at Gallipoli and later on the Western Front. Their dedication to duty and tenacity saw them rise quickly through the ranks to attain commissions as Lieutenants. Both brothers suffered serious trauma and shell-shock, but after recuperation, courageously returned to the battlefield. Samuel was killed first. Eleven months later, his brother, Robert, was also dead.

Prior to war, their short lives were closely intertwined. Despite differences in personality, the brothers possessed a close bond enhanced by their shared adventurous spirit. Friends and family always regarded them as a pair, fondly labelling them 'Big Mac' and 'Little Mac.' Sam was so named because he stood seven centimetres taller with a slightly larger build. He was a quieter man with a serious disposition and took the role of responsible older brother. In contrast, Robert, 17 months younger, with blue eyes and dark complexion, was known for his easy-going, charming, jovial nature.

The brothers spent their childhood and early adult life in Liverpool,

England. Born in 1886 and 1888, at nearby Birkenhead, the boys had a privileged upbringing. Their father, Robert McKenzie, in partnership with his father and brother, owned a successful umbrella manufacturing business known as 'E.M. Crawford's'. The family lived in Wallasey, a fashionable residential area for successful Liverpool merchants. Their home, "Redfern", in Lyndhurst Street,[1] was a short walk from the popular seaside promenade of West Brighton. For the brothers and their younger sisters, Edith and Mary, "Redfern" provided many wonderful childhood memories. Later, as the family business prospered, a second residence, "Aubrey House," was purchased in the equally prosperous suburb of Wavertree.[2] The family's affluence also allowed the boys an excellent education at one of Liverpool's most respected grammar schools, the Institute High School for Boys.[3]

Although childhood years were undeniably happy, as teenagers, the Crawford children endured much sorrow. Their father developed a rare sickness known as pernicious anaemia. Although easily treated today, in the 1900s, it was fatal. Helplessly, Samuel and Robert watched their father's slow and agonizing physical and mental decline. He passed away in 1904, aged 44 years.

Their mother's large inheritance of almost £28,000 (equivalent to more than £3 million today) secured a comfortable future but, as Sam and Robert grew into young men, they were eager to assert their independence and escape life in Liverpool. As a 15-year-old, Sam left home to enlist in the 8th Kings Liverpool Regiment stationed at Warrington, east of Liverpool.[4] He enjoyed military life but, after completing his seven years' service, new challenges were sought. Lured by advertisements that promised untold opportunities in far-away America, Sam departed on the ship "Coronia" for New York on 27th April, 1909. Although his immigration papers stated he migrated as a farmer,[5] upon arriving in America, Sam returned to what he was familiar with. He firstly worked with the Transport Service of the US Army and later became a member of the Canadian militia.[6]

Meanwhile, Robert gained work with one of Liverpool's many shipping companies and, by 1912, had become a senior officer working as a ship's purser. His energetic and outgoing nature ensured his success and popularity with both stewards and passengers. Valuable leadership skills were also gained that would later be crucial to his role in the war.

The First Ashore

When not at sea, until 1913, Robert continued to live at his mother's home, "Redfern". In Liverpool, he was an active member of the Harmonic Lodge of Freemasonry[7] and also shared his brother's interest in military affairs by becoming a volunteer in the local army reserve, Liverpool's Scot's Regiment.[8]

At the end of Sam's fourth year in America, the promises of a prosperous future had not eventuated. He became disgruntled and was eager to avoid another bitterly cold Canadian winter. After some correspondence, he made plans with Robert to start a new life together in Australia. Sam paid for his passage by working as a deckhand on the ship "Makura" departing Vancouver for Sydney on 6th August 1913.[9] In contrast, four weeks later, Robert left England as a saloon passenger on the comfortable P and O liner, "Medina".[10]

The brothers reunited in Sydney, but their reunion was disappointingly brief. Job opportunities and connections in Australia compelled them to go their separate ways. Sam headed north to Brisbane to work as a commercial traveller while Robert had contacts in Adelaide and the offer of a position with the Adelaide Steamship Company.

Yet despite this setback, life in Australia began well for the brothers. At Wilston in Brisbane, Sam rented a room with the Davis family and was accepted almost as a member of their family. The friendship and support of Mr. and Mrs. Davis and their two daughters, Daisy and Ivy, would become crucial for both brothers during the war years. In Adelaide, Robert resided with the influential Holland family at their "Woodhurst" home in Millswood. Thomas Holland, a solicitor and a prominent Adelaide citizen, had been the mayor of Unley and was an important leader of Freemasonry in South Australia. Robert's stay with the Holland family was short but, during that time, their daughter Hilda, developed a special fondness for the handsome young Englishman.[11]

Robert began work almost immediately as a ship's purser. He was fortunate to obtain a position on the "Grantola," one of the Adelaide Steamship Company's most popular interstate passenger steamers. In 1914, the ship was grandly described as *'a modern passenger liner, being lighted by electricity and fitted with wireless apparatus.'*[12] As well as the prestige of working on such a fine ship, for Robert, an added benefit was its itinerary along the east coast with brief but regular stops in Brisbane.

In July 1914, he was particularly excited to receive some extended time in Brisbane. After that month's trip to Cairns, the "Grantola" went into dock for an overhaul. Robert disembarked in Brisbane on 28th July with the expectation of spending several weeks with his brother. He was blissfully unaware that days later, life would change irrevocably. On 5th August, when Australia officially entered the war, Robert's ship was immediately requisitioned and suddenly, he was unemployed.

However, there was no despondency. The McKenzie brothers were proud Empire men who greeted the news of war with great enthusiasm. The next day, they were among the first at the Town Hall to place their names on the register of volunteers and, twelve days later, on 18th August, when the official recruiting process opened at Blackall Street, Petrie Terrace, Sam and Robert became some of the first members of the Queensland contingent of the new Australian Imperial Force. It was an exciting time.

Events moved rapidly. Four weeks later, the brothers embarked with the 9th Battalion embarked on the "Omrah", the first troopship to leave Queensland for war. Their destination was Egypt, where, for four months, in the scorching desert sands, a repetitive routine of tough, intensive military training was endured. The brothers were moved from C Company to A Company and became part of Lieutenant Duncan Chapman's Number 3 Platoon.

At the fateful Gallipoli landing on 25th April, they sat, with fear and excitement, together in the lead boat in the Number 1 tow with the rest of Chapman's men. At about 4.30 a.m., before the first rifle was fired, Sam and Robert scrambled ashore and took refuge under the shelter of the cliffs. There, they watched as boat upon boat arrived under a deadly rain of Turkish gunfire. When the call came, 'Come on Queenslanders! Come on the Ninth!' with bayonets fixed, Robert and Sam joined the heroic charge up the steep slopes.

Their exact movements and actions immediately after leaving the beach remain unknown. However, sometime during the fierce fighting on the first day, Robert sustained a shrapnel wound to his right leg. Late in the day, he was evacuated to a hospital ship and transported to Cairo, where he remained in hospital for four weeks. Sam faced the beginning of the Gallipoli campaign without his brother's support, but comforted by the knowledge Robert survived the landing and was now safely removed from the ordeal.

The First Ashore

The first week was a horrifying test of endurance as the Anzacs fought desperately to keep their tenuous foothold. By the 29th, Sam, like most others, had gone four nights with little sleep. He was in the last stages of exhaustion when orders came for the remnants of the 9th Battalion to muster on the beach. Sadly, only half of the almost 1000 men who landed answered this call. At the muster, 19 officers and 496 other ranks were recorded as casualties.[13] The 9th's loss was enormous, but there was no time for rest or sorrow. Turkish snipers and unpredictable shrapnel fire were relentless. Nowhere was safe. Trench digging became the chief preoccupation. Sam tried to stay positive, but began to doubt his chance of surviving. On 5th May, he penned a short will, leaving all his possessions to his mother.[14]

By the time Robert returned to Gallipoli on 23rd May, the situation in the trenches was deplorable. Water was scarce, the heat intolerable and a horrendous stench of death pervaded the air as thick swarms of flies menaced the hundreds of unburied bodies. Fortunately, the next day, sense prevailed. An armistice was called so burials could occur.

Sam was grateful for Robert's return. The brothers gained strength from each other and were once again inseparable. Command even regarded them as a pair. They were both promoted to Corporals in the same company on the same day in early July. However, as the months passed, the strain of continuous service impacted them differently. Sam became weary and less enthused by battle. In contrast, Robert, who had not endured the first difficult month of the campaign, was more energized and determined. After his promotion to Corporal, he earnestly sought further leadership roles and, on the 4th August, took on the enormous responsibility of Sergeant Major of A Company.

Robert's overzealous dedication to duty alarmed Sam. He watched as his young brother pushed himself to exhaustion. By late August, with weakened health, Robert fell victim to the epidemic of dysentery sweeping through the Battalion but, aware the high number of evacuations was dangerously weakening the army's strength, he stubbornly refused to leave the battlefield.

However, days later, the choice was no longer his. While the Battalion was strengthening its defences on 3rd September, the Turks shelled their position. Robert took a bullet to his left wrist and left leg. These severe wounds mercifully forced his removal from the

Peninsula. He was taken on board the hospital ship "Salta", trembling, confused and in a pitiful condition. Six days later, at the hospital in Alexandria, while treating his bullet wounds, doctors noted he suffered severe dysentery and was in a serious neurotic state.[15] Robert's selfless dedication to duty had resulted in his complete nervous breakdown. Official recognition of his gallantry and selflessness was noted in the 9th Battalion War Diary, dated 22nd September, and his superior officers also submitted his name for the Honours List.[16]

Recovery was a slow process. After a month in a hospital in Alexandria, followed by three weeks in Cairo's 1st Australian General Hospital, Robert's pain remained considerable. His leg was not healing, and his trembling and confusion persisted. As well, he suffered severe headaches and could not sleep. Medical officers diagnosed severe neurasthenia (shell-shock) with a recommendation that he be immediately returned to Australia. For Robert, this decision was devastating. Return to Australia removed him from his family in England. Their care and nurture was desperately needed. Also, separation from his platoon and his brother added to his anguish. Robert worried incessantly about their fate.

The long six-week voyage to Australia further impeded his recovery. On the third day at sea on the crowded hospital ship, "Kanowna", Robert's high temperature and unrelenting pain forced doctors to reluctantly operate. They explored the wound cavity for foreign matter and inserted a drainage tube but, three weeks later, little improvement was noted. His thigh wound was still discharging freely and there was some evidence of a staphylococcus infection.[17] Regrettably, the necessary vaccine was not on board, which meant this infection remained untreated until he reached Brisbane.

Meanwhile, at Gallipoli, the day after Robert was wounded, Sam gained additional responsibilities. Hesitantly, he took on his brother's role as Sergeant, becoming Temporary Sergeant of No 2 Platoon.[18] With courage and resilience, he carried this added burden of leadership throughout the last two months of the Campaign. The horrors continued but, somehow, Sam managed to remain physically unscathed.

His survival was an incredible feat of endurance. Sam left Gallipoli with the rest of the 9th Battalion on 16th November, 1915 as one of the few 'original' Anzacs who endured the entire campaign without a wound, illness or evacuation. From the 1000 strong 9th Battalion that landed on 25th April, and the 500 reinforcements that followed in the first few weeks, only 93 other men could boast the same unbroken period of service. Sam became a member of a select group whose courage and endurance was recognized with a unique honour known as the 'Kilcoy' or 'Butler Medal'.[19] Although proud of his achievement, he also left Gallipoli extremely battle weary and exhausted.

In Australia, Robert's strength had slowly returned. By mid-April 1916, his leg was completely healed. There were some bouts of anxiety and loneliness, but his mental health had improved considerably. After being discharged from Kangaroo Point Hospital, four weeks' leave was spent alone at the Pacific Hotel in Southport. In a letter to Daisy Davis, Robert complained, *'I have to talk to myself for company.'*[20] The fate of his brother and mates on the battlefield was a constant worry. He felt useless and frustrated by the inabilities that prevented him from returning to the war.

As Robert convalesced at Southport, Sam moved with the 9th Battalion to the Western Front in northern France. There was some satisfaction that finally they would face the German enemy, but Sam also felt apprehensive. Soon he would experience an abrupt and ugly introduction to this new phase of the war. On 19th April, the men moved to within a couple of kilometres of the front line in a supposedly quieter area known as the "Nursery". The sound of intermittent shell fire seemed menacingly close, but the presence of French civilians still living nearby reassured Sam that this sector was relatively calm and safe. On arrival, the Battalion worked through most of the night fortifying nearby trenches. They returned to their new billets, a group of farmhouses and outbuildings near the small village of Rouge-de-Bout, for rest on 20th April. It was dinner-time, exactly five minutes past, when the Germans unleashed an unexpected and terrifying artillery attack. The first three shots went wide, but the next one directly struck one of the huts.[21] As men frantically raced to help their mates trapped inside, more shells rained down. Several men were killed instantly, and many more were horribly wounded. Bodies were blown to pieces and made unrecognisable. Another shell exploded against the brick wall of a billet where a large group of C Company was sheltering. At the end of the tragic day, 25 men were dead and 51 were wounded.

During the terror and chaos, rather than seeking shelter, Sam displayed exceptional courage and selflessness. Repeatedly, he risked his life to help the wounded and dying. His gallant actions and meritorious conduct were mentioned in Despatches on 21st April. *'Sergeant Samuel A McKenzie at Rouge de Bout, on 20th April 1916, during the shelling of 9th Battalion billets, whilst under heavy shell fire, continuously rendered invaluable help in the removal and tending the wounded.'*[22] Military Orders on 29th August, 1916, also officially recognized and promulgated appreciation of his gallant conduct.[23]

Unfortunately, heroism came at a cost. Sam left the horror at Rouge de Bout feeling 'done in.' A compassionate CO realized this and, mercifully, weeks later, when some of the 9th was given leave in England for the first time, he made sure Sergeant McKenzie was chosen. With haste, Sam travelled home to the care and love of his family in Liverpool. It was a tearful and disturbing reunion. Sam was barely recognizable to them. His exhausted and haggard appearance was shocking. Days later, the extreme fatigue that he had been suppressing for so long, could no longer be contained. Sam suffered an almost complete breakdown. On 8th May, his family sent an urgent cable to army headquarters in London stating that he had fallen seriously ill at his home in Liverpool.[24] Leave was mercifully extended to four weeks, but this was an insufficient time for any kind of recovery.

A deeply distressed mother farewelled her son in early June. She realized Sam remained seriously unwell and feared the worst. He reached the front in France as his Battalion was carrying out a series of daring diversionary raids. Although eager to take part, it was obvious to all that Sam was unfit for active duty. Two days later, he was admitted to the field hospital and removed from the frontline. The hospital in Boulogne diagnosed 'debility,' the broad World War 1 term used to describe mentally and physically exhausted soldiers. A more accurate diagnosis today would be Post Traumatic Stress Disorder. It would take almost seven weeks for Sam to regain his strength.

As he began his recovery in France, on the other side of the world, Robert completed the last days of his convalescence. After six months in Brisbane, he was tired of the endless idle days and desperate to re-join his brother on the frontline. Finally, in June, medical officers deemed him fit for active service. However, Robert was disappointed.

Instead of returning to the Western Front as expected, on 1st July command sent him for two months' officer training at the newly established school at Duntroon in Canberra. While most men regarded selection for Duntroon as a proud achievement, Robert saw it only as an unnecessary, frustrating and shameful delay to performing his proper duty. He wrote on 15th July, *'I regret not being able to get away with the re-enforcements …… I shall feel almost too ashamed to own up to it.'*[25]

His first weeks at Duntroon were difficult. Robert resented the army's decision to keep him in Australia and lacked any motivation to succeed. He was also not confident of his abilities and, at the end of the second week, admitted that it was extremely unlikely he would pass the course. As well, he felt out of place among the young trainees at Duntroon. Their youthful naivety caused him constant annoyance as he observed, *'War has as yet not touched them.'* To him, these privileged young men seemed ignorant and self-absorbed, *'no one seems to take an interest in it (news from the front). No rush for the latest news, just a discussion as to whether the war will be over before they get their commissions. Poor things, they imagine … that the war will soon be over.'*[26]

Added to Robert's discontent was separation from his dear Brisbane friend, Daisy Davis. In one of his first letters from Duntroon he wrote, *'Another week has passed, making it a fortnight since I left you and it seems years.'*[27] Robert and Daisy's friendship grew in 1916, when Robert was repatriated to Brisbane. The only people he knew in the city were the Davis family of Wilston, with whom his brother had lived. It proved a fortunate contact. Mr. and Mrs. Davis and their daughters showed him great kindness during his recuperation at Kangaroo Point Hospital and, after his discharge, they invited him to live with them at their home "Romos" in Wilston. Although 18-year-old Daisy was already engaged to another man, a special fondness and friendship developed that would sustain Robert through the difficult times ahead.

During the first three weeks at Duntroon, Robert failed almost every course but, slowly, as the training continued, his confidence grew. Weeks later he reflected, *'I call myself a fool for being as I was in the first weeks but somehow I could not help it ……. made me realize that I was not then fit to return to the front and in that physical condition take charge of men.'*[28] In the second half of the programme, his marks improved markedly. His battlefield experience allowed him to excel at the more advanced field work. '*I have the advantage of the others in that.*' '*Since we have started the advanced work I have passed high up in everything except shooting which is still a bit shaky.*'[29] At the end of the course, there was every indication Robert would be a first-class officer.

Buoyed by his unexpected achievements at Duntroon, he returned to Queensland, eager for an overseas posting. Large casualty lists now appeared regularly in the newspapers. Each day, he fearfully perused them and, with feigned confidence, assured Daisy, '*Big Mac and I will see some more.*'

Meanwhile, in France, Sam's mental health improved, and he was discharged from hospital. While Robert was training at Duntroon, on 29th July, he returned to the front as part of reinforcements urgently required after the battle for Pozieres. The battle had been successful, but the casualties were enormous. Sam joined the survivors in the village of Berteaucourt where a re-structuring of the Battalion was taking place. After losing so many officers, positions had to be quickly filled, and Sam was an obvious candidate. Outwardly, his strong commitment to duty effectively masked his health issues and, after seven weeks' absence from the front, he appeared strengthened and revitalized. Therefore, on 5th August, Sam was promoted to 2nd Lieutenant.

Days later, orders were given for the 9th's return to the frontline. While the Battalion had been resting at Berteaucourt, the Germans re-captured Pozieres Heights and were now pushing forward to Mouquet Farm. With little experience in his new role as a Lieutenant, nervously, Sam led his men towards the battle. For the first time, he passed by the ruins of Pozieres. Not one building remained, and the surrounding landscape was totally destroyed. As they moved through Sausage Valley, closer into the line at Mouquet Farm, their path was blocked by an increasing tide of soldiers with horrific wounds heading back to support lines. Sam's unease grew markedly.

The hell of Pozieres was quickly reborn at Mouquet Farm on 20th August. For almost 48 hours, the 9th's front line came under a continuous barrage of heavy shell fire. Debris and death rained down upon Sam and his men as trenches crumbled. Men were buried alive, and the roar of shells was deafening. Many soon became shell-shocked. In this horror, Sam gallantly attempted to push his platoon forward. On the second day as they moved through the trench, a devastating shrieking shell exploded amongst them. Standing closest to Sam was Sergeant Denis Ward of 'H' Company. With brutal ease, the shrapnel ripped open the Sergeant's chest. He was alive but *'past all hope.'*[30] For Sam, mercifully, death came more quickly. His body was torn apart by the direct hit. He died instantly.

In Australia, for almost a month, Robert remained oblivious to his brother's fate. At Toowoomba army camp, with officer training completed, he continued to wait for his deployment and anxiously planned for the day he and Sam would be reunited. On 23rd September, Robert's world was shattered when the 220th Casualty List was released by the government censor.[31] Suddenly, Robert felt incredibly alone. More than a month passed before he wrote again to his dear friend, Daisy. On 1st November, he lamented, *'I have not been in the condition to write to you ...... I am such poor company now little girl, people soon get tired of me.'*[32]

Yet, despite overwhelming grief, Robert's resolve to return to the front did not diminish. Throughout October, he made persistent appeals to his superior officers. *'I wrote Captain Bell last Saturday, reminding him I was here and asking to be sent to the front.'*[33] His motivation was no longer simply patriotic duty. Now his brother's death needed to be avenged.

Finally, his orders arrived. On 17th November, Robert embarked with the 23rd Reinforcements, 9th Battalion on the troopship "Kyarra" for war. Their destination was England, where five more weeks of training was carried out at Dunnington on the Salisbury Plains. Although the delay frustrated Robert, the opportunity he received to spend some time with his grieving mother and family consoled him.

Robert arrived in France on 1st April, 1917. Despite his extensive preparation, more than a year had passed since he last saw active service, and he felt some trepidation. In freezing and wet conditions, the Battalion began their long march back to the frontline on 4th April. It took two days for them to reach their new position in a relatively quiet area near Lagincourt. To the north, the Germans were causing devastating damage at the 1st Battle of Bullecourt, inflicting 3,300 casualties and taking 1,170 Australians prisoner. They then turned their attention on the 9th Battalion and the rest of the 1st Division, who were precariously holding a dangerously thin line of almost 11 kilometres to the south. Realizing the Australian weakness, the

Germans launched a huge raid that aimed to capture all nine villages in the area, including Lagincourt.

An hour before dawn on 15th April, 26 German battalions attacked, forcing the 9th and three other Australian battalions into retreat. The village of Lagincourt was quickly lost. However, at 7.30 a.m., Robert and the other Lieutenants of the 9th and 20th Battalions, despite being outnumbered, bravely led their men forward in an unexpected counter-attack. The Germans were taken by surprise and soon found themselves caught between the advancing Australians and their own barbed wire while being hemmed in by Allied Artillery. A fearful slaughter followed. Hundreds of Germans were killed and 147 prisoners were taken. By mid-morning, the Australian front was re-established, and the Germans were pushed back behind the Hindenburg Line. For Robert, although the success of Lagincourt boosted his confidence as a Lieutenant, it also revealed the genuine horror of the Western Front.

After being relieved, the exhausted Battalion moved to the sunken roads nearby Morchies where, for the next week, Robert and his platoon worked each night fortifying the defence line. Working conditions in the continuing cold and wet weather were miserable and, with no escape from the dampness and mud, Robert's health soon suffered. He was admitted on 19th April to the 47th Casualty Clearing Station at Vareness with infective enteritis and diarrhoea. The next ten days in hospital allowed him some time for reflection. In a letter to Daisy, he wrote, *'if I go (die) it does not matter so much'*. He revealed his despondency as he struggled with the reality of war, *'it seemed funny for me to be trying to kill people again.'*[34]

The Second Battle of Bullecourt was about to begin when Robert returned to the front. On the third day of this great offensive, the 9th was ordered forward to take over the left flank. With enemy shells bursting about, Lieutenant McKenzie led his men into the line. As they neared the battle, the horror they met was shocking. On top of the trench on either side were dead bodies that had been hastily thrown there to clear the passage. In some places, the trench floor was so choked with the dead, Robert and his men had no option but to walk over them.

Throughout the night of the 6th May and into the next morning, Robert and his men were engaged in brutal fighting. With an objective to capture nearby trench positions, fierce bomb throwing battles were carried out along the narrow trenches. Eventually, 600 metres were captured, but the cost was again huge. Twenty-six 9th Battalion men lost their lives and 135 men were wounded.

Robert's exhausted platoon left the frontline on 8th May and moved to nearby Bapaume for two weeks' rest. Sleep was difficult. The rumble of guns and the lights on the horizon were constant reminders of the continuing horror at Bullecourt. When new orders arrived on 22nd May, there was enormous relief. The Battalion was sent to Ribemont, sixty kilometres south, far from the action where, mercifully, they would begin four months of training. This was the longest and most complete period of rest given since the war began.

The 9th moved north back into battle on 6th August, 1917. Wet weather continued and again they suffered deplorable conditions in muddy trenches. Robert's letters revealed his despair at the never-ending horrors, *'One has to do a lot of make believe you know to look outwardly happy in a mud-hole like the one I am writing this from.'*[35] Stoically and selflessly, he accepted his destiny, *'We are just about to go into another stunt, one of the biggest yet, and a lot of us are not coming out. It is alright if men like myself stop up there for good, because you see I am not engaged or married but there are others it is better for them to live.'*[36]

Robert led his men into battle once more. They arrived at Chateau Segard Camp, near Menin Road, on 18th September. The rain was heavy and, under the cover of darkness, in the early hours on the 20th September, the Battalion moved forward stealthily. Unfortunately, German flares detected their position and, at 4.20 a.m., while passing through Chateau Wood, a heavy barrage fell upon them. It lasted 20 minutes, and many men were hit. At 5 a.m., there was a second bombardment that included gas-shells. Casualties were again high. All company commanders and half of the junior officers were lost. Robert was severely wounded. With multiple shrapnel wounds, he was taken to the 10th Casualty Clearing Station, where, for many hours, he courageously held onto life. The following day, at 7.20 p.m., his fight was lost. The gallant young Lieutenant was buried on the battlefield with a full military service.

The McKenzie brothers lie together in Flanders' fields, 100 kilometres from each other. Robert was interred at the Lijseenthoek Military Cemetery (Plot 23, Row B) and Sam was buried at buried at Pozieres British Cemetery (Plot 1, Row H, Grave 20).

Private William Alexander Pollock

No. 316, C Company (later A Company),
9th Battalion

In many ways, Private William Pollock was more prepared for Gallipoli than other soldiers in the first boat ashore. He was older, not blinded by the enthusiasm or naivety of youth and, as a Boer War veteran, he knew the deadly reality of war. Also, twelve years' service in the British Army made him a skilled and confident soldier. Sadly, age and experience did him naught good at Gallipoli.

William was an Irishman, born on 26th September, 1877, in the small hamlet of Lismacarol, south of Londonderry, where for centuries, his family had farmed. Regrettably, during his childhood, the idyllic countryside, with its picturesque woodlands, wildflower meadows and quaint thatched cottages, was marred by troubled times. Rural areas became volatile and sometimes dangerous places to live as impoverished Irish farmers mobilized against an unjust system of landlordism. Sectarianism was also widespread and often brought William's family into conflict with authorities.[1]

Reluctantly, when William was about 14 years old, the Pollocks were forced to leave their tenanted farm near Killennan. They moved to a rented home at 20 Dungiven Road in Waterside, a Protestant suburb in Catholic Londonderry. William's father continued to work outside the city as a farm labourer while his mother and sisters found work as seamstresses in Londonderry's thriving clothing industry. William also gained his first job at the city's largest tannery and boot factory, Mr Harper's Fountain Hill tannery.[2] It was unpleasant work that required strong young lads to prepare and move heavy hides through noxious tanning pits. Work conditions were dangerous and extremely unhealthy and the pay was small, but for the children of tenant farmers, there were few other options apart from emigration or employment in the military.

In 1896, seventeen-year-old William chose the latter. He moved to Glasgow, where he enlisted in the 3rd Battalion of Glasgow's Highland Light Infantry.[3] His life changed dramatically, but William relished the opportunity for adventure and two months after enlisting, he also fulfilled a childhood dream. The renowned Irish regiment, the Royal Inniskilling Fusiliers whose parades William often admired as a child, began recruiting in Glasgow. He applied immediately for transfer and, on 22nd January, 1897, was overjoyed to be accepted as a Private in the 2nd Battalion.[4]

Proudly wearing the Irish Fusiliers' uniform, he returned with his new regiment to Ireland. As a bonus, he completed his military training at Omagh's St Lucia Barracks, less than 60 kilometres from his parents' home. Although it was a comfort to be near home, William grew restless. He was thirsty for adventure and longed for an overseas posting.

Two years later, on 12th January 1899, his hopes were realized. The 2nd Battalion received a posting to India. William was thrilled, but he soon found the reality of life in India was not as exciting as expected. A repetitive and tiresome routine of garrison duty dominated his life for the next three years.

An escape came when, in January 1902, his Regiment moved to join the 2nd Boer War. Unfortunately, the dullness of India was suddenly replaced by a savage guerrilla war. His Battalion was given the dangerous responsibility of manning mini-forts known as blockhouses. They acted gallantly by effectively impeding the movement of the Boers at strategic points across the veldt and, thus, contributed to bringing the war to an earlier close. They also achieved notable service in the Pietersburg district under Colonel Colenbrander, with their efforts also receiving praise from Lord Kitchener.[5]

While William was proud of the Fusiliers' gallant actions against the Boers, the war's murderous ordeals left harrowing scars. He witnessed huge casualties, with almost 200 of his battalion killed and over 300 wounded. He also watched helplessly as many fellow soldiers suffered slow, painful deaths from diseases such as typhoid. When victory was attained, 25-year-old William had enough of war and was eager to leave South Africa.

After an unpleasant posting to Egypt's desert, in October 1904, his company was ordered home. William had served five years overseas and was pleased to serve the rest of his time in Ireland. Much had changed during his absence. His brothers had also joined the military and now only his widowed mother, his sisters and grandmother lived at Dungiven Road. They provided for themselves by working long hours as seamstresses. It was a harsh existence. Fortunately, William's modest military income plus a South African War Gratuity enabled him to provide them some support.

After his time with the Fusiliers expired in January 1909, William returned to live in mother's home. However, transition from military life was difficult. Very few work opportunities existed in Londonderry for a 32-year-old man without a trade. Any labouring jobs he gained were not secure or well paid. Also, as the only son living at home, the responsibility for looking after his aging mother was a heavy burden. William felt trapped. He watched with envy when his adventurous sister, Bella and her daughter, Annie, migrated in 1911 to Australia. They established a new and prosperous life in Brisbane, and William desperately wanted to join them.

Two years later, an opportunity arose. After his brother, Joseph, wed in 1913, he and his bride established a home in Glasgow and invited William's mother to live with them. Free of responsibilities, William acted quickly. He purchased a third class fare on the steamer, "Waipara" for Brisbane and departed London on the 5th November, 1913 with 350 equally enthusiastic immigrants.[6]

When his ship docked at Musgrave Wharf, South Brisbane on New Year's Eve, 1913, his sister and his niece were waiting anxiously to greet him. Their reunion was joyous. They bombarded William with questions about home, while he listened intently to Bella and Annie's enthusiastic tales of Australia. Bella had gained a job as a stewardess on a coastal passenger vessel[7] out of Brisbane and his niece worked a Brisbane barmaid. That night, the Pollocks loudly celebrated the New Year and the start of William's new life. Fortunately, they were blissfully unaware of the dark events that 1914 would bring.

With Bella and Annie's help, William quickly settled into Brisbane. Work as a labourer was swiftly found and lodgings were obtained at 1 Hope Street, South Brisbane, close to his sister's comfortable home,

The First Ashore

Durham Cottage, opposite Musgrave Park.[8] William was very content. He enjoyed the warm weather, easy-going lifestyle and the many opportunities available to working-class men like himself. The dream of owning land or property, an impossibility for him in Ireland, was now within his reach.

Regrettably, less than seven months after arriving, all aspirations and plans came to an abrupt end. On 5th August, Australia entered the war and William's life changed forever. Without any reservation, he volunteered immediately. Although almost excluded by his age, his previous military experience made him a valued recruit in Australia's new army. He was accepted into the 9th Battalion and posted to C Company (later A Company).

Life in Australia's new army was not what William expected. The initial chaos and disorganization at Enoggera camp, as 1000 enthusiastic volunteers flooded in, was in stark contrast to the strict routine and stern discipline he had known in the British Army. The irreverence and egalitarianism were also unfamiliar and greatly enjoyed. Sunday afternoons became William's favourite time. The camp took on a carnival-like atmosphere as friends and family arrived to picnic with the recruits. Bella and Annie often visited and were William's greatest fans. Dressed in his uniform with his perfectly manicured moustache, William was their dashing hero.

After only 33 days at Enoggera camp, the 9th Battalion left Brisbane on the "Omrah", the first troopship to leave Queensland for the war. A brief stay followed in Melbourne and, from there, they embarked for Albany, Western Australia, to join the largest convoy of ships Australia had ever seen. With a cargo of 30,000 men and 7800 horses, this huge flotilla of 33 ships left Australian waters on 1st November. William felt optimistic that the war would quickly end and he would soon return.

Shortly after arriving in Egypt, his optimism was stifled by devastating news. William's brother, Joseph Pollock, who enlisted in the Inniskilling Fusiliers, had been killed in France while participating in one of the war's first battles, the Battle of the Ainse. (His death occurred on 14th September, but was not reported until 14th October.)[9] William was overcome with grief. Suddenly, the war was no longer an exciting adventure. He now carried an intense need to avenge his brother's death.

William was eager for battle and frustrated by the 3rd Brigade's long stay in Egypt. The next four months at the desert camp at Mena passed slowly. As an experienced soldier, he found the repetitive regime of long marches and endless drills exhausting and unnecessary. He was battle ready and this long training period was an interference to his real purpose which was to fight Germans and bring the war to a speedy end.

When orders were finally received in March for the 3rd Brigade to join the war, William was elated. He and his mates sang loudly as they marched the 10 miles from Mena camp to the Cairo train station. From Alexandria, they were transported to the Greek island of Lemnos, about 55 kilometres from the Dardanelles. Although disappointed that their destination was not France, William sensed the enormity of the task ahead. Four weeks were spent on Lemnos, and each day, more transport ships arrived.

Finally, on 24th April, the details of their mission were revealed. William's A Company was transferred to the warship "Queen" about midday and, at 2 pm, their warship led a magnificent armada from the harbour on a voyage to the Turkish coast. William had waited more than six months for this day. Even Brigade-Major Brand's blunt warning that the 9th Battalion's honour of leading the landing party would require a great sacrifice of life could not dampen his spirits.

That afternoon, a church service was held on the quarter-deck, and William found some time for reflection. With loud bold voices, the soldiers sang the hymns "Nearer my God to thee" and "God be with you till we meet again". The words of these, plus "Auld Lang Syne", held powerful poignancy. William could not help but think of his brother. In the evening, the crew of the "Queen" treated the men to a concert followed by a hearty hot meal. William tried to get some sleep, but sleep was difficult. As he viewed his mates resting on the deck, he wondered how many would see daylight after tomorrow.

At midnight, the troops were awakened. The night air felt heavy with tension. Silently they left the "Queen", climbing down rope ladders into the rowboats waiting below. They carried out the exercise with well-rehearsed precision and, by 2.35 am, every man had disembarked into his allocated tow. William and the rest of A Company filled the rowboats of the two tows on the starboard side of the ship.[10] He joined men from No. 3 Platoon and a selection of scouts in Lieutenant Chapman's boat in No. 1 Tow.

The battleships then began their slow final advance with the tows towards the Turkish coast. At about 3.30 a.m., a point was reached where the battleships would be detected if they proceeded further. Anchors were dropped and from the bridge of the "Queen", the order softly pierced the air, *'Go Ahead and Land!'* Sailors lined the deck and, with a waving of hats, gave a silent cheer. By now, the moon had set, and it was very dark. Not a word was spoken in the crowded rowboats as the tows quickened their speed.

As they neared the shore, William listened intently for the sound of the enemy. The suspense was palpable. In the shallower water, the steamboats cast off their tows. Rowers quickly took the oars and quietly moved the boats the last few hundred metres towards shore. Still, there was not a sound. Their boat grounded, and William dashed for the cover of the beach. Suddenly, almost as a relief, the tension was broken. A single gun sounded, followed by a rapid explosion of rifle fire. As more boats grounded, the beach quickly descended into chaos and confusion. Without hesitating, overpowered by adrenalin, William joined his mates in a heroic charge up the slopes.

Like so many others, the next details of William's actions remain unknown. Four days later, the remnants of the 9th Battalion returned to the beach for a sombre roll call. From the 1000 strong battalion that landed, only ten officers and 419 other ranks answered the call.[11] Private William Pollock was not among them. His body was never found. Evidence given to the Field Service Enquiry held on 8th June, 1915 concluded he was killed in action on 25th April, 1915.[12] William's last possessions, a small brown paper parcel containing cards and photos, were dispatched to his mother in Scotland.[13]

William was robbed of his dream of a happy and prosperous life in Australia. The gallant Anzac had enjoyed only nine months in Brisbane. At the war's end, his family honoured his sacrifice and fulfilled the dream. His only surviving brother, Robert and his sister Bella migrated to Australia (Bella for the second time). They established families in Brisbane whose descendants live throughout Queensland today.

The life of Private William Pollock is commemorated on the Australian War Memorial's Roll of Honour and on Panel 31 of the Lone Pine Memorial to the Missing at Gallipoli. He is one of 3,268 brave Anzacs killed at Gallipoli who have no known grave.

Private Archibald Henry Reynolds

No. 134, A Company, 9th Battalion
(later Sergeant, 3rd Echelon, Service Number 1171)

Private Archibald Reynolds differed from the other soldiers in the first boat in many ways. Besides being one of its youngest members, he was from Tasmania and, as a 4th generation Australian with a convict heritage, he was perhaps more Australian than any of the Anzacs in that boat. While Archie shared the same fierce patriotism and eagerness for battle as other Anzacs, he spent only one day on the battlefield. His significant contribution to the war effort occurred through his valuable work with the 3rd Echelon.

Born in 1895 at Triabunna on Tasmania's picturesque east coast, Archie was the youngest child in a large, well-respected and prosperous family. His father, Edwin Reynolds, operated a passenger and mail service that ran stage-coaches between Spring Bay and Hobart.[1] As the family business grew, a new home was established at Glenorchy, outside Hobart, where Archie completed his schooling. He was a capable academic student who also had strong athletic skills. A prized possession was a Silver Medal awarded for running.[2]

At the completion of two years' High School education, Archie was fortunate to obtain work as an accountant's assistant at Hobart Savings Bank. With enthusiasm and diligence, he quickly rose through the ranks and, within five years, he was a bank teller and clerk, earning almost £100 per year.[3] His future seemed secure, but, like many young men, Archie was restless with a thirst for adventure and new opportunities. A chance meeting one evening on the train home from work changed his life. A friend's brother, who owned a Queensland cattle station, casually made an offer of work. Archie was captivated by his description of outback life in Queensland and accepted immediately.

He resigned his bank job to become a Queensland stockman. However, on the sea voyage north, Archie's impulsiveness caused these plans to be quickly abandoned. His cabin mate, an adventurous American travelling to Brisbane to start a photography studio, persuaded Archie to join his business venture. After disembarking in Brisbane, the pair rented a city shop at 245 George Street[4] and established a studio that used comical backdrops and specialized in quick-finish photography with a guarantee that prints would be ready within 10 minutes. It was frivolous and light-hearted work that contrasted starkly with the seriousness of Archie's previous bank job. In Brisbane, he enjoyed the new direction his life was taking him.

Regrettably, war changed everything. Charged with patriotism and eager for adventure, Archie rushed to enlist. He hurriedly returned to Tasmania on 19th August[5] but discovered Tasmania's recruitment quota was already filled. He decided to return to Queensland and was back in Brisbane on the 31st August.[6] Less than a week later, Archie signed his enlistment papers and became a member of the 1st Reinforcements of Queensland's 9th Battalion.

Despite his bountiful enthusiasm, adjusting to military life brought some unexpected challenges. As a teenager in Hobart's local Citizens' Forces, Archie had gained some familiarity with military life, but this was more serious. Upon entering Enoggera camp, he was issued with a uniform, a groundsheet and two blankets. No longer was there the luxury of a bed or a pillow and, at first, he found the ground a bit hard to sleep on. Privacy also ceased to exist, as Archie shared his Bell tent with 15 other recruits. The exhausting daily regime of training exercises and long route marches presented more challenges.

A fortnight later, the Reinforcements left Enoggera for the large military camp at Broadmeadow outside Melbourne, where another four weeks of rigorous training was endured. On 21st December, with much excitement, Archie finally embarked on the troopship "Themistocles" for overseas service. Their first port of call was Albany in Western Australia, but disappointedly, no one was allowed ashore.

Weeks later, they arrived in Colombo, Sri Lanka. By then, Archie was desperate for some shore leave and his larrikinism could not be contained. He and a few good mates went AWOL. They absconded by clambering from the ship down a rope into one of the many small local crafts moored nearby. It was a daring and dangerous escapade but rewarded by a memorable day wandering the streets of Colombo. Archie's first wish was to have *'a good Cuppa'* of Ceylonese tea.[7] Later, after having photos taken in a rickshaw, the foolhardy tourists returned to the wharf where an escort waited to take them to a very disgruntled Colonel. The cost of the misadventure was a £4 fine. However, Archie declared it a good day.[8]

Upon disembarking in Egypt on 9th February, sadly Archie was forced to fare-well many of his good mates. At Mena Camp, outside Cairo, the Reinforcements were dispersed into different 9th Battalion companies. Archie was assigned the Battalion's A Company. Weeks later, on 28th February, they embarked on the "SS Ionian" for the Greek island of Lemnos. Like the rest of the Anzacs, Archie felt disappointment. He was eager to get to France to take part in the war against the Germans, but found himself on an extremely uncomfortable six night voyage to an unfamiliar destination. He travelled in the overcrowded, unventilated No.5 hold where soldiers slept on an uncomfortable iron deck. The rancid smell of the ship's previous cargo of horses also caused many troops to become seasick.

Fortunately, because their cargo ship was ill-equipped to carry soldiers, the 9th Battalion was allowed to land at Lemnos. For five weeks they camped on the island, carrying out fatigue duties such as unloading supplies and the construction of a jetty. Although always busy, Archie and his larrikin mates again found time for mischief. When one of the dixies (large iron pots) containing tea was emptied, it was mysteriously refilled with a couple of bottles of local wine. Archie concluded it to be *'a very pleasant change of diet.'*[9]

On Lemnos, preparations for the Gallipoli campaign proceeded slowly. Archie hoped action was imminent when, on 8th April, the Battalion left Lemnos to re-embark on another overcrowded troopship, the "Malda." However, for two weeks, they waited restlessly on board. Sagging morale was lifted a little when their first pay in five weeks, £1 15s per soldier, was received. With plenty of time and nothing else to spend this money on, 'two-up' games became popular. Archie joined the fun but

The First Ashore

incurred little luck. By the end of the two weeks, he recalled the games' ring-keepers had collected more gold sovereigns than they could carry.

Much anticipated orders were finally received on 24th April. Archie's A Company, with B Company, were transferred to the battleship, "Queen" and, at 2 p.m., their ship led the huge armada of warships and transports from Lemnos' Mudros Harbour. With pride and nervous apprehension, Archie stood on the deck and watched the inspiring sight. On-board, final furtive preparations for the landing were being made. According to Archie, *'we were issued with 120 rounds of ammunition, 3 sandbags, 3 days' rations of bully beef and ANZAC wafers and, of course, a rifle.'* He lamented the wafers were *'about 4 inches in size and nearly as hard as cement.'*[10] Meanwhile, the British crew of the "Queen" bestowed special treatment on the Australians. There were gifts of cigarettes and tobacco and, in the evening, a concert was held, followed by a hot meal where the men were invited to eat as much as they wanted.[11] For Archie, sleep was impossible.

At midnight, the ship was awakened. After enjoying a mug of hot cocoa, with precision and speed, the 400 men of the 9th Battalion's A and B Companies disembarked. Silently they climbed down rope ladders into the row boats waiting below. Archie found manoeuvring the ladders in the dark with a heavy pack was an uneasy task. *'Our gear weighed more than ourselves.'*[12] Waiting below, the landing crafts were tied in groups of three connected to a steam tow-boat, a pinnace, which would bring them through the darkness towards the shore.

Anxiously, Archie sat jam-packed with his platoon in the leading boat of No. 1 Tow. Not far in front, his good mate, signaler Private Jim Bostock, sat at the bow beside Lieutenant Duncan Chapman. As their steam pinnace chugged quietly across the water, the Turkish coast slowly became more visible. Archie earnestly searched the skyline for signs of the enemy. Within 50 yards of the beach, the pinnace cast off its tows. The rowers took over. Now the only sound was the splash of their oars. Fear and suspense were overwhelming. It seemed the Turks were not there. Their boat hit the beach but, incredibly, the morning remained silent. After hearing the command, *'All out!'* Archie recalled Lieutenant Chapman and Jim Bostock were the first to land and *'I was not very far behind.'* After jumping overboard into water waist deep, with a heavy water-logged uniform and pack, he made a frantic dash across the beach. Then the Turkish rifle fire began.

Huddled by the shelter of the cliff, he watched as battalions and companies came ashore and became hopelessly mixed on the narrow beach. It was obvious the landing had occurred in the wrong location. Amid growing chaos and confusion, orders to form up into platoons were ignored. Archie recalled, *'The only order I remember was to pull our packs off and stack them on top over one another. We were then able to climb up the hill. That was the last I saw of all my possessions.'*[13]

As the hail of bullets intensified, running through Archie's mind were the Battalion's original orders to move forward quickly and keep going at all costs. A call was made, *'Come on Queenslanders! Come on the 9th!'* and, with bayonet fixed, he charged wildly up the steep slope. The terrain was difficult and contact with most of his platoon was quickly lost. Yet their advance moved at great speed. At first, it seemed the Turks were on the run. Within 30 minutes, Archie had reached the level area above the beach, the summit known as Plugges Plateau. This was to be a mustering point where soldiers could re-group before going further. However, when Archie arrived, the situation was disorganized. There was a lack of command and Archie could not wait. With wild enthusiasm and pumped with adrenalin, he pushed on. A mixture of Scouts from the 9th, 10th and 11th Battalions had already arrived on the Plateau and were following orders to move forward quickly to clear a path for the main body. Keener soldiers like Archie followed them in what some historians refer to as 'a premature advance.'[14]

Very early in the day, Archie left Plugges Plateau and moved into Shrapnel Valley and then onto the Second Ridge and beyond. His recollection was that he reached a point where he *'could see the Black Sea. It was never seen again by our boys.'*[15] Several historians, including N.K. Harvey, recorded that, before 8 a.m., small parties from the 9th and 10th Battalions crossed Legges Valley and arrived at the Third Ridge, where in the distance they viewed the waters of the Dardanelles.[16] It is probable Archie belonged to one of these brave advance parties.

Sadly, a change of orders early in the day sealed their fate. About 6.30 a.m. Colonel Sinclair-Maclagan decided the Third Ridge could not be taken and ordered troops to dig in on the Second Ridge. Archie noted, *'Those that followed dug in on the Ridge.'* These new orders left his group and others isolated, far ahead of the main line, to face the Turkish counter-attack alone. In the afternoon, *'As our boys got fewer, the Turks began to advance.'* Despite suffering high casualties stubbornly, these small advance parties held on. Through their gallant actions, they slowed the Turkish advance onto the 2nd Ridge, which gave the rest of the Anzacs valuable time to dig in. However, the sacrifice was great. *'As our boys were getting fewer the Turks advanced. I collected three wounds, my left side and right foot and got blown up by a shell.'*[17]

In great pain and unable to walk, Archie crawled his way to the safety of an old Turkish trench. *'I left my rifle and ammunition for the Turks and managed somehow to get back.'*[18] Stretcher bearers fortunately found him and safely returned him to the beach. From there, he was ferried to the overcrowded hospital ship, "Gascon". Its capacity was about 400 but, that day, they took 557 wounded soldiers on board. With no room available inside, Archie received a mattress and a small space on the ship's open deck. He remembered falling asleep looking at the stars while a warship fired shells across the ship towards shore.

It took four days for the "Gascon" to reach Egypt. Archie was admitted to the Australian General Hospital at Mena but, days later, when the hospital reached capacity, he was transferred to a new hospital established in the old Ghezirah Palace in downtown Cairo. This was a grand setting but, according to Archie, the heat, mosquitoes and flies were *'the limit'*.[19]

Despite three months in hospital, Archie's foot remained damaged. He carried a painful and permanent disability which, fortunately, also rendered him unable to march. Deemed unfit for active service, on 17th July 1915, he was transferred to the 1st Australian General Hospital at Heliopolis to work as an admissions registrar.

His good fortune continued. Five months later, by chance, he met an old friend from Hobart who was able to arrange his transfer to the army's pay office at Cairo. The new position suited his skills well, and it pleased him to leave the tragedy and sadness of the hospital environment. After reporting for duty on 1st December, he also gained promotion to Corporal.

After six months' service at the pay office, on 8th May, 1916, a transfer was received to Administrative Headquarters in Horseferry Road, London. It was a relief to leave Cairo's noise and heat. Archie was also excited to be in London. His Australian identity and heritage were strong, but he still regarded England as the mother country and

London, the heart of the Empire, was a place to be revered. Also, he revelled in the large fraternity of Australians stationed in London. Two of the most popular meeting places were near his workplace at Horseferry Road. A few steps away were the War Chest Club and further up the street was the Anzac Buffet. Whenever possible, Archie would leave his office duties to slip across the road to partake in tea, read Australian newspapers or converse with mates from home.

After three months' of service in London, on 12th August, Archie received another important posting. He was transferred to the Australian Records Section, Third Echelon of the General Headquarters, based in the city of Rouen in France. The Third Echelon was the hidden war machine that was crucial to the army's success. The Records Section, where Archie was assigned, carried out extraordinarily significant work. It was responsible for meticulously recording what happened to every Australian soldier on all battlefields. The accuracy of their record keeping determined the deployment of reinforcements and important functions such as food rationing and issuing of supplies. With great effort and compassion, they also attempted to provide families back home with details of wounded, sick, missing and killed loved ones. In 1918, General Birdwood congratulated the men of the Australian Records Section, 'All honour to the men whose duty lay where glory did not often pass but who fulfilled that duty for duty's sake.' Archie applied himself diligently and, a few months after transferring to the 3rd Echelon, he was promoted to Temporary Sergeant. After two years of dedicated service as Rouen, on 4th October, he was transferred back to Administrative Headquarters in London. Archie regarded himself as fortunate as five weeks later, when the Armistice was declared, he was able to witness the city of London celebrate. The memories of the joyous pandemonium that erupted in Trafalgar Square and in front of Buckingham Palace were never forgotten.

A month later, very welcomed orders were received. Archie's long overseas service of four years and 35 days entitled him to 'Special 1914 Leave' and on 9th December, with 1300 other veterans, he returned home on the troopship "Leicestershire." In Melbourne, an enthusiastic crowd of approximately 3000 people celebrated their arrival. Street barricades could barely prevent the veterans from being mobbed as they disembarked. Among them were 111 Anzacs, including Archie, who had served at Gallipoli. Distinguished by their red, white and blue rosettes, they received special honour. The Age reported, *'At Port Melbourne and at many points along the way, they were regaled with flowers, fruit and 'smokes'.*[20]

From Melbourne, Archie and the 202 Queenslanders in the contingent made a two-day train journey to Brisbane. At Central Station, another magnificent welcome honoured them. After a motorcade parade through city streets, there was a large dinner reception, attended by the Mayor, government ministers and high-ranking military officers. At the dinner, the Minister for Education delivered a most poignant speech. He gave a pessimistic and stark warning to the veterans, *'I am not so hopeful as I would like to be regarding the prospects of all of you returning to work again.'*[21]

Archie soon learnt the harsh reality of the Minister's words. The post-war economy was in poor shape. As well as a rising cost of living, there was a severe job shortage. Despite his extensive clerical experience, over the next decade, Archie could not find secure employment. In early 1919, he travelled to Adelaide but discovered unemployment rates there were worse than in Brisbane. By May, he was desperate and forced to apply to the Repatriation Board for sustenance payments.[22] Enrolment in a vocational training programme studying book-keeping led to short-term work as a clerk at Adelaide's Repatriation Department but, six months later, Archie was again unemployed.

With little prospect of gaining an office job, he made the bold decision to try his luck at rabbit trapping. In the 1920s, a government rabbit bounty and a lucrative market for rabbit carcasses and skins made the rabbit industry one of Australia's largest employers. Newspapers reports and exaggerated accounts of sensational earnings encouraged veterans. For instance, in 1920, a newspaper reported a trapper at Molong received £21 for a single week's catch.[23] Influenced by such stories, Archie moved to Narromine in New South Wales.

He soon discovered the reality of rabbit trapping. It was hard work; the income was often unreliable, and working conditions were isolated and unpleasant. But with few options, he stuck with it. Archie worked in the Narromine and Peak Hill district from 1921 to 1923. Astutely, he saved his earnings and by 1924, he had sufficient funds to purchase a car and finance a 'car for hire' business in Peak Hill. Regrettably, profits from this venture did not eventuate.

Dispirited, his hunt for secure employment continued. Finally, in

1927, perseverance was rewarded. An application for a position in the State Public Service was successful. On 27th June, Archie began work as a clerk with the Main Roads Board in Castlereagh Street, Sydney. Finally, he attained a job that suited his skills and provided security and a reliable income. Life seemed to improve for Archie. He established a home at Carter Road in the northern beach suburb of Brookvale and met Carol Tate, a widow who lived nearby. At the age of 37, after living alone for so many years, Archie took on the responsibilities of husband and stepfather. Their marriage was a happy union, but, tragically, it did not last. Less than four years later, while holidaying in Tasmania, Carol died unexpectedly. Devastated by the loss, Archie moved to live alone in a small rented flat at Neutral Bay.

Fortunately, four years later, he met Olga Mullane, a saleswoman from Manly. After marrying in 1940, a new home was purchased at 32 Greycliffe Road, Queenscliff, north of Manly. This residence, within walking distance from the beach, became their cherished home for the next four decades.

Archie continued his job with the Main Roads as a clerk in the city. He completed 30 years' service but, by the age of 63, bad nerves and a painful arthritic foot made the daily commute to the city too difficult. He was forced to retire. Without the benefit of an aged pension, he relied on a small income he gained from casual gardening work in his Queenscliff neighbourhood. Over the next ten years, Archie became a popular and well-known gardener in the local community.

Unfortunately, the last decades of Archie's life were also marked by a long and frustrating battle with the Repatriation Commission. Like so many other wounded veterans, he believed his war service qualified him for financial help when needed. When his application was denied in 1954, Archie refused to accept the Commission's decision. Over the following years, he made ten more applications and mounted numerous appeals. When, a partial pension was finally obtained in 1963, Archie remained unsatisfied. He felt aggrieved by the process and continued his constant lobbying of politicians, pressing for a better deal for all veterans. At the approach of the 50th anniversary of the Gallipoli landing, the 70-year-old Anzac made a direct plea to Prime Minister Menzies. He cited the need for medical and hospital care for all surviving World War 1 veterans.

The First Ashore

'......*A commemorative avenue of trees is being planted at Canberra in memory of those Anzacs who have passed on. May I suggest that we give a little thought to those few 'Gallant Anzacs' who are still with us...... there are many of the few left no doubt, who are finding life burdensome through financial troubles, apart from ill-health.*'[24]

Like many other veterans, Archie's final years were marred by ill-health and financial difficulties. A full war pension and repatriation benefits were finally granted in 1973. He was 78.

When Archie died on 19th November, 1986, he was the last surviving soldier from the First Boat Ashore. The proud 'Original' Anzac was 91 years old.

Sergeant Archie Reynolds was cremated at the Northern Suburbs Crematorium, Sydney.

Private William James Rider

No. 317, A Company, 9th Battalion
(later Lance Corporal, 9th Battalion)

Age should have excluded William James Rider from enlistment in World War 1. At 38, he was older than the 1914 enlistment regulations allowed. Yet his strength and endurance equalled any younger recruit. He survived more than six continuous months on the Gallipoli peninsula and also every action that the 9th Battalion took part in on the Western Front. Sadly, four years and two months of overseas service took an irreversible toll on his health and wellbeing.

Bill was born in Liverpool, England, but had few memories of the home country. In 1878, two years after his birth, Bill's father, an unemployed tailor, left Liverpool to seek a better life in Australia. He went ahead of the family, arriving at Moreton Bay in 1878.[1] His plan was to find work and set up a home so that Ann and the children could follow soon after. Unfortunately, this took almost three years. Bill's mother rented rooms in a crowded tenement building at 27 Clare Street in Liverpool and supported her sons by working long hours as a paper bag maker.[2] Life was tough.

Fortunately, in 1881, the family was able to re-unite. Annie left England with Bill and his brother Nalus (Cornelius) in the summer on a perilous sea voyage that took three months to reach Australia. On the crowded ship, sickness was rampant and resulted in the deaths of two adult passengers and six children.[3] It was with enormous relief that the Riders disembarked in Brisbane on 26th October 1881.[4] On the docks at Kangaroo Point, William Senior waited anxiously to greet his young family and take them to the home he had established at Dalby. Bill and his brother were in awe of their new surroundings. The wide open spaces of the Darling Downs were a stark contrast to the crowded slums of Liverpool.

The First Ashore

A year later, Bill's father gained a position as a tailor at the popular Toowoomba store, Penny and Beirne.[5] The family left Dalby and purchased a home on Church Street, Toowoomba. This address became the setting for a happy childhood and remained the family's home for over three decades. The boys enrolled at Toowoomba South Boys State School,[6] and later Bill was a student at East Toowoomba State School. Although he was not a strong academic student, he enjoyed school. A special prize was awarded for his near perfect attendance at East School.[7]

Regrettably, school life ended abruptly for Bill. In 1890, the sudden death of his father meant the 13-year-old had to leave school and find a job to help support his family. For the next seven years, at various locations in the district, he worked as a labourer.

As he neared adulthood, Bill became restless and eager to establish his independence. Like many young people, he was drawn to city life. Brisbane's euphoric celebrations to mark the 1901 inauguration of the Commonwealth of Australia had captured his imagination. He also was eager to join one of the city's popular militia groups. Like many young men of the time, Bill held a strong interest in military matters. He was especially fascinated by the amazing new weaponry and large artillery, such as powerful Nordenfeldt, multiple barrel guns and the Hotchkiss revolving cannon, recently installed at the mouth of the Brisbane River. Eager to be involved, he left Toowoomba to find work in Brisbane. Almost immediately, he enlisted in the Queensland regiment of the Royal Australian Garrison Artillery stationed at Fort Lytton.[8]

Although training, military exercises and weekend camps at Fort Lytton occupied almost all leisure time, Bill also found time in Brisbane for an unfortunate romance. He fell in love with Mrs Mary Jane Hanson, who lived with her elderly husband and their two children on busy Leichhardt Street, Spring Hill.[9] In pre-war years, this bustling street, lined with grocers, fruiterers, butchers, boot-makers, tobacconists and four hotels, was the perfect setting for a secret dalliance. Bill and Mary maintained discreet secrecy, but in 1896, Mary fell pregnant. A devastating public scandal followed. Although their illegitimate daughter, Grace Ruth, was baptized with the Rider surname, she grew up as a member of the Hanson family. Bill and Mary's relationship did not endure. Three years later, when Mary was widowed, she remarried another man.[10]

It took almost 10 years for Bill to find love again. In 1908, Louisa Jane Blank, a young country girl, left her family's dairy farm at Deep Creek, near Esk, to find work in Brisbane. Soon after, she met Bill. A relationship blossomed and the young couple established a home together in Ernest Street, South Brisbane. In the pre-war years, an unmarried couple living together was frowned upon. Bill was keen to avoid more scandal so he and Louisa posed as husband and wife. She appeared on the 1912 electoral roll as Mrs Rider.

Two years later, the declaration of war prompted the nature of their relationship to change. On the day before signing his enlistment papers, Bill hastily proposed marriage to Louisa, and the couple wed in a simple ceremony held at the Mission House, 452 Leichhardt Street on Sunday, 23rd August.[11] An evening of celebration followed, and early the next morning, Bill joined his mates in the long queue at the recruitment office. He took his oath to serve on Monday, 24th August, less than a week after recruitment began.

After farewelling his bride, he and the other volunteers moved immediately to the new military camp at Bell's Paddock on Brisbane's outskirts. Four weeks later, they embarked on the troopship, "Omrah" for war. Naïvely optimistic, Bill believed it would be all over within 12 months. Regrettably, four years and two months would pass before he saw Louisa again.

Bill's long and grueling battlefield service began at Gallipoli. After landing with the first boat ashore, he endured almost seven continuous months on the Peninsula. As the deadly campaign continued, he joined a macabre game to see who could stick it the longest. Bill was one of the winners. Out of the original 1000 members of the 9th Battalion and 500 Reinforcements, only 6 officers and 88 other ranks survived six or more consecutive months on the Peninsula. It was an extraordinary feat of endurance that was recognized by the award of a unique unofficial honour, the 'Kilcoy' or 'Butler Medal'. (The family of the Battalion's medical officer, Colonel A.G. Butler, and the residents of the Doctor's hometown, Kilcoy funded and designed the medal.)[12]

When Gallipoli ended, Bill's battalion returned to Egypt. They expected a period of recuperation but instead, on the 25th January, they were marched, with a train of 80 camels, to the sandy ridge of Gebel Habieta deep in the desert. For six weeks, their new mission was to fortify the eastern defence of the Suez Canal by digging trenches in moving sand. It was an almost impossible task, but Bill applied himself well and, on the 8th March, received a promotion to Lance Corporal.

When orders finally came for the Australian infantry to join the war in France, Bill was elated. Finally, he would leave the desert and fight Germans and help bring the awful war to a close. Unfortunately, foolhardy and irresponsible behaviour prevented his departure. The 9th Battalion left for France without him.

For many soldiers, Gallipoli's horrors and killings had inspired a recklessness, and a confused sense of morality. Bill was not immune. After foolishly visiting brothels in Egypt, he contracted a venereal disease. 15% of the AIF suffered this disease during the war but, despite its almost epidemic proportions,[13] the condition brought immense shame and stigmatization. As well, Bill felt guilt for deserting his mates on the battlefield. His name was placed on a special register and, for the disease's duration, the army stopped his pay, including the allowance that was sent to his wife. He feared Louisa's reaction.

Regrettably, the army considered venereal disease to be a disciplinary as well as a medical problem. Rather than a normal hospital ward, Bill was admitted to the Detention Barracks at Cairo's Abbassia Infectious Hospital, a facility that operated more like a prison than a hospital.[14] There, he was subjected to ghastly, embarrassing and extremely dangerous treatments. Penicillin did not exist. Instead, gonorrhoea patients received urethral syringings. Twice daily, using a large metal syringe, powerful antiseptics such as Argyrol (a silver nitrate compound) and Benetol (a toxic compound similar to carbolic acid) were injected into the urethra and bladder.[15] Bill also suffered numerous applications of caustic substances to the genitals. All treatments were painful, with serious long-term side effects.

At the end of 20 days at Abbassia, Bill was extremely pleased to leave Egypt. He arrived in France on 29th May, eager to be reunited with his mates. Disappointed, he was instead sent to Etaples, a notorious transit camp on the French coast. Raw recruits and soldiers returning from hospital were sent here for rigorous training before deployment to the front. It was an extremely unpleasant place, renowned for the bullying inflicted by training officers. The British war poet, Winifred Owen, who was at Etaples with Bill, gave the camp's brutal training ground its nickname, the 'bull ring.' In a letter home, Owen wrote, '*on all faces in that camp; an incomprehensible look.... It was not despair, or terror, it was more terrible than terror, for it was a blindfold look, and without expression, like a dead rabbit's.*'[16] Most soldiers spent two weeks at Etaples but, for unexplained reasons, possibly recurring ill-health, Bill remained there for a torturous six months.[17]

During this time, he witnessed profound injustice and cruelty. A notable incident on the 29th August destroyed his faith in the military system. An Australian, Private Alexander Little, was quickly arrested after he delivered a torrent of verbal abuse to a British officer who turned off the water to his shower. On his way to the punishment compound, four Australian mates intervened and, for their actions, each soldier was court martialled and sentenced to death by firing squad. Fortunately, the Australian army did not condone the death penalty for its soldiers. Three of the four sentences were reduced. However, Australian Jack Braithwaite had enlisted in the New Zealand army. The mood of Bill and other Australians at Etaples verged on rebellion when Jack was executed on the 29th October, 1916.[18]

After enduring six months at Etaples, Bill was pleased to move into the frontline. He arrived on the 15th December to join the 9th Battalion at Flers, where they were enduring deplorable conditions. Europe was suffering one of its coldest winters and, as well as freezing temperatures, weeks of rain had turned the battlefield into a sea of mud. In most trenches, soldiers stood constantly in mud at least 30 centimetres deep. Their feet became numb, swollen and sometimes gangrenous. Incidents of scabies, frost-bite, and diseases like typhus were common. In these horrid conditions, Bill's already weakened health worsened rapidly. Within days of arriving at Flers, he was diagnosed with trench feet and also 'debility', a general term used to describe physical and mental exhaustion. He spent the next three weeks in hospital.

When he returned on the 6th January, the 9th was resting at Dernacourt. The wet weather had ended but temperatures remained bitterly cold with heavy falls of snow. For the rest of the month, they remained in the village of Albert. As always, there were training exercises, but during this time, Bill and his mates were able to re-build their strength.

In mid-February, the Battalion moved nine kilometres north east of Pozieres to a system of trenches known as 'The Maze.' Anxiously, Bill prepared himself for his first battle on the Western Front. For four days and nights, with practically no sleep and few rations, he and his mates fought gallantly. Their objective was to engage enemy soldiers who were withdrawing to their newly prepared Hindenburg Line.

Two weeks later, the heavy fighting continued. On the 6th April, Bill moved with the 9th Battalion to the frontline at Lagincourt where Australia's 1st Division was attempting to hold an 11 kilometre front. Nearby, at the 1st Battle of Bullecourt, the Germans were inflicting significant damage on the Allied Forces. When concluded, the enemy turned their attention to the Australian line. In the pre-dawn darkness on the 15th April, twenty-six German battalions launched a massive attack which forced the 9th and three other Australian battalions into immediate retreat. The village of Lagincourt was quickly overrun, but the Australians refused to accept defeat. With incredible bravery, the 9th and 20th Battalions mounted a fearless counter-attack. Although greatly outnumbered, they re-established the Australian front. Bill's participation in this amazing victory did much to lift his disgruntled morale.

More brutal close combat began on the night of 6th May as Bill took part in a second attempt to take Bullecourt. In narrow trenches, under heavy fire, his 9th Battalion lost another 26 lives and incurred 135 casualties in order to capture 600 metres of trenches.

Mercifully, on the 8th May, the exhausted men left the frontline. They moved to Ribemont, sixty kilometres away, where for the next four months, they entered a period of training, their longest and most complete rest since entering the war. During this time, Bill's health improved markedly. Although he realized the war was far from over, he felt more prepared for what lay ahead. The successes at The Maze and Lagincourt had boosted his confidence and restored his faith in military command. As well, his identity as an 'Original Anzac' had become a source of great pride.

The granting of two weeks' leave in England, beginning 1st September, also lifted his spirits. Finally, after more than two years of war, he had the opportunity to experience the heart of the Empire and visit its famous landmarks. Leave also enabled him to travel to Liverpool, the home of his parents, where he reconnected with uncles, aunts and met cousins for the first time.

On his return on the 15th September, the 9th Battalion had moved from France to Belgium. Preparations were being made for the advance on the Menin Road Ridge, one of the first offensives of the 3rd Battle of Ypres. Bill found the deafening, incessant noise of British guns bombarding the German defences unnerving and steeled himself for another ordeal. The 9th's advance began after midnight on 19th September. The objective was to take Anzac Ridge, east of Ypres, and the enemy's deadly cement pill boxes in front of Polygon Wood. They moved under the cover of darkness, but German flares lit the sky and quickly detected their position. At 4.20 a.m., for 20 minutes, a heavy barrage of German artillery rained upon them. A second bombardment that included gas shells followed at 5 a.m. Many men were hit. Bill's nerves were severely shaken but, gallantly, he and the remnants of the 9th pushed on. Under the cover of a thick morning mist and behind a perfect creeping barrage of artillery fire, they made progress. By the afternoon of February 20th, the edge of Polygon Wood was reached and all objectives successfully taken. Sadly, the cost was enormous. 35 lives were lost and 149 soldiers were wounded, with another 56 missing. Bill regarded himself as very lucky.

The Battalion remained in the area for the next few months, moving in and out of the frontline. Bill's next major engagement, the Battle of Broodseinde, took place on the 4th October. This was another tough objective, but once again, after advancing behind the usual creeping artillery barrage, the troops bravely took Broodseinde Ridge.

As 1918 began, Bill feared the war would never end. It seemed each horrific battle was followed by another in a seemingly never-ending cycle. He entered every encounter fuelled with adrenalin but, afterwards, always felt the same draining sadness. The long periods of inaction in the trenches also created idle time that allowed his mind to dwell and lament on the life he left behind. He missed his wife, his family and Brisbane very much.

The first months of 1918 began well in a quiet sector at Messines. However, Bill's foreboding and fears quickly returned. On the 1st March, the Battalion marched back into the frontline and, five days later, the Germans unleashed a bombardment of gas-shells that rained upon them for almost four hours. The men suffered terribly, but worse was to come.

Three weeks later, the Germans' Spring Offensive forced an unexpected Allied retreat. The sacred ground, gained in 1916, through the sacrifice of thousands of lives, was lost. For the first time, Bill believed defeat was possible. With the enemy rapidly advancing through Belgium, the 9th Battalion was quickly sent north to help defend the important railway junction at Hazebrouck. Their first objective was to capture the village of Meteren, east of Hazebrouck. On 23rd and 24th April, they made an ambitious attempt against the ring of German machine guns surrounding the village but, without artillery support, it was impossible. Twelve men lost their lives and 30 were wounded.

The 9th Battalion remained in this sector until late July, carrying out frequent raids against the German frontline and outposts in a continued effort to help defend Hazebrouck. Each dangerous action inflicted more casualties and mounting stress. A minor operation on the 20th June advanced the line 200 yards but resulted in six deaths and 18 soldiers wounded.

Bill was exhausted. A brief respite of two weeks' leave in Paris was received at the end of June, but when he returned, the Battalion was already back on the frontline preparing for another important attack. The new objective was the village of Le Waton, and spearheading the advance was No.1 Platoon and Bill's No.3 Platoon. With speed and great courage, the enemy strong-posts were overrun, and they successfully captured the village. For this outstanding achievement, the platoons gained much admiration.

Weeks later, the last phase of the war, the Allied offensive, started. For Bill, there were two more significant battles to face. At Crepy Wood, on 9th August, he nervously pondered his fate. After arriving during the night, daylight revealed a frightening expanse of flat, open ground between them and their objective. Without cover, Bill knew this would be a bloodbath. At 8 a.m., they moved forward, and the Germans responded as expected with heavy machine gun fire. Many mates fell, but Bill and the Battalion bravely continued their advance until they finally drove the Germans from Crepy Wood. The next day, with their strength at little more than 300 and without sleep, the advance continued. Attacks, counter-attacks and fierce fighting persisted until, finally, late in the night on the 15th August, the Battalion was relieved. Eight days later, the exhausted remnants of the 9th moved a few kilometres north to face the enemy again. Incredibly, despite their weakened state, near the village of Chuignes, more important territory was taken.

Mercifully, it was Bill's last battle. In September, he received an unexpected reprieve when he became one of the first lucky recipients of two months' special leave in Australia. Bill's happiness and relief were hard to contain. On the 14th September, with 800 other 'original Anzacs' who had volunteered in 1914, he left the war on the troopship "Kaiser-a-Hind".[19]

Four days from Australia's coastline, on 11th November 1918, the ship's wireless received a two-word message, *'Unconditional Surrender!'* The reaction on board was spontaneous. Joyous pandemonium erupted on every deck. Using anything that could make a noise, Bill joined his mates in jubilant revelry. Although it was a 'dry' ship, their boisterous antics and singing continued well into the night.[20]

When they reached Australia, the country was still celebrating. In Freemantle, Melbourne and in Sydney, enormous crowds celebrated their return. A special train conveyed the Queenslanders from Sydney to Brisbane, and at every station they passed through, there were more celebrations. For Bill, the stop at Toowoomba held special significance. In the crowd were his mother and family and friends. At Brisbane, thousands filled the streets as the city staged one of its biggest welcome home celebrations. Louisa waited nervously on the crowded platform at Central Station for a glimpse of the husband whom she had not seen for over four years. There was only time for a brief tearful reunion before Bill joined the other Anzacs in a motorcade procession through crowded city streets. That day, Bill was buoyed with optimism about the future.

However, adjusting to post-war life was a hard task. Bill's mental scars were severe. Although surrounded by the goodwill of friends and the loving support of his wife and mother, he felt alone. Like many other veterans, he found the experience of war was impossible to share. Family and friends could never understand the horrors, the unrelenting nightmares and the emotions running through his head. When Bill was discharged from the army on the 24th January 1919, his post-traumatic stress and combat fatigue remained hidden and untreated.

Stoically, he attempted to carry on. Finding secure employment was a problem. At 42 years of age, with faltering health and only labouring skills, he had to compete with thousands of younger returning veterans for fewer and fewer jobs. During the first five years after his discharge, life for Bill and Louisa remained very unsettled. Their first home was on Logan Road, near Nile Street, at Woolloongabba. A year later, they moved to 172 Heal Street in the Valley and the following year, they rented a double room at 66 Gotha Street, Fortitude Valley.[21]

Life was tough, but Bill persevered using the same strength and resilience he had shown on the battlefield. As his health rapidly declined, the couple became eager to move to the suburbs. Fortunately, Louisa was thrifty and, by 1925, there were sufficient funds to place a deposit on a small home at 48 Sixth Avenue in Windsor. The Queenslander, with its traditional verandah, stood in a peaceful tree-lined avenue within easy walking distance of the tram and train. It was an idyllic setting for the last years of Bill's life.

Throughout the war, Bill had exhibited great strength and resilience. He took part in almost every battle fought by the 9th Battalion, enduring great trauma, multiple gas attacks, illness and debility. The 'Original Anzac' was a steely survivor, but war left him with a dark legacy of irreversible damage. On the 24th February, 1932, he was admitted to the Brisbane Hospital with acute fatigue and breathing difficulties and passed away later that day.[22] His early death at the age of 56 is counted among more than 8,000 ex-servicemen who died prematurely in the post-war years.[23]

Corporal William John James Rider was buried at Toowong Cemetery on the 25th February, 1932. His grave is located at 10-66-5.

Private James Roy Speirs

No. 364, A Company, 9th Battalion
(later 1st Australian Division Salvage Company)

"Jimmy Speirs was still going strong when I saw him last."[1]

These reassuring words, written three months after the Gallipoli landing, fortunately, still rang true at the end of the war. With immense toughness and resilience, Jim endured four months at Gallipoli and three years on the Western Front. He returned home without suffering physical injury and with a resolute determination that the sacrifice of so many fallen mates would not be forgotten.

Like many of the first volunteers, Jim was not Australian born. His first home was Scotland. Born in East Glasgow on 5th December, 1879, the only child of John and Mary Speirs, Jim grew up in the tough working-class suburb of Calmachie, where crime and poverty were major problems.[2] After finishing school, Jim was indentured as a carpenter. He successfully qualified in this trade, but jobs were hard to find in East Glasgow.

20-year-old Jim searched, instead, for a better life as a seaman. He believed work on the large Glaswegian merchant ship, "Pass of Brander," with its four mighty sails, promised a life of adventure. However, the reality was different. The small crew of the "Brander" laboured long hours for little pay. After the ship arrived in Gladstone in central Queensland in 1900, because of inadequate port facilities, they worked for several torturous and back-breaking weeks unloading the cargo of 3000 tons of heavy steel rails. Jim knew the life of a mariner was not for him.[3]

Fortunately, jobs abounded in Gladstone in 1900. The cargo of steel rails was for the construction of the railway line to Rockhampton, a project that would employ over 400 men.[4] Jim's carpentry skills, in particular, were in demand, as many wooden rail bridges had to be constructed. An attractive pay rate of 10-12 shillings a day for qualified tradesmen made Jim's decision easy. He joined the railway's team of carpenters and, for the next two years, worked on the construction of Gondoon Street Bridge, Calliope Bridge and the Police Creek Bridge.[5]

He enjoyed Gladstone's small and friendly community, and, as an active member of the district's Waratah Football Club and the Gladstone Rifle Club, soon became a popular and well-known resident. The Rockhampton rail project provided secure, well-paid employment for many years and, when completed, he moved to the construction of the Gladstone to Boyne railway line. Jim's first home was at Allot 15 in Jaroon Street, but later he moved to Woodstock in south Gladstone, and then to nearby Calliope River.[6] By 1913, after completing more than a decade of work on the railway lines, Jim decided he needed a change. He turned fishing, his favourite leisure time pursuit, into a full-time job. As a self-employed Gladstone fisherman, he created a comfortable and rewarding lifestyle.

Despite this, a year later, when war arrived, Jim did not hesitate. He was a proud Briton who believed it was his duty to serve King and country. With mates George Burgoyne and Hubert Welsh, Jim was one of the district's first three volunteers. Gladstone farewelled the trio with great fanfare. The local newspaper described the day as the largest social event that the town had ever seen. Countless Union Jacks and Australian flags decorated the length of Gondoon Street. At a colourfully decorated Oddfellows Hall, the Gladstone Brass Band entertained an enormous crowd as rousing and enthusiastic renditions of patriotic songs filled the air. The extraordinary display humbled Jim and his mates.[7] With great pride, they left the next day by train for the Enoggera army camp in Brisbane.

Three weeks later, as a member of the 9th Battalion's C Company, Jim embarked on the "Omrah" the first troopship to leave Queensland for war. The destination was Mena Camp, Egypt, where, for the next four months, he participated in a daily regime of rigorous drills and military exercises which transformed him into a tough, physically fit soldier. At Mena, Jim also became a member of A Company and joined Lieutenant Duncan Chapman's No.3 Platoon, assuring him a role in the advance party at the Gallipoli landing.

On the 25th April, 1915, Jim was an oarsman in the Lieutenant's boat. His letter, written to Brisbane's Telegraph newspaper, proudly recounted his experience of the landing and strongly declared Lieutenant Chapman was the first man ashore.

> *'The four boats containing A Company, in common with the rest of the storming party, were taken in tow by a steam pinnace and taken as close as possible to the shore. Then she cast off and a few strokes of the oars put the bow ashore.*
>
> *Lieutenant Chapman was right forward, and hopped over, and was followed quickly by the rest. Somewhere about 17 men were out of the boat before the first rifle shot rang out. They sure made up for lost time after that, for the air seemed pretty full of bullets for a bit. But we got there. I did not see Lieutenant Chapman till four days later, when what was left of the 9th mustered on the beach.*
>
> *Talking over the landing afterwards, it was the opinion of most of my cobbers that Lieutenant Chapman was the first man ashore by a small margin. .... B Company boats were under fire 100 yards from the shore, and as a number of A Company men were ashore before the firing started, I think that is proof positive that our boats made the landing and that Lieutenant Chapman was the first man ashore.'*[8]

At the landing, like so many others, Jim soon lost contact with his commanding officer and most of the platoon. Little knowledge exists of his movements on the first day except that he joined a small group that pushed far inland and that luck remained by Jim's side. Queensland newspapers in 1915 reported all members of Gladstone's Waratah Football Club except one were wounded during the first weeks of the Campaign.[9] That one soldier was Jimmy Speirs.

He served over three months at Gallipoli, taking part in numerous raids and dangerous attempts to break the Turkish line. However, on 21st August, the most prevalent illness of the trenches, diarrhoea, caused his evacuation to the hospital ship "Gloucester Castle". For the next three months, he was hospitalized on the nearby islands of Imbros and Lemnos.[10] Such a long recovery period suggests a more chronic condition. Often diarrhoea was only one symptom of a soldier's general collapse. For instance, many ailments associated with post-traumatic stress disorders remained unrecognized. Although Jim's condition was serious, he was also fortunate. Illness prevented his return to Gallipoli. He rejoined the 9th Battalion on the island of Lemnos on the 14th December, 1915, the day before the Peninsula was evacuated.

Jim finally entered what he regarded as the 'real' war on the Western Front in April 1916. The Battalion was first posted to a fairly quiet area a few kilometres south of Fleurbaix. However, in the summer, the big offensive, the Battle of the Somme, brought Jim and his mates to Pozieres. Their first battle was for this small village on strategic high ground in the Somme valley. It became a horrific nightmare. For two days, artillery blasted the area and then at midnight on 23rd July, 1916, the 9th bravely advanced into No-man's-land. Moving with speed, Jim's company attacked on the extreme right of the front line. Swiftly, with close combat, the village was taken, but the battle continued for four days. Repeatedly, the Germans counter-attacked and delivered an almost continuous artillery bombardment. It was estimated that howitzer shells, at one point, were landing every three seconds. A soldier described the horrors, '*All day long the ground swayed and rocked backwards and forwards...... men were driven stark staring mad.... Any amount of them could be seen crying and sobbing like children, their nerves completely gone.*'[11] Pozieres shattered the strongest men. The Battalion suffered severely with almost 40% casualties. The ordeal stayed with Jim forever.

After Pozieres, there was very little time to recuperate. Within weeks, the Germans regained Pozieres Heights and, on the 19th August, Jim and his mates were ordered back into the frontline. At Mouquet Farm north of Pozieres, another heavy German artillery barrage greeted them with shells falling on their trenches throughout the day and night. On the 21st and 22nd, the Australians launched their attack. Although Jim's A Company was placed in reserve, about 1000 yards from the Farm, their position did not shelter them from the terrible shelling. Again, Jim narrowly escaped death. His mate, Private Bob Proudfoot, stood a couple of metres away when killed. Jim reported,

'I was with him at the time...... the Germans were shelling heavily. He and I were in a bit of a dugout together, and I had just gone a few yards along the trench when a shell burst on the corner, and when the dust

cleared, poor Bob sung out 'They've got me, give me a hand somebody.' I went back at once but he was quite unconscious and died shortly afterwards. He did not suffer for he was unconscious within half a minute of being hit. I intended to take his papers to send to his people, but orders came for us to get back.'[12]

After Mouquet Farm, while still processing the trauma, Jim moved north with the 9th Battalion to face new perils on the front line at Flers. One of Europe's worst winters was beginning and weeks of rain had turned the battlefield into a sea of mud. In most trenches, soldiers moved in mud that was almost 30 centimetres deep. Frost-bite, gangrene and trench-feet became common problems. Flers pushed Jim to the limits of his endurance.

Despite a brief respite of two weeks' leave in England in early December, he entered 1917 exhausted and battle worn. It was to be his hardest and most challenging year. In the first six months, three major battles were faced and then came the trials of the Passchendaele offensive. At their first engagement in February at the Battle of the Maze for four days and nights, the Battalion gallantly advanced to take a complex of trenches ten kilometres from Pozieres. Then, in April, although outnumbered, they helped defeat the Germans at the Battle of Lagincourt. These two triumphs boosted Jim's confidence and the lagging morale of the Battalion but the fighting that followed the next month was more brutal. At the 2nd Battle of Bullecourt, in order to gain approximately 600 metres of damaged and useless trenches, over 150 casualties were incurred.

Although Jim survived the first half of 1917 without physical injury, by July, he sought any opportunity to escape the dreadful life of an infantry soldier. The newly formed 1st Australian Division Salvage Company drew his attention. By 1917, severe shortages of raw materials made it necessary to re-use and repair all items that could be re-covered from the battlefield, and these new salvage companies became crucial to the war machine. Jim could not believe his luck when he received his transfer from the horrors of frontline fighting. However, as a salvager, he soon discovered a new set of gruesome and deadly dangers. With a strength of about 60 men, ten horse-drawn wagons and eight motor lorries, Jim's Salvage Company scoured the battlefield for any items of value.

They worked within range of German artillery fire, often close to the front-line and therefore were constantly at risk. After scouts were sent out on perilous missions to locate the salvage, Jim and the carrying parties followed, usually under the cover of darkness, to recover the items. Muddy battlefields made their work particularly hazardous as horse-drawn wagons laden with salvage easily bogged. The records of weekly salvage returns reveal the enormity of the salvagers' task. In one week, ending 21st December, 1917, the list of salvage collected covered four handwritten pages. It included 1200 rounds of ammunition, 1600 shell cases and, sadly, many personal items.

Respirators	701	Mess tins	292
Hats	570	Boots (pairs)	1251
Steel helmets	495	Water bottles	205[13]

Casualty rates for salvagers were high. Enemy artillery constantly shelled the transport lines used by salvagers, and German aeroplane bombers made their dumps, wagons and lorries priority targets. During Jim's first three months as a salvager, he experienced two mustard gas attacks, one aerial bombing, and multiple artillery shelling.[14] Even when his company was stationed far behind the front line, they were not immune from attack. In August 1918, their salvage yard at Weincourt, eight kilometres from the front, was heavily bombed. Two of Jim's mates were blown to pieces, and many others were wounded.[15] This constant danger, combined with the morbid and horrific nature of salvaging work, had a profound effect on Jim's psychological wellbeing.

Jim served 15 long and exhausting months with the Salvage Company. Three weeks before the Armistice, on 13th October, he finally received a reprieve. As an 'Original' Anzac with more than three years of active service, Jim was granted two months' Special Anzac Leave in Australia. Overjoyed, on 23rd October, he left the war on the troopship, "Durham".

When the "Durham" arrived in Australia, the country was still celebrating the end of war. After disembarking in Melbourne, with 52 other 'Original' Queensland Anzacs, Jim travelled by special train to Brisbane. When they arrived at Central Station at 4 p.m. on Christmas Day, the surrounding streets and the station yards were densely packed with cheering crowds. The District Military Band greeted their arrival with a loud rendition of "Home Sweet Home". After many emotional reunions on the platform, the soldiers left in a triumphant motorcade that proceeded through almost every city street. *'Cheers, hand-grips, salutations, confetti, and flowers greeted the heroes as they were slowly driven through the streets...... What these men had helped to do to bring about a "Peace Christmas" appeared to be fully realized by the cheering crowds.'*[16]

The magnificent welcome filled Jim with optimism. He eagerly returned to Calliope River, outside Gladstone, with the hope of quickly re-establishing his pre-war life. Sadly, this would not occur. The dark legacy of war left Jim restless and, for the next decade, his life remained unsettled. At Calliope River, there were no jobs. Instead, he settled for itinerant work wherever it was available. By 1920, he had moved to the nearby Mt. Larcom district. Five years later, disgruntled and frustrated by his inability to find reliable work, he re-located to Coorooman Creek,[17] north of Rockhampton. At this popular fishing spot, he was able to alternate casual labouring jobs with his much loved pastime of fishing.

Although the solitary life at Coorooman Creek suited his new temperament, as the years passed, Jim still could not find contentment. He yearned for happier times and became nostalgic for his Scottish birthplace. Earnestly he saved for a sea passage to Scotland and, after much frugality, arrived there in early December, 1923. It was a wonderful tonic to return to the comfort of family and, for six months, he lived with his parents at 237 Dukes Street.[18] However, Glasgow was not as he expected or as he remembered. As time passed, the stark contrast to his lifestyle in Australia became more evident. To his surprise, Jim felt pangs of homesickness. The experience of Gallipoli and the Western Front had forged a sense of comradeship and a fierce connection to Queensland. By May 1924, he realized his future was in Australia. Reluctantly, Jim farewelled his elderly parents and returned to Gladstone.

For the third time, with a renewed focus and determination, he re-started his life in Gladstone. A home was established at Yaroon Street and he returned to work as a fisherman.[19] His mates at the local RSSILA provided important support and comfort, but fishing remained his sole passion. While Jim's life improved, it remained solitary. He never married, but the prospect of a lonely future was avoided in 1929, when, after the death of his father, he persuaded his mother to leave Glasgow and join him in Australia. It was a wonderful, rewarding reunion. They established a new home at Oaka Lane and, over the following years, Jim's wellbeing benefited significantly from his mother's love for her only son. Australian life also suited Mrs. Speirs. She became a very popular resident of Gladstone. Upon her death in 1941, although having lived in Gladstone for only 11 years, she was praised as 'an old Gladstone identity' who possessed 'a charming disposition and was loved by all who knew her.'[20]

Jim spent the remaining 20 years of his life in Gladstone. He became well known throughout the Gladstone community for his fishing and his dedication to the RSL and veteran welfare. Outspoken in his advocacy for soldier repatriation, in the early 1920s, he joined the National Democratic Council of Queensland, an anti-socialist, loyalist political party that aimed to assist returned soldiers.[21] He was also a founding member of the Gladstone RSSILA and a tireless worker who was elected many times to its Sub-branch committee.[22] Active membership was also maintained with the 9th Battalion Association and the Omrah Association. Throughout his post-war life, duty, mateship and the Anzac tradition were ideals that Jim held very dear.

In early December, 1945, the 65-year-old 'Original' Anzac fell ill. He was admitted to Gladstone Hospital and, days later, suffered a fatal heart attack.

The grave of Private James Ray (Scotty) Speirs is in the Gladstone Cemetery at Position 47, Row 4, Section C, 1818A.

Private Frederick Thomas

No. 388, C Company, 9th Battalion
(later Sergeant, A Company, 9th Battalion)

Before 1914, Frederick Thomas showed little interest in military life. He was a tough young lad, enjoying his life in the Queensland bush. After landing with the first boat ashore, Fred endured six continuous months on the Gallipoli Peninsula and, later, more than two years in the frontline trenches on the Western Front. He proved he was a resilient, determined and courageous fighter. Sadly, his long war service was torturous. It changed him forever.

As a young man, Fred envisaged his future would be in Queensland's remote outback. His parents, John and Margaret, after migrating from Wales in 1889, settled in the small and isolated railhead town of Mitchell, 600 kilometres west of Brisbane. For 25 years, his father worked as the railway's lengthsman, responsible for the upkeep of the local Mitchell line. It was a hard, solitary life with few comforts. However, the Thomas family came to enjoy the vastness of the western plains and the challenges of outback life. Five children were raised at the family home at the 2 Mile Bend (373 Mile Gate) outside of town.[1] Fred, born on 12th October 1891, was the only son and a much favoured child. He attended Mitchell State School, where he relished the role of protective brother to his four younger sisters.

When Fred finished school at the age of 13, he packed a swag and became an itinerant labourer. It was an opportune time for employment in the Mitchell-Roma district. Vast areas of crown land were recently opened up for settlement and there were many new cattle and wheat properties desperately needing workers. Moving from property to property was not an easy lifestyle, but outdoor work suited the young teenager well and transformed him into a physically strong

The First Ashore

and mentally resilient bushman. He gained attributes that would later be crucial to his survival in the war.

For 10 years, Fred was content with outback life. Yet, when Australia entered the war, he did not hesitate to give it all up. He joined Mitchell's extraordinary rush to enlist. From a district population of less than 1600 people, 46 young men volunteered in the first three months of the war.[2] This disproportionate contribution continued and, by 1918, 51 families from the district had lost a son or husband.[3]

Fearing the recruitment officer at Roma was only accepting volunteers with experience in the citizen militia, Fred rushed to Brisbane to enlist. He entered the new camp at Bell's paddock, Enoggera, on 2nd September and was assigned as a private in 9th Battalion's C Company (later to be A Company). For the lad from the bush, the camp's size and bustling urgency was overwhelming. Although not yet two weeks old, over 1000 eager volunteers had already set up tents there. After rudimentary training, five weeks later, Fred left with the 9th Battalion for war on the troopship "Omrah". The speed of their departure seemed reckless, but Fred remained undaunted. He could only see adventure, travel and new experiences ahead.

Upon arriving in Egypt on 4th December, spirits remained high. Egypt's sights and exotic activities were intoxicating. However, the next four months were also challenging. Sandstorms, scorching heat and cold desert nights became features of Fred's life at Mena camp. Also, for six days, every week, he took part in a gruelling regime of intensive military training which involved day long route marches through desert sand, monotonous drills and exercises, endless parades and repetitive lectures.

By February 1915, Fred was very eager to leave the desert. The months of training boosted his confidence as a soldier and he was impatient to enter the battlefield. Although the army's move to the Greek island of Lemnos was not what he expected or hoped for, Fred sensed something big was about to happen.

After seven weeks on Lemnos, on the morning of Saturday, 24th April, Fred's A Company was transferred, with B Company, to the warship, "Queen". His spirit soared when, later that day, their ship led a huge flotilla of warships, destroyers and transports from Lemnos to the Turkish coast. He listened intently to General Hamilton's message that they would be the covering force and that *the whole world will be watching your progress.*[4] That night, sleep was impossible.

At about 1.30 a.m., soldiers mustered on deck and, with well-rehearsed precision, began their disembarkation, down rope ladders, into the rowboats waiting below. In groups of three, the boats left the warship, each group towed by a steam pinnace. Fred and the rest of Lieutenant Duncan Chapman's No. 3 Platoon were positioned in the first of the three boats of No.1 Tow. As they moved towards Gallipoli, the silence in each boat grew eerily acute. 50 metres out, the land's outline became visible, and the tows were released. The rowers took over. With each stroke of their oars, Fred felt his heart race faster.

His boat ran aground on the pebbly beach at about 4.30 a.m. Incredibly, the morning remained silent. Lieutenant Chapman gave a muffled order, "All OUT!" The men responded as quickly as possible, but disembarking over the rowboats' high gunnels was difficult. They scrambled ashore, struggling in waist deep water. When the sound of a single Turkish rifle pierced the air, about half were on the beach. In an instant, a deadly rain of bullets followed.

As they landed, battalions, companies and platoons quickly became mixed. It was obvious the landing had occurred in the wrong place. The orders were to cross open ground and attack the first ridge, but ahead there were only cliffs. During mounting chaos and confusion, Fred attempted to remain calm. He answered the call, *'Come on Queenslanders! Come on the 9th!'* and joined the charge up the steep slopes.

The soldiers from Lieutenant Chapman's first boat suffered considerably at the landing. Three were killed and eight wounded. During his brave advance inland, Fred also became a casualty. A Turkish bullet pierced his left arm.[5] Bleeding and in pain, he found his way back to the beach where he was taken on board the hospital ship, "Galeka" and evacuated to Egypt.

It took four weeks for the wound to heal. Fred returned to Gallipoli on 23rd May, with renewed strength, but was shocked by the situation he met. The stench of dead bodies filled the air and, because of a lack of sanitation and clean water, sickness was rampant. The extreme anxiety and stress that was etched on the faces of his mates shocked him. For six months, Fred endured Gallipoli's ordeals.

Surviving such a long period on the Peninsula was a feat that few men achieved. From the 9th Battalion's approximate 1500 men, who landed at Gallipoli in the first few weeks, only 6 officers and 88 other ranks survived more than six consecutive months.⁶ As one of these steely survivors, Fred received a small unofficial medal known as the 'Kilcoy' or 'Butler Medal'. It was a unique honour, funded and designed by the citizens of Kilcoy, the hometown of the Battalion's medical officer, Colonel A.G. Butler. There were only 94 recipients.

From Gallipoli, the 9th Battalion returned to Egypt. They moved to the sand dunes at Gebel Habeita on the east side of the Suez Canal, where, for the next two months, their orders were to dig trenches in the shifting dunes. The work was exhausting, but Fred was used to manual labour and he enjoyed the chance to work without the fear of shrapnel or gunfire. Also, at Habeita, on 29th February, he proudly received promotion to Temporary Corporal.

The next month, the 9th moved to France. Fred eagerly looked forward to joining what he regarded as the 'real war' against the Germans, but quickly learnt he was facing a formidable enemy. Two weeks after arriving at Fleurbaix, a quiet area south of Armentieres, the destructive might of the German artillery rained down on the 9th as it rested in seemingly peaceful billets. 50 to 60 shells fell upon them, killing 24 and wounding 48.

While in the line south of Fleurbaix, Fred's first active deployment involved a series of important raids that aimed to distract enemy attention from preparations for the Battle of the Somme. According to war historian, Charles Bean, the most brilliantly executed of these was a 9th Battalion raid on the 2nd July, carefully planned and commanded by Captain Wilder-Neligan. Volunteers were called for, and Neligan selected the best 160 men. Corporal Fred Thomas was one of these. In the planning, the Captain took meticulous precautions to ensure surprise and speed. The raiders' hands, faces and bayonets were blackened and chewing gum was issued to prevent coughing. He also warned anyone who left the attack to attend wounded colleagues would be court martialled.

At 11.50 p.m., Fred and the raiding parties moved into No-man's-land. He and another mate from the first boat ashore, Corporal Ted Teitzel, were in the Right Flank Party, commanded by the popular Captain Benson.⁷ Ahead, in the darkness, they faced 300 metres of crater-ridden landscape, with wire entanglements barring their way. Slowly and stealthily, progress was made by using heavy canvas mats flung on top of the wire. Fred's Right Flank Party lost its direction and advanced in a curve but, fortunately, met little hindrance. At 2.03 a.m. precisely, when all were in position, about 50 yards out from the German trenches, Neligan gave the signal. Supporting artillery opened their barrage and, with shells screeching overhead, Fred and his mates bravely rushed forward. By 2.12 a.m., all three raiding parties had entered the German trenches and were engaged in fierce fighting. The enemy was taken by surprise. Fred's Right Flank Party captured four and killed many. 21 German prisoners plus a German machine gun were taken. It was a great triumph, but, as always, the cost was high. 21 Battalion men were wounded and nine killed, including Fred's commanding officer, Captain Benson. Fred sustained a wound to his right knee, but bravely clawed his way back to the Australian line.

After only four days' recuperation, on 6th July, he re-joined the Battalion as they moved south to take part in the Battle of the Somme. His leg still pained, but the success of Neligan's Raid filled him with confidence, pride and a renewed energy. On 19th July, the 9th Battalion reached Pozieres, the site of the fiercest and bloodiest battle Fred would ever encounter. Exhausted, they arrived at 2 a.m. and took billets in old German trenches in Sausage Valley outside the small village. Despite the late hour, the Germans greeted their arrival with a heavy bombardment of gas shells. For Fred, this first encounter with clouds of deadly gas was an eerie experience. In the darkness, the shells burst all about him with only the sound of a slight 'pop', but he soon learnt this quietness was a cruel deception. Pain followed instantly as lungs and skin were attacked. In the days that followed, there were many more gas attacks.

Several British Battalions had already attempted to capture the small village of Pozieres and failed. It was now the Australians' turn. In the early hours of the morning on 23rd July, Fred's A Company moved cautiously into No-man's-land to a battle that quickly became hell on Earth. For four days and nights, a relentless German artillery rained upon them. The ground swayed and rocked under a bombardment that was more intense than any other experienced in the war. At one point howitzer shells were tearing up the ground at the rate of one every three seconds. Men were buried men alive. Some were blown to bits. Those who survived suffered intense trauma. Fred left the battlefield shell shocked and dazed.

After Pozieres, the Battalion regrouped in the nearby villages of Berteaucourt and Albert. Heavy losses meant many positions of command had to be quickly re-filled. Having proven themselves on the battlefield, Fred and his mate Ben Kendrick were promoted to Temporary Sergeant. Fred was extremely proud but also aware that command of a section of 40 men was a heavy burden to carry into battle.

Only three weeks after Pozieres, although depleted and traumatized, the Battalion returned to the frontline. Their new objective was Mouquet Farm, a shattered farmhouse on top of nearby Pozieres Ridge. At the head of his own platoon, Fred marched fearfully through Sausage Valley, passing the ruins of the village they had fought so hard to take. As they neared the frontline, the stench of the unburied dead grew stronger and the narrow trenches became congested by a constant stream of horrifically wounded men heading away from the battle.

At Mouquet Farm, on 19th August, another terrifying hell began. Once again, the Germans devastated the Australian line with a heavy barrage of shellfire that continued relentlessly for almost 48 hours. Trenches collapsed and again men were buried alive. The sound was deafening. *The wants of the troops were not many; none of them ate anything, as they were too shaken by the shell-fire. Cigarettes and drinks of water supported them for the three days they were here.*[8] By the 22nd August, Fred and his men were totally exhausted. Some were shell-shocked. At about 8 p.m., mercifully relief arrived. Over three days, the Battalion lost 27 lives with 125 men wounded and 12 men missing.

After the ordeals of Pozieres and Mouquet Farm, the shattered Battalion moved north. They re-entered the frontline on 9th November, 1916 at Flers, 25 kilometres south of Ypres and began another gruelling test of endurance. Europe was experiencing its most severe winter in 25 years and conditions in the trenches were atrocious. Frostbite, trench feet, respiratory disease, gangrene, and scabies soon were common ailments. Fred fell ill soon after arriving at Flers and spent a week in hospital with a fever of unknown origin.

Fortunately, two successful operations in the spring of 1917 brought a boost to the severely lagging morale that Fred and all the Battalion were suffering. After four days and nights of gallant fighting, a complex of trenches, known as 'The Maze', was successfully captured. Seven weeks later, at Lagincourt, Fred played a significant role in another important triumph. Before dawn on the 15th April, a massive German attack forced four battalions, including the 9th, into retreat. The village of Lagincourt was quickly lost but, despite being hugely outnumbered, the 9th and 20th Battalions refused to accept defeat. A swift counter-attack was mounted and, in the fierce fighting that ensued, Fred's platoon and company took a prominent role. One platoon member later recalled, *'Bluey, Fred Thomas, led our platoon calmly, and we had good shooting at 200 yards and we accounted for many Huns.'*[9] The village of Lagincourt was retaken, many prisoners captured, and the Germans were pushed back behind the Hindenburg Line.

Fred left Lagincourt, relieved and proud. In the stress of battle, he had displayed strong and steady leadership and gained much respect from his platoon. However, there was little time for reflection. On 6th May, the Battalion moved forward again and, for two days and nights, Fred once more led his platoon in brutal fighting against a storm of grenade and bomb explosions. In this second attempt on Bullecourt, his Battalion took less than 600 metres of damaged trenches for a cost of 25 lives and 136 wounded.

Mercifully, on 8th May, 1917, the exhausted 9th was relieved from the frontline. Two weeks later, they began four months of training and relief. This was the longest and most complete rest that Fred had received in two years of war. To his delight, more respite came in September with the granting of two weeks' leave in England. Although he was homesick for Australia, the boy from Mitchell relished the chance to visit London, the heart of the Empire. He was also eager to look up family and visit his parents' birthplace in Wales.

When Fred re-joined his platoon in Belgium on 22nd September, preparations were being made for yet another tough engagement. This time, the objective was the high ground at Broodseinde Ridge, which would hopefully open the way for an ultimate attack on Passchendaele Ridge before winter. The Australians moved forward in a well-planned advance behind a creeping barrage of artillery. 40 men from Fred's Battalion died, 2 went missing and 108 were wounded, but the operation was a success. Once again, Fred was a lucky survivor.

His next mission brought another close encounter with death. After a brief rest, the 9th returned to the front line at Tyne Cot, near the ruins of Passchendaele. As they advanced, Fred's platoon became perilously trapped in no-man's-land. Forced to shelter in shell holes, their fate seemed sealed. Desperately, B and C Companies attempted to save their mates. They launched a brave counter-attack, a well-timed manoeuvre, which briefly distracted the Germans by allowing the trapped soldiers sufficient cover to escape no-man's-land. Fred could not believe his luck at surviving another close call.

Fred was now at the edge of collapse. As he entered his third year of war, it seemed he was caught in an endless cycle of battles and horrific ordeals, and he wondered how much more he could endure. Some brief relief came at the end of November with two weeks' leave in Paris, but on the 30th December, a much greater consolation was granted. Fred was selected for attachment to the 1st Training Battalion in England. For the next six months, he was removed from the front and stationed at the military training camps at Sutton Veny and Codford on England's Salisbury Plain. The calm of the English countryside became a re-energizing tonic.

The Battalion was in northern France when Fred re-joined them on the 9th July. They were about to enter a frontline operation described by Battalion historian, Norman Harvey, as *'one of the most successful and exciting of those engaged in by the 9th.'*[10] While an attack was being made on nearby Meteren, the 9th Battalion planned to take the village of Le Waton. Without a supporting artillery barrage and in broad daylight, Fred's A Company bravely led the advance across the wheat fields. Using a strategy of hasty, surprise attacks from the flank and rear, they succeeded in quickly overrunning enemy gun-posts. Their speedy capture of Le Waton gained Fred's Company much admiration. Fred was again energized by the success.

As the 'Big Push', the last offensive of the war was about to begin, the 1st Division, including the 9th Battalion, moved south. As the Battle of Amiens began, the 9th Battalion was sent to make an assault on the German line north of the village of Lihons. When they arrived on 8th August, Fred fearfully surveyed the battlefield. To reach their objective at Crepy Wood and the German line beyond, a large, wide open expanse of flat ground had to be crossed. With much trepidation, Fred moved forward with his platoon. As expected, in the open field, they were easy targets for German machine guns. Many soldiers fell, but Fred and the rest of the 9th valiantly pushed on. Fierce fighting continued for the next four days as attack and counter-attack were made. The Battalion lost one third of its men, but the Germans were driven from Crepy Wood.

A week later, with depleted numbers, the fighting ability of Fred and his mates was once again tested. Fred was exhausted. It was his third significant battle in two months. They advanced on 23rd August along the slope of the Somme River through Luc Wood to Froissey Beacon. Despite suffering a heavy bombardment of gas and 8inch shells, important territory was taken, as well as many prisoners. Mercifully, it was Fred's last engagement.

While preparing his mind and body for the next ordeal, he received unexpected orders. A new special 'Anzac Leave' gave original 1914 volunteers two months' leave in Australia and Fred was chosen as one of the lucky first recipients. He could not believe his good fortune. With two mates from the 'first boat ashore', Bill Rider and Dave Kendrick, he embarked on the troopship, "Kaiser-a-Hind" on 14th September, 1918, for Australia.

Four days before reaching home, the war ended. When their ship arrived, Australia was still celebrating. Everywhere, huge patriotic crowds gathered to welcome them. From Sydney, the Queenslanders took a special train onto Brisbane, and at every station through which they passed, there was another amazing reception. When their train arrived on Monday afternoon on 25th November, thousands gathered at Central Station. The enormity of the spectacle overwhelmed Fred. From the station, a military band led the veterans' motorcade in a triumphal procession through colourfully decorated city streets. From every vantage point, people pushed and shoved to get a glimpse of the Anzac heroes. A newspaper reported *'Men and boys cheered, and many women and girls wept for very joy as the worthy representatives of Australia's famous army passed by.'*[11]

Although grateful for Brisbane's extraordinary reception, Fred was desperate to leave the city and return to Mitchell. With two other local boys, also 'Original Anzacs', John Carlyon and Francis Callow, he boarded the first overnight train. In their hometown, an enthusiastic crowd of family and friends waited eagerly.[12] Prominent on the small platform were Fred's father and his adoring sisters. Their pride was hard to contain. Fred returned as a local celebrity, a hero of Gallipoli and the many battles of the Western Front. He stepped from the train, handsome in his Sergeant's uniform, beaming with joy but also unprepared for his new status within the community. The public attention was awkwardly accepted. His only joy was to be back with his family.

There was so much to catch up on. In his four years away, many things had changed. His eldest sister, Flo, was now a nurse at the Mitchell Hospital and Jane had married a Roma grazier. As his sisters unloaded their stories, he listened intently, but, unexpectedly, he found the normality of their lives was now foreign to him. Also, their many questions about the war were impossible to answer. He could not share or re-visit those horrors, and his stony silence was misunderstood. Suddenly, Fred felt isolated and confused. Unable to connect with the people he loved, he was angry and bewildered. The dream of returning to his old life, that sustained him in the trenches, somehow had been taken from him. War had changed everything.

Over the following days, the district continued to fete Fred as a hero. In early December, the members of Roma's Oddfellows Lodge held a special meeting to honour their lodge brothers, John Carlyon, Fred Thomas and Francis Callow, with a night of songs, recitations and speeches.[13] He appreciated the accolades, but Fred knew there was no glory in war. The attention he was receiving made him feel increasingly uneasy. He longed for the company of his old mates from the 9th Battalion and their unspoken understanding.

Immediately after the family's Christmas celebrations ended, Fred left for Brisbane. He rented a room in Thomas Street, South Brisbane,[14] and searched for employment. However, jobs in the city were scarce. Eventually, low-paid work was found in the nearby small town of Toogoolawah as a saw-mill hand.[15] Unfortunately, there he became embroiled in a messy industrial dispute. Fred was elected the saw-mill's union representative in an unfair dismissal dispute that led to strike action. Using the same self-assured leadership skills he displayed as a Sergeant in the war, he earnestly attempted to get a satisfactory result for his workmates.[16] The ugly dispute created much ill-feeling and when resolved, Bill, tired of conflict, was eager to move on.

He returned to Brisbane and to the comradery of his old 9th Battalion mates. Three friends from the 'first boat ashore', Cecil Holdway, Eli Coles and Harry Hansen, were working as conductors and motormen for the Brisbane Tramways Company. With their help and encouragement, Fred joined the Tramways as a motorman. It became his job and life for the next 20 years.

A room was rented on Commercial Road at Fortitude Valley but, later, job security enabled him to move to more comfortable lodgings at Wilberforce Flats at 422 St Pauls Terrace.[17] Although he lived alone, Fred led a busy life that focused on work and the fraternity of his Anzac mates. He became a stalwart of the 9th Battalion Association and other veteran associations. He was a founding member of the Omrah Association, established in 1934 to preserve the spirit of comradeship among the Anzacs who left in 1914 on the troopship "Omrah". At their first annual meeting, with other 'first boat ashore' mates, Andy Fisher and Ben Kendrick, Fred was elected to the Reunion Committee.[18] He was also a committee member of the 9th Battalion Association from 1947 to 1950, responsible for organizing Anzac Day commemorations and reunions.[19]

Anzac mates and Anzac projects dominated his work and social life, and it seemed Fred would remain a bachelor. However, in 1944, at 52 years of age, he surprised everyone. Fred wed Margaret Jennings, the widow of a close workmate and fellow war veteran, William Jennings. Their marriage brought a tremendous change in lifestyle and provided Fred with much comfort. It was a happy union that lasted almost 30 years. The couple lived at the Jennings family home at Henderson Street, Bulimba, and later at 43 Barrinia Street, Manly.

Unfortunately, like many other veterans, at an early age, Fred suffered declining health. Three years after their wedding, illness forced him to leave his job at the Tramways. He attempted to return to the workforce in 1949 with a less demanding city job as an office clerk with the Lands Department.[20] However, his health continued to worsen and retirement was forced upon him.

He and Margaret moved to Manly. With the help of Margaret's sons, they built a two-bedroom cottage at 43 Barrinia Street and enjoyed a quiet life by the sea. However, as Fred became more incapacitated, he relied heavily on his wife for care and support. Sadly, Margaret suddenly died in February 1975. Left alone, Fred moved to a nursing home at Pleasantville Private Hospital in Lindum but, less than six months later, on 30th July, 1975, he died. Fred was 83.

The First Ashore

Friends and family remembered him as a good mate, a courageous soldier, a leader and a resilient survivor. His toughness during four years of active war service was remarkable. After six months at Gallipoli, Fred fought in almost every major action that the 9th Battalion was involved in. His battle honours included Flers, Lagincourt, Pozieres, Mouquet Farm, Broodseinde, Le Waton and Froissey Beacon. In his post-war life, the 'Original' Anzac worked to uphold the Anzac tradition of service and mateship. With the help of Anzac mates, he overcame the dark legacy of war and built a satisfying life.

Sergeant Fred Thomas was cremated at Albany Creek Crematorium on 1st August, 1975.

Private Samuel Aubrey McKenzie (SLQ)

Private Robert McNiel Crawford McKenzie (SLQ)

Private William Alexander Pollock (SLQ)

Private Archibald Henry Reynolds (RAHS)

Private William James Ryder (SLQ)

Private James Roy (Scotty) Speirs (SLQ)

General Buller, 9th Battalion mascot. (Mrs L G Holdway)

Private Fred Thomas (Thomas family album)

Lieutenant F.G. Haymen (SLQ)

Scout Sergeant Fred Coe (SLQ)

Lance Corporal Edward Teitzel (SLQ)

Private William (Bill) Cleaver (SLQ)

Private Fred Uden (SLQ)

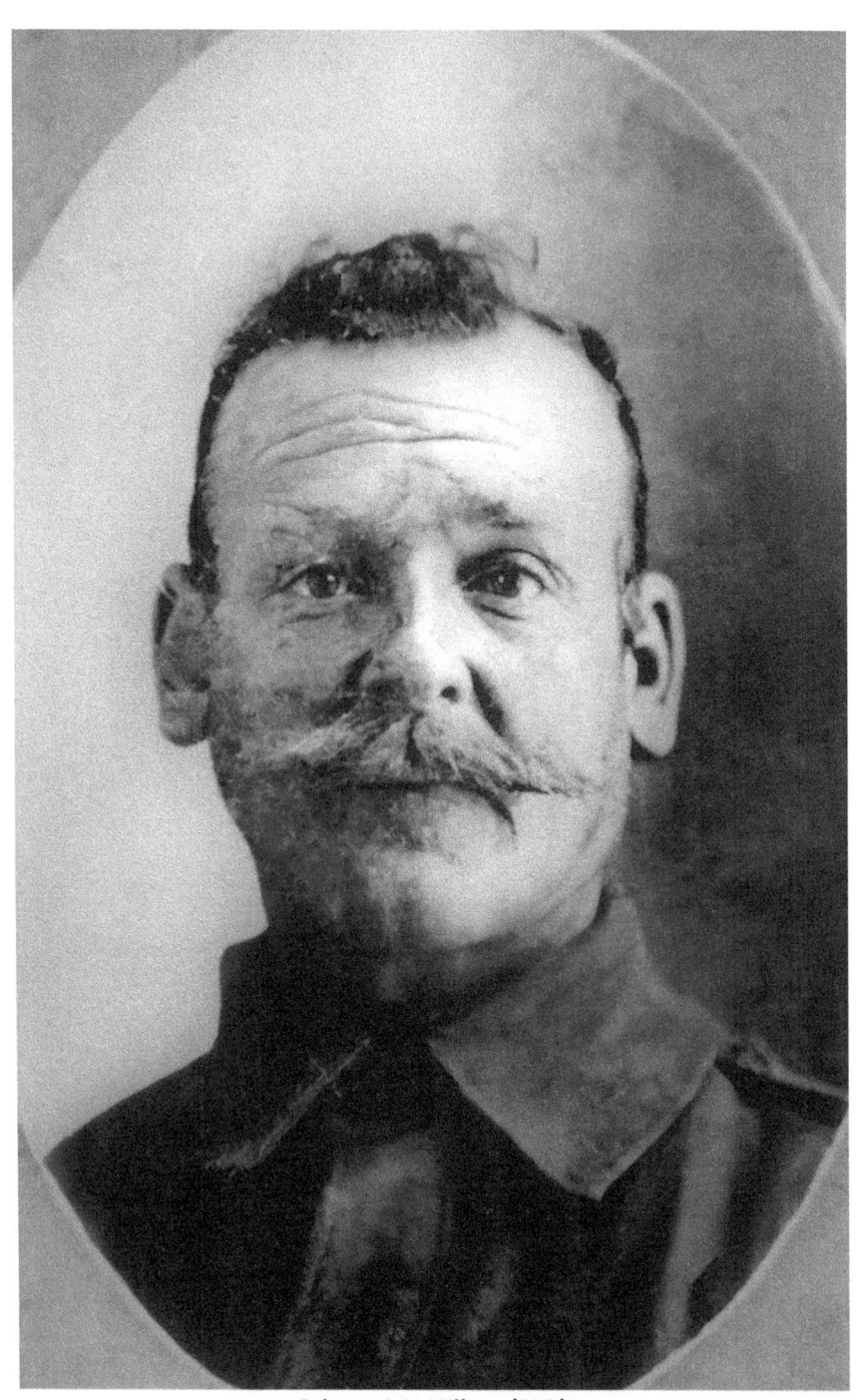
Private A.K. Wilson (SLQ)

9th BATTALION SCOUTS

Lieutenant Frank Granville Haymen

9th Battalion

The courage of Scout Commander Lieutenant Frank Granville Haymen was immense. After landing with the first boat ashore, he bravely led a group of soldiers to a point far beyond the forward line. His selfless actions and fearless leadership helped stem the enemy's advance near Lone Pine. At the end of the day, he died so his mates could live.

Frank's selflessness was surprising for a young man whose upbringing had been extremely privileged. His family was wealthy, well-known and highly respected in pre-war Brisbane. Frank's father, Marmaduke Haymen, was the General Manager of the Queensland National Bank and his mother, Florence, was a Brisbane socialite, daughter of one of the city's most successful merchants, Ernest Goetz.[1] The Haymen family mixed with the State's wealthiest and most important people. Marmaduke and Florence were frequent guests at receptions and dinners hosted by early Queensland governors such as Sir Henry and Lady Norman, and Lord and Lady Lamington.[2]

Born on 14th September, 1891, Frank was their eldest child. Although born in Toowoomba, he grew up in Brisbane at "Grafton," the family's River Terrace home at Kangaroo Point. Nearby, his grandparents lived in a grand, two-storey mansion, named "Hilderstone". Built by Ernest Goetz, with lavish gardens running down to the river, this was one of Brisbane's most impressive homes and became a favourite childhood playground for Frank and his siblings.

The family's success afforded Frank an excellent education. He started school at Bowen House,[3] a fashionable city preparatory school for boys in Ann Street. A high school education followed at the equally exclusive Brisbane Grammar School, where Frank and his brother, Charles, were students from 1905 until 1907. Although Frank attained excellent results in mathematics, he was not a strong academic student. In the 1907 Junior examination, he achieved five C grades and one 'A' result for arithmetic.[4] More notable were his achievements on the sports field. Frank possessed a passion for sport and outdoor pursuits. He especially loved cricket and proved to be a very competent batsman on the Grammar School's cricket team. Also, at a young age, he developed a strong interest in military matters and was a keen member of the School's Cadet Corps, where he proudly attained the rank of Corporal.[5]

At the end of 1907, tragedy visited the Haymen family. Frank's younger brother, Charles, contracted typhoid fever and, after a three-week battle, died at the Haymen's River Terrace home. The loss devastated Frank. He and Charles were almost the same age. They played in the same school cricket team and belonged to the same Cadet Corps. He lost a best friend and a brother.

After the funeral, Frank did not return to school. At 16 years of age, his life took a new direction. He found work as a cadet surveyor,[6] a job that was well suited to his love of the outdoors. He applied himself enthusiastically and completed the four-year cadetship by the time he was 19 years old. His ambitious plans for the future were, however, thwarted by a new *Land Surveyors Act*, introduced in 1908, which stipulated surveyor qualifications could not be authorised until the applicant was 21 years old.

While waiting, Frank sought new challenges. The new age of engineering, that was transforming life through exciting developments associated with electric lighting, the telephone, railways and motor cars, captivated him. Astutely, he believed an engineering qualification combined with his surveying qualification would open the path to career opportunities and a promising future in Queensland's rapidly developing economy.

On 12th March 1912, Frank enrolled in the Faculty of Engineering at Brisbane's new University of Queensland.[7] The University in George Street's Old Government House was only 12 months old, and overflowed with optimism and innovation. At 18 guineas per year,[8] tuition fees were extremely expensive, but for Frank, this was not a problem. Its small campus of 150 students assured him very individualized learning. Frank joined 21 students studying in the Engineering Faculty.[9]

The university became a great joy in Frank's short life. He joined almost every sporting club and became a well-known and popular figure on campus. As well as playing in the University cricket team,[10] he competed in the university's lawn tennis tournaments and represented the University Rifle Club in A grade competition.[11] He was also a keen rower. In faculty boat races, he took the position of bowman for the Engineering crew.[12]

Frank's many university commitments consumed his time but his interest in military matters took precedence. On 25th March 1912, just days after enrolling in his Engineering course, he was proudly commissioned as a Lieutenant in the prestigious Australian Intelligence Corps, 1st Military District. The A.I.C. sought smart young men, like Frank, with surveying and mapping skills to gather information about topography and military resources within Australia. In the year before the war, AIC Lieutenant Haymen took part in military camps that surveyed and strategically mapped the Bauple-Tiaro district[13] and also the country surrounding the 'Redbank Camp'.[14]

As the world moved closer to war, his work with the Australian Intelligence Corps grew substantially. A temporary secondment to the 7th Infantry Moreton Regiment[15] also consumed much time. Study and career goals became less important and, by the end of his second year at university, Frank's academic results were less than satisfactory. One subject was failed and a supplementary exam was required.[16] Regrettably, his third year exams were never completed.

Two days before Australia joined the war, Frank was mobilized to Thursday Island. Two German cruisers and a powerful Japanese cruiser had been sighted near the island and, in response, on 2nd August, the government moved 700 men from Townsville's Citizens Forces to form a garrison there.[17] Details of Frank's orders remain unknown. His role in this new garrison can only be speculated.

When he left Brisbane by train on the night of 4th August, the atmosphere in the city bristled with excitement as rumours of impending war were spreading. At Central Station, the popular university student received a hero's farewell. The Telegraph reported,

A demonstration on the part of 20 or 30 students of the Queensland

The First Ashore

University attracted some attention in the main streets of the city last evening. The squad attended at the Central railway station to bid farewell to one of their number (Lieutenant F.G. Haymen), who left by the northern mail train, en route for Thursday Island, to which place he has been ordered as a member of the Intelligence Corps. As the train left the station, cheers were given and patriotic songs sung. The squad then marched down Edward Street, singing "Rule Britannia", the "Marseillaise," and cheering every person in uniform.[18]

Upon reaching Thursday Island, Frank was alarmed by the degree of anxiety and uneasiness within the community. All men were busily engaged in digging trenches and fortifications. Frank realized important work needed to be done, but he was desperate to return to Brisbane. While he travelled north by train, Australia had officially declared its involvement in the war and, in Brisbane, Queensland's contingent of the First Australian Imperial Force was being hurriedly put together. Frank wanted to be involved and, although orders were given for no adult males to leave Thursday Island,[19] by the beginning of September, he had found his way back.

On his return to Brisbane, Frank applied immediately for a commission in the new A.I.F., and, on 5th September, he entered Enoggera camp as Lieutenant to the 9th Battalion's E Company. The next two weeks passed quickly as earnest preparations were made for the Battalion's departure for war. The young Lieutenant's excitement was hard to contain as he looked forward to the glorious adventure he believed lay ahead.

Upon reaching the desert camp at Mena in Egypt, four months of crucial military training began. Transforming Australia's undisciplined and largely inexperienced army of volunteers into an efficient fighting force was a daunting challenge for young officers like Frank. At just 22 years of age, he was younger and possessed less life experience than most of the men under his command. Many of his platoon had been resourceful, independent bush men unused to regulation and authority. Others were veterans of the Boer War and, therefore, possessed actual combat experience. Yet Frank was not daunted. He worked hard to earn the respect and confidence of his men and, as testimony to his success, he later received command of the Battalion's Scouts.[20]

As part of the final preparations for the Gallipoli campaign, a contingent of 9th Battalion Scouts was formed.[21] Frank's pre-war experience with the Australian Intelligence Corps and his skills as a surveyor made him an obvious choice as Scout officer. At the landing, his scouts were to fulfill important objectives. Upon reaching the beach, they were to move forward quickly, locate and eliminate Turkish guns and snipers, and clear the way for the rest of the covering force to follow.[22] Anzac commander, Lieutenant-General Birdwood, referred to them as 'special groups to deal with snipers.'[23] In many regards, success depended upon them.

At the landing, Frank sat at the bow of the leading boat of the No.1 Tow. Next to him was Scout Sergeant Fred Coe and opposite company commander, Lieutenant Chapman. As they approached the coastline, they crouched low in the boat, not knowing what to expect. Their anxiety increased as the morning darkness remained silent. When metres from shore, the steam boats released the tows, and the rowers took over. It was approximately 4.30 a.m. when Frank jumped into waist-deep water and scrambled across the gravelly beach. He and most of the Scouts were sheltering under the cliffs, busily taking off their packs, when the silence was broken. A single shot sounded, and within seconds, a deadly rain of Turkish gunfire followed it.

Despite the many testimonies and substantial evidence that Lieutenant Duncan Chapman was the first man ashore, one member of the first boat had a different recollection. Private Frank Uden, a Battalion Scout, who was well known to friends and family for his keen eye and attention to detail, loudly and publicly proclaimed in 1933, *'Mr. F. Kemp, whom I knew as Sergeant Coe, says that Lieutenant Chapman was the first man ashore. I imagine that if Mr. Kemp thinks back he will see that he has made a mistake. It was Lieutenant Haymen, our scout officer, who was first ashore.'*[24] Undoubtedly, the two Lieutenants were positioned at the bow of the boat and would have disembarked closely together.

As the first wave of 1500 men came ashore on a beach frontage of only 800 metres, battalions, companies, officers and men became hopelessly mixed. Frank, a surveyor and mapmaker, immediately was aware the landing had occurred in the wrong place. The steep inclines, obstructing their way, placed them many kilometres from their principal objectives - the capture of the guns at Gaba Tepe and guns on the Third Ridge at Andersons Knoll. Soldiers, expecting flat topography, were confronted by steep rugged cliffs and there was a mounting bewilderment about what to do next. Frank realized it was imperative that his Scouts move quickly and not join the confusion. With determination and courage, he attempted to stay true to original orders. While other troops hesitated, taking shelter from the fierce rifle fire coming from the cliffs above, Frank led his scouts on the scramble up the slopes.

Within 30 minutes, they were atop of the knoll and on Plugge's Plateau. However, during the frantic move from the beach, all formation was lost. The hostile terrain of prickly scrub and the bewildering maze of gullies and ridges divided the men and hid them from each other. Communication was soon lost. The scouts became scattered but continued to move forward, often blindly, in isolated groups. Some groups, such as Scout Sergeant Coe's, went to the left while Frank moved across Plugge's Plateau towards 400 Plateau, diligently attempting to follow the 9th's original orders to secure the right flank on the 3rd Ridge.

At first, it appeared the Turks were retreating. Plugge's Plateau was secured and 400 Plateau quickly captured. While some soldiers waited to regroup on Plugges, the scouts with small advance parties continued on, reaching the 2nd Ridge and beyond. Unfortunately, by mid-morning, with increasing intensity, Turkish machine gun fire swept through the bushes. The build-up of Turkish forces on the 3rd Ridge had begun. Soon shrapnel was bursting every few minutes. Without reinforcement and consolidation, the progress of Frank's and other advance groups halted.

As the Turkish counter-attack grew stronger, before noon, Lieutenant Haymen was sent forward on a perilous mission.[25] Already, the Turks were forcing many small advance parties on the edge of the 2nd Ridge and beyond into retreat. These positions needed to be held. They were providing an effective screen to the enemy and giving the main bodies of the 9th and 10th more time and opportunity to dig in on 400 Plateau. When news came that some of the advance parties, under Lieutenant Boase and Thomas, were in danger of being cut off, Major Charles Brand (3rd Brigade HQ Staff) responded quickly. He ordered Frank with about 50 men forward to assist.

They reached Boase and Thomas' position as they were retreating from an intensifying and devastating Turkish assault. Rather than join the retreat, bravely, Frank pushed his men forward to a position in front of a gully, known as The Cup, where Turkish field guns had been captured earlier in the day. They attempted to form a rough line about 50 yards in front of the captured guns, but communication was almost impossible and quickly their action became disorganized. Frank's men came under fire from three directions from a seemingly invisible enemy. The noise and frequency of shrapnel bursts strained their nerves. Every five minutes seemed like an hour. Losses were heavy.

In this dire situation, Frank took comfort that the machine-gun section of the 9th Battalion was nearby. Commanded by his old schoolmate from Brisbane Grammar, Lieutenant Joseph Costin, the gunners were stubbornly holding the isolated crest a short distance above Frank's position. All morning, with only two machine-guns, they had courageously been drawing the fire of Turkish guns on themselves.

In the afternoon, tragedy unfolded. One of the few survivors, Lieutenant Fortescue of the 9th Battalion, provided an account of the disastrous events that occurred.[26] Just before midday, while attempting to find the firing line, Fortescue and his small group of soldiers came across Lieutenant Costin's position. Costin informed him he did not know where the firing line was or the whereabouts of the rest of the 9th Battalion. His only knowledge was that Haymen and a few men were in the captured Turkish gun position further down the hill. Using Costin's directions, Fortescue moved his men forward to join Haymen's group. About this time, the Turks established their mountain battery on the 3rd Ridge near Scrubby Knoll and, with heavy guns, began their deadly work, pounding The Cup and the Lone Pine area. Fortescue found Haymen making a valiant stand in front of the captured Turkish gun position at The Cup. Sadly, only 15 of his original 50 men remained. They were sheltering in the gully's shoulder but, soon after Fortescue arrived, with the enemy shelling intensifying, the combined group was forced to move into the trenches of the captured gun-pit. This desperate move had deadly consequences as a determined Turkish General Sefik escalated his efforts to recapture his lost gun battery.

Haymen and Fortescue found themselves in a dire situation, isolated and without support. Lieutenant Fortescue's recollection was vivid.

> 'Haymen had his line of about fifteen men out in the open. We came to the conclusion that gun-pits were nasty places to be and were drawing a good deal of fire, but …..as they provided some protection against the shrapnel we stayed in them. This settled, we began to wonder where we were. Maps were by no means clear and were absolutely incorrect; we could not pick up our position on them at all. Haymen was sure there was nobody to get in touch with, or anybody on either flank. There were some people to the right because we could hear them firing, but did not know whether they were our people or the enemy. We could see people moving on the hill to our left rear, but could not tell who they were. I had binoculars, but they had got full of salt water when we jumped into the water and were no good. The shelling got very bad.'[27]

As the day progressed, circumstances worsened. Crucial support from the Machine-gun Section was lost. In the early afternoon, a Turkish shell destroyed the gunners, killing Lieutenant Costin. The lone survivor of his Section, Sergeant Alexander Steele, bravely attempted to carry on with the one remaining machine-gun but his position was impossible. When opportunity allowed, he heroically carried the machine-gun to Haymen's party in the gun-pit. Lieutenant Fortescue recalled the impossible decision that they then faced,

> 'Costin had got blown up with one of his guns, so Steele brought the other one down to where we were. ….. We were right out in the cold (or rather in the hot), a long way from our main position, and whatever people were near us they did not seem to love us much. We could not stay here indefinitely. What were we to do? To get back we should have to go up the slope of a hill that was being pelted with fire. There were as many wounded men as whole ones, so to attempt to get these back would make a certainty of our being all wiped out. To wait until night was to run a big risk of being entirely cut off. To get back immediately with the fit men and leave the wounded to the mercy of the enemy was a perfectly sensible thing to do–really the only thing to do under the circumstances–but we couldn't do it. We stayed where we were. The afternoon seemed a miserable thing without beginning and without end.'[28]

Lieutenant Frank Haymen did not have to face the problem of organizing a safe retreat. According to the diary of Lance Corporal Frank Loud, he died just before dusk. When *'the Turks were coming over the next hill in swarms'*, the Lieutenant and his men had no option but to leave the gun-pit trench. While taking refuge behind a mound, Frank stood up, perhaps to assess the situation or give direction. *'He was standing up and fell on top of me.'*[29] A sniper's bullet had hit him in the chest. He died instantly.

It was a heroic end. Frank's tenacious actions and leadership that afternoon had significantly slowed the Turkish advance onto the 2nd Ridge. As a result, the 3rd Brigade was given valuable time to dig in on 400 Plateau. Even when totally isolated and in danger of being cut, he courageously refused to retreat. After the war, Turkish General Sefik reflected on the bravery of men like Frank, *'The enemy was not only stubbornly persevering in not letting Kanlisirt (Lone Pine) go and give up the guns but they were also executing counter assaults. The enemy was demonstrating fortitude and obstinacy in retaliation and resistance.'*[30]

Frank's body lies in an unknown grave. As night fell, during the desperate withdrawal from The Cup, there was no time to retrieve his body. His name is memorialized on the Lone Pine Memorial (Panel 30) in Gallipoli's Lone Pine Cemetery. In Frank's hometown of Brisbane, the Anzac Memorial in Keating Park, Indooroopilly honours his memory and the Brisbane Grammar School commemorates his sacrifice in its ornate War Memorial Library. One of 12 spectacular stained glass windows is dedicated to the brief life of Lieutenant Frank Granville Haymen, 9th Battalion AIF.

Scout Sergeant Frederick Charles Coe (aka Fred Kemp)

No. 1010, C Company, 9th Battalion

Scout Sergeant Frederick Coe held the unusual distinction of volunteering twice to serve in World War 1. After being repatriated to Australia as medically unfit, with headstrong determination, he falsified his name and immediately re-enlisted. His notable achievements at Gallipoli were a source of great pride. Fred was one of the first to step ashore and, on that fateful day, he made a valiant stand that helped save the left flank. Regrettably, his brave service and dedication to duty received little reward. War inflicted injury, sickness, disillusionment and disappointments that eventually brought his life to a sad conclusion.

Life for Fred began in 1885 at Lowestoft on England's idyllic east coast. However, he spent most of his childhood in the bustling south London suburb of Brixton where his stepfather, John Charles Coe, had a hairdressing shop on Cornwall Road, and his mother, Harriet Coe, nee Kemp, worked as a fancy goods dealer.[1] Fred and his brother, Ernest, were raised as John Coe's sons, but both boys were fathered outside their mother's marriage.[2] Family life was strained. His mother worked hard to save for the day she could escape life in Brixton.

Fred left the family home before he was 15. He escaped by enlisting in the army. At the turn of the century, boy recruits were still being accepted to serve chiefly as drummer boys or buglers. Fred, a slightly built, blue eyed, fair-haired teenager, was a perfect candidate. He signed a 12 year contract with the Dorsetshire Regiment and ten months later, found himself in India, serving at Ferozepur in the Punjab.[3] For a young boy, adjustment to military life in such an exotic location so far from home was a daunting experience. However, the army became Fred's new family. It provided important role models and gave him an education and skills that he would not have achieved in Brixton. By the age of 18, Fred had moved to the rank of private and joined the mounted infantry at Ambala in India.[4]

Three years after Fred joined the army, his mother and brother also escaped Brixton. In 1904, they migrated to Australia and started a new life in North Queensland. Despite having little experience of farming, the pair jointly purchased a 129 acre farm at Smithfield, near Redlynch Station, just outside of Cairns. Their bold venture struggled, but Fred's mother was a determined woman who aimed to re-unite her sons. She worked hard growing and selling vegetables[5] and saved frugally. Incredibly, within three years, she could pay for Fred's passage to Australia plus the £25 penalty payment for his early release from the British Army.[6]

Fred arrived in Cairns in 1908, eager to be with his family and to start civilian life. However, his mother and brother barely recognized him. The awkward, skinny teenager who left their Brixton home was now 23, fit, educated, well-built and a confident young man with an assertive air. In the British army, he became a skilled horseman and also a competitive fighter in the boxing ring but, now he looked forward to being a farmer. To repay his mother, Fred agreed to work on the farm without wages for the next 18 months.[7]

He was given charge of the garden and immediately set about expanding cultivation. Over 20 acres of scrub were cleared and planted with bananas. Fred worked long hours and soon the farm was productive but, sadly, his timing was unfortunate. Cheap overseas bananas flooded the Queensland market, forcing prices into steady decline. With confident bravado, Fred joined the campaign to fight these unfair trade practices. Using his excellent communication skills, he became a prominent leader and vocal advocate for the local growers. In 1912, his well-crafted letters protesting against the importation of bananas from Fiji appeared in newspapers in Brisbane and Cairns.[8] As the Cairns representative, Fred also attended the 1912 Royal Commission enquiry into the failing North Queensland banana industry.[9]

Fred also became well known throughout the region because of his prowess as an amateur boxer. While in the British army, many believed he had the potential to make boxing a professional career and, in Cairns, his fights were attracting large crowds. In 1910, with his typical boldness, Fred publicly challenged the reigning Queensland champion,

Percy Simmonds, to a fight. Prize money was put up and substantial bets were placed. Their fight, which was held at the Cairns Shire Hall on 1st October, drew much interest, but the event turned out to be a humiliating farce. Newspapers described it as the *'greatest fiasco ever seen in the hall.' 'Simmonds pummelled him... Coe evidently being too dazed to defend himself.'*[10] The police had to intervene. Although unproven, it seemed, before entering the ring, Fred had been doped. He later explained,

'When I entered the dressing room, I was as fit as a man could be. How it occurred I do not know. I went to sleep, and from that till I was roused to go into the ring I remember nothing ... On going to shake hands I felt myself going off. Simmonds' gloves appearing in a blur...'[11]

For Fred, there were serious consequences. Besides the financial loss that he and his family incurred, his pride and reputation were severely damaged. Simmonds' refusal to have a re-match meant the chance of a boxing career was gone for Fred.

More disillusionment followed. Over the following years, the Coe farm sank further into debt. As a consequence, the family cohesion, which Fred had desperately sought and cherished, fell apart. Relations with his brother became increasingly strained and, by July 1912, the family was living apart. Fred's mother kept ownership of the farm, but left Smithfield to establish a new home at Mungana, west of Cairns.[12] Her disappointment turned to shame when, a month later, Fred was charged with physically assaulting his brother. At his appearance in the Cairns Police Court, private family details were made public and published in the Cairns Post under the unsavoury headline, "A Family Squabble. Washing Dirty Linen."[13]

The following year, Fred's life continued to spiral downwards. Twelve months after leaving the farm, his mother, Harriet Coe, died unexpectedly. The shock was devastating and compounding his grief was the awful realization that the farm, that he had worked so hard to build, would be sold. Without sufficient funds to purchase the property, Fred was evicted. He left Smithfield in early 1914. More calamity followed. Months later, Fred became embroiled in a sordid scandal when the secret affair he had been conducting with Mrs Louis Grasset, the wife of a local fisherman, became public knowledge.[14] It seemed Fred's troubles and disappointments were never-ending.

By 1914, he was desperate to escape the mess his life had become. Although, ten years before, he was pleased to leave the British Army's rigid discipline, Fred now found himself eager to return. Unsurprisingly, when Australia entered the war on 5th August, Fred was one of the first volunteers. He travelled immediately to the nearest recruitment office at Townsville. Previous service with the British Mounted Infantry meant an immediate posting to the 2nd Australian Light Horse Regiment, C Squadron. Just three days after recruitment opened, he departed North Queensland with the region's first contingent of volunteers on the steamer, "Bombala."

The comradery and patriotic celebration that surrounded the North Queensland contingent's departure buoyed Fred's spirit. He felt optimistic. However, upon reaching Brisbane, there was more disappointment. The army had already reached its recruitment quota for Light Horsemen. Fred was frustrated that his skills as a horseman would not be utilized. Reluctantly, he accepted his transfer to the 9th Infantry Battalion's E Company, but his despondency was short-lived. In the infantry, Fred's eight years' experience in the British army was recognized and promotions quickly followed. He enlisted with the rank of Lance Corporal and, six weeks later, he became Corporal. On the voyage to Egypt, he was made Sergeant.

After disembarking in Egypt, Sergeant Coe diligently guided his platoon through a gruelling regime of military training. Each day was tiresome and repetitive but, at the end of four months, Fred was confident his men were a physically fit and tough fighting force. From Egypt, in February 1915, they moved to the Greek island of Lemnos for a further final seven weeks of training.

While on Lemnos, in every battalion, scout contingents were being formed. In the 9th Battalion *'the Scouts were put together again under Sergeant Coe.'*[15] As these men would play a vital role in the upcoming campaign, scouts were carefully selected from various companies for their superior qualities or skills. As a Scout Sergeant, Fred carried heavy responsibilities. The infantry training manual in use at the time of Gallipoli stipulated in military engagements, *'a rule, that bodies of infantry feel their way and protect themselves by scouts pushed out several hundred yards.'*[16] Anzac commander, Lieutenant General Birdwood's instructions for the landing specifically mentioned the scouts' importance. *'If troops were fired on at the start, they should 'move on', preceded by special groups to deal with snipers.'*[17]

In each of the first row-boats of the first landing wave, places were reserved for scouts to enable them the best opportunity to be first ashore.[18] In the lead boat of No.1 Tow, with Lieutenant Duncan Chapman's No.3 Platoon, Fred sat with a small group of scouts. Sitting beside him at the bow of the boat was Scout officer, Lieutenant Frank Haymen,[19] and opposite was Lieutenant Chapman with his signaller, Jim Bostock. Other scouts at the bow were Lance Corporal Tietzel, Private Wilson and Private Uden.

In an important letter to Australia's official war historian, Dr Charles Bean, Fred recalled his experience of the landing. This recount would become Bean's primary evidence for determining who was first ashore.

'We touched shore, and Lieutenant Chapman was the first man ashore. I followed him, and we all got ashore. Private A K Wilson was taking my pack off when the first shot rang out: a pause: then 7 more....'[20]

As no other Anzacs reported being on the beach before the first rifle shot, Bean concluded Fred's account to be true.

On the small Anzac Cove beach, as more boats came ashore, organization was quickly lost. Battalions, companies and platoons were hopelessly mixed. It was quickly obvious the landing had occurred in the wrong place. Soldiers had been told to move forward over open ground but were confronted with cliffs. Amid the growing confusion, Fred quickly gathered some scouts and, in an effort to remain faithful to instructions, immediately charged up the steep slopes.

Upon reaching Plugge's Plateau, the summit of low scrub above the beach, it seemed the Turks were on the run. Some soldiers waited to regroup, but Fred continued to move his scouts forward. While Lieutenant Haymen, Private Uden and most other members of the first boat moved towards the right, for an unknown reason, Fred's small group moved to the left. He recalled, *'The Scouts and myself went on for a couple of miles and cleared the ridges.'*[21] They reached far inland. *'We cleared the 2nd Ridge by 10 o'clock'*[22] and arrived at the extremely important high ground around the summits of Baby 700 and Battleship Hill, crucial to the landing's success.

An intense battle ebbed and flowed here throughout the day.

Bean recorded the line on the seaward flank, changed five times between 7.30 a.m. and 3 p.m.[23] Fred and his small band of men bravely joined other isolated advance groups from various battalions, and fought valiantly against overwhelming odds. Incredibly, they held on and Fred proudly boasted their actions helped save *'the left flank on Sunday at Anzac–Captain Bean knows that to be true because of the proof I gave him and he accepts nothing that is not proven.'*[24]

Upon arriving in the vicinity of Baby 700 very early in the day, Fred and his scouts pushed on and, by 9 a.m., the south-east slopes of Battleship Hill were reached. They were almost within about 400 metres of the summit when a strengthening Turkish advance forced a rapid withdrawal. On returning to Baby 700,[25] Fred's group joined some survivors from Captain Tulloch's 11th Battalion Scouts[26] who were bravely attempting to hold the slopes.

For many hours, this band of men tenaciously held on, but the Turks were determined to push the Anzacs from the high ground. At about 1 pm, two Turkish battalions from Mustafa Kemal's 57th Regiment swarmed across the main range. Fred recalled, *'at 2 o'clock we got it heavy. We were on the extreme left flank, and at 2.30 the Turks put six battalions on to us.'*[27] The hill was quickly lost. Fred and the other survivors streamed back to the narrow saddle of land, 'the Nek,' that connected the First Ridge with the plateau top.

While retreating, he came across 9th Battalion Company Commander, Major Sydney Beresford Robertson, with a small group of 9th Battalion men. The Major was the only 9th Battalion officer who fought on the far left flank that day. Soon after he left the beach, he gathered together approximately 95 soldiers,[28] a mixture of men from 9th, 11th and 12th Battalions, for an advance on Baby 700. Bean described their heavy fighting on the seaward side slope as *'one of the most stubborn fights of the day.'*[29] By 11 a.m., Robertson's determined stand was forced into retreat. His men were driven back to the Nek, and according to Private S.J. Divett, by 1 p.m., only 15 of the original group were left.[30]

It was after 2.30 p.m. when Fred met Major Robertson and these survivors at The Nek. By then, some of Captain Lalor's 12th Battalion men had joined them and Fred estimated the combined group comprised about 70 soldiers.[31] To his consternation, when he arrived, the Major and these men were *'sitting down smoking and eating'*, unaware of Kemal's approaching force. Fred hastily imparted his important intelligence. *"Good god, sir,"* he said to Major Robertson, *"Aren't you preparing for the counterattack?"* Stunned, Robertson replied, *"What counterattack?"* (Fred told) him that the Turks were coming on in their thousands.'[32]

For Major Robertson, further retreat was not an option. He knew if the left flank was lost, the Turks could easily enfilade the Anzac's centre and right flanks. Therefore, at about 3 pm, he mounted a final valiant attempt to advance.[33] However, by then, the Turkish battery on Scrubby Knoll was increasingly drenching the Nek with artillery fire. Every minute, the situation became more desperate. According to Fred, Major Robertson did his utmost to get reinforcements, but Turkish artillery prevented any regiments reaching them.

Late in the afternoon, the Major gave Fred orders to hold a Turkish trench on the extreme left of the Second Ridge. With only 32 men, it was an impossible, almost suicidal, task. Shrapnel fire was now horrendous. It was one of Major Robertson's last orders. At about 4.30 p.m., while rising from the cover of shrubs, he was fatally hit. Fred recounted the tragic loss of leadership, *'(Major Robertson) was bowled over by a burst of shrapnel, and died as a brave gentleman. Lieutenant Rigby got a bullet soon afterwards and shrapnel completed his short career as a soldier.'*[34] Another nearby survivor, Private Divett recalled, *'my haversack was taken clean off my back by a lump of shrapnel, which continuing on its way, struck Major Robertson behind me.'*[35]

With all leadership gone, Fred's isolated band attempted to carry out the Major's order. Stubbornly, they held on. However, the Turkish counter-attack continued to intensify and their hold on the trench rapidly failed. Fred wrote, *'At half-past 5, out of the 33 (soldiers) in the trench on the left, only two were left, and we were forced to retire, expecting death at any moment.'* All appeared lost when, at the last moment, they heard New Zealand reinforcements moving towards them. *'Then down below, we heard the glorious cry ring out, "Come on, the Otago Regiment!" Shall I ever forget it?'*[36]

As darkness fell, Fred and the remnants of his group surrendered their position and joined the New Zealanders, who were holding a corner of the 2nd Ridge, nearest to Baby 700. *'Up they came, and we dug in …. and with Major Dawson's men held the enemy.'* Over the next two days, the actions of these Anzacs became legendary. With only about 150 New Zealanders and Australians, under the leadership of New Zealand's Major T. H. Dawson, this corner, later known as Quinn's Post, was famously held. Fred recalled, *'Throughout the night, Dawson's men kept up a continual battle-every man shouting orders of some sort or other. The Turks were thus led to believe that a considerable force confronted them...... bluff and courageous spirit saved the day.'*[37]

Fred was fortunate to survive the landing with only a slight bayonet wound to his left knee. However, two days later, an attack of severe dysentery brought him to the edge of collapse. Fred was taken on board the troopship "Mashobra", and evacuated to Egypt where, on 3rd May, he was admitted to No. 2 General Hospital at Zeitoun, outside Cairo. Ten days later, he was discharged and sent back to Gallipoli. This was far too soon. In the trenches' unsanitary conditions, his acute dysentery quickly returned and, on the 1st June, he had to be evacuated again. But this time his condition, complicated by severe anaemia, was much more serious. For the next three months, Fred remained in hospital on Lemnos and later in Cairo and Alexandria.

While convalescing, he reflected on the sacrifice that he witnessed at the Gallipoli landing. As one of the six survivors from Major Robertson's group, he believed it was his duty to speak for those *'who consequently cannot speak for themselves .... To give their friends an idea of what they did.'* From his Cairo hospital bed, for the Brisbane newspapers, he penned a detailed account of the heroic deeds of Major Robertson and Lieutenant Rigby and the men who fell with them while defending the corner of the Second Ridge near Baby 700.[38]

After three months' treatment in Egypt's hospitals, Fred's condition failed to improve. In an extremely weak state, he was invalided to England and, on 24th September, admitted to South General Hospital in Edgbaston. The cause of his acute anaemia remained undiagnosed, but slowly some strength returned. By October, he was deemed fit for light duties and attached to the Army Depot at Abbey Wood in S.E. London.

After almost eight months in England, Fred finally re-joined his unit on the front, near Armentieres, on 14th May, 1916. From Gallipoli, he learnt the horrid reality of war, but it did not prepare him for what he met in France. Conditions were more deplorable than he could have ever imagined. As well as contending with heavy German artillery, machine guns and gas attacks, in the muddy trenches there were lice, sickness and the stench of rotting bodies. Fred mused the rats grew as big as cats. Two weeks after arriving, he wrote in a letter home, *'Last night it was a veritable hell.'* He described *'the terrible fire'* concentrated on them and revealed *'just a few yards away are a few of my regiment sleeping with a little white cross above them, chums through India, and chums in death.'* Although his letter detailed horrors, its tone remained fiercely patriotic and optimistic. With his typical bravado, Fred mocked the heavy German artillery bombardment, *'The terrible fire they concentrated last night on our line (was) a tremendous waste of ammunition..... The moral effect is practically nil on our boys.'* He also refused to dignify 'fear' with a name, referring to it instead as that *'indescribable something'*. *'The big shelling seems to make them* (soldiers) *jocular outwardly, though all have an indescribable something which never shows itself outwardly, but is inwardly felt throughout the whole bombardment.'*[39]

Towards the end of May, the enemy intensified their artillery attacks. At dusk, on Tuesday, May 30th, a terrific bombardment of trench mortar bombs and artillery was let loose that continued through the night. As howitzers pounded away hour after hour, the German infantry launched a devastating raid on nearby 11th Battalion trenches. 9th Battalion soldiers quickly moved to assist, and it was during this action, Fred was hit. A machine-gun bullet smashed his left arm, fracturing his radius and ulna bones. Although it was a serious injury, Fred eagerly looked forward to his return to battle. *'I got smacked with a machine gun that night… My arm is going good, and I shall be back in the firing line by another month. I hope for the big smash.'*[40]

However, Fred's damaged arm was slow to mend and other medical complications associated with his long history of anaemia worsened. For five months, at three different English hospitals, doctors tried various treatments, but his weakness and anaemia remained severe. On the 7th November, Fred was deemed unfit for further frontline service. He was discharged from hospital and transferred to the 69th Battalion for duty in England.

During this time in England, he discovered love. Fred met 18-year-old Kate Beatrice Jackson, a London girl who lived with her parents at Islington. After a whirlwind romance, on 23rd November, 1916, two weeks after his discharge from hospital, the couple married at the Islington Registry Office.[41] When a son, Peter, was later born,[42] Fred became a proud father. Family time became a treasured asset, causing him to frequently overstay his leave. In May, as punishment for going AWOL, Fred was demoted to Private with a substantial pay cut. However, he remained incorrigible. In July, he was absent without leave for another four days.

That month, his health problems worsened dramatically. Fred returned to hospital with chronic anaemia but, for the first time, they diagnosed a cause. Doctors deemed he was suffering ankylostomiasis, a disease created by hook worms which he probably acquired when in Egypt in 1915. The diagnosis gave Fred some hope, but his condition grew worse. Over the next four months, at five different hospitals, various treatments were tried without success. It was, therefore, decided in December 1917, Fred should be repatriated to Australia for discharge from the army.

The decision was a disastrous blow for Fred and his family. Four days before Christmas, 1917, he farewelled his wife and baby and reluctantly boarded the hospital carrier "Persic" for Australia. When the ship docked at Capetown, Fred was unwell and deeply morose. In desperation, he devised an attempt to return. Knowing that the "Persic" was due to sail at daybreak, Fred went AWOL and remained absent all night, hoping as punishment he would be sent back to England. He reported for duty at 12 noon the next day, well aware the "Persic" had already sailed. Regrettably, his ploy did not work. Fred was re-embarked on the next ship for Australia.

He arrived in Brisbane angry and depressed. Other soldiers were welcomed home with happy and emotional family reunions, but he felt acutely alone. He missed his family greatly. Adding to his woes was a court summons to appear in the Townsville Supreme Court as co-defendant in a divorce case between Florence and Louis Grasset.[43] The extramarital affair he had in North Queensland before the war returned to haunt him. He despaired at his situation and resolved to return to his English wife and child.

Without money for a fare, the only possible means of reaching them was on a troopship. Therefore, using his mother's maiden name, Fred created a new identity and, on 20 September 1918, he re-enlisted into the 8th Queensland Reinforcements as Frederick Kemp, a labourer living at Brisbane's YMCA. His enlistment papers revealed his disgruntled state of mind. Fred vehemently stated he had 'NO' relations and 'NO' friends, and that he no longer believed in God. Two weeks after enlisting, Fred's health problems returned. He was hospitalized at Enoggera Camp with a stomach problem but the seriousness of his condition and his past medical history remained hidden.

It seemed his clever plan worked and he would soon be re-united with his family. On 7th November, he embarked with the Reinforcements on the troopship, "Carpentaria" for England. However, he did not reckon on the war ending so soon. Four days after they sailed, Armistice was called, causing the "Carpentaria" to be immediately recalled to Australia. For the second time, on 28th November 1918, Fred was discharged from the army.

Despite the setback, Fred was not willing to give up on his family. He immediately made plans to bring them to Australia. The government offered free sea passage for war brides and families, and Fred anxiously applied. After a four month wait, in April, 1919, Kate and Peter's fares were finally approved. Fred was relieved and elated but, sadly, unprepared for his wife's response. Kate refused the free passage.[44] Perhaps the move from parents, siblings and friends was too daunting, or perhaps she still hoped Fred would return to England. For whatever reason, Fred's wife and son remained in London. He would not see them again. Their last known address, dated 1918, was 26 Lowman Road, Holloway, London.

The years that followed were tough ones. While bearing the emotional cost of losing his family, Fred also found it difficult to adjust to civilian life. Jobs were scarce. The Soldier Settlement Scheme provided opportunities to return to banana farming, but he was no longer physically able. His recurring anaemia and the weakness of his wounded forearm limited his ability to carry out manual labour. Frustrated by his condition, Fred's confident manner slowly disappeared.

With few other options, he sought help from a Returned Soldiers Repatriation Fund scheme that placed wounded veterans on small, manageable poultry farms. He was granted a few acres at Wattle Street, Tingalpa and, to cover the cost of building a house and purchasing poultry stock, a loan, repayable over several years, was also made available.[45] The project gave Fred's life purpose and, with optimism, he set about building his farm.

Regrettably, as the years passed, contact with his wife and son dwindled and was eventually lost. Eight years later, on 1st November 1926, Fred re-married. His bride was a country girl, Florence Ellen Keeble, from the small farming community of Rosewood. With her help, a valiant attempt was made to make the Tingalpa farm a success. They worked long hours, but poultry farming produced only a modest income. To make ends meet, despite his ill-health, Fred found a part-time job as a wharf labourer on the Howard Smith's Wharves near the Story Bridge. It was dangerous work unsuited to his physical condition. On 8th March, 1929, while unloading cargo, a sling of packing cases fell from 30 feet above, pinning him to the floor. It severely crushed his chest and, if not for the quick response of frantic co-workers, Fred would certainly not have survived.[46]

When he left hospital a month later, his ability to do manual work was much more limited. He attempted to continue the poultry farm, but struggled physically and financially. Finally, in 1934, during the Great Depression, he had no option but to walk off his farm. Regrettably, about the same time, his marriage to Flo also collapsed. By 1940, Fred had no knowledge of his wife's whereabouts.[47]

When he abandoned his farm, Queensland's unemployment rate was soaring at 30%. With no chance of securing a job, Fred survived these years by joining a government relief work scheme operating from Caloundra that offered unemployed workers intermittent low paid work. Unfortunately, his health continued to decline. By 1937, Fred could no longer carry out labouring work. For the next three years, he lived off a dole payment of just eight shillings per week.

At the age of 55, Fred found himself in a desperate situation. Without savings, assets or family support, his working life was over and his eligibility for an aged pension remained 10 years away. Fiercely independent and always proud, Fred previously refused to apply for a war pension but, now, there was no option. Optimistically, he believed he qualified for what he called the 'burn-out pension.' He gained his severe anaemia during his war service in Egypt and, from the trenches of France, he carried a permanent arm disability.

The Repatriation Commission's response to his 1940 application was brutal and quick. It deemed Fred's 'burn-out' was not because of the war and that his wounded arm warranted only a 10% Disability

Pension. Fred felt deeply betrayed. Tersely, he let the Repatriation Commission know his disappointment and proudly informed them that their help was not wanted. '*I have lived three years on the dole 8 /- and owe no man.*' He closed the letter with a mocking thanks, '*So thanking you for your kindness and trouble.*' In a footnote of despair, the Commission's decision was scorned with one last argument, '*I held and saved the left flank on Sunday at Anzac, Capt. Bean knows that to be true .... Surely that was worth the Burnt out pension.*'[48]

Fred was a broken man. The insurmountable tide of disappointments, personal loss, ill health, and injury had beaten him. The once proud bravado and confidence of a brave and gallant Anzac were gone. During his last years, he led a solitary life at Cleveland where he irked a small income fishing and crabbing. By selling his catch in the pubs in the Cleveland area, he supplemented his meagre 10% pension.

Fred took his last fishing trip on 5th May, 1944. The 59-year-old set out in fine weather on a routine crabbing trip but, mysteriously, never returned. Seven weeks later, his body was retrieved from the mangroves on Coochie Mudlo Island, near Cleveland. Because of the advanced state of decomposition, a cause of death could not be determined. The inquiry simply concluded there was no need for further investigation.[49] Fred, an experienced fisherman, had fallen overboard and drowned. It was a sad and lonely end to a damaged life.

Sergeant Frederick Charles Coe was buried in the Anzac section of the Lutwyche Cemetery, Brisbane. (Grave 23, Portion 7, Section 85)

Lance Corporal Edward Teitzel

No. 691, F Company, 9th Battalion
(later Corporal, D Company)

Twenty years after the war, Edward (Ted) Teitzel was described as *'a good man gone to pieces.'*[1] On the Gallipoli Peninsula, he survived six months and seven days of continuous service and, on the Western Front, fought bravely as a 9th Battalion scout. After suffering two wounds, multiple gassing and much trauma, in 1918, Ted returned home determined to overcome the dark legacy of war and provide for his young family. The task was formidable.

Born at Bundaberg on 12th September 1891, Ted Teitzel had an unsettled childhood. His parents, Charles and Mary, were constantly on the move in search of new opportunities and a better life. At the time of his birth, the family lived at the Barolin Marine Township (Burnett Heads).[2] Five years later, they moved to Gladstone, where Ted and his brother Henry started school at South State.[3] Three years later, when Ted's father obtained a five acre mining lease on the Gympie goldfields,[4] the rough life of the goldfields was not considered a suitable environment for young boys. Eight-year-old Edward and his two younger brothers were sent to live with their grandparents. Their Grandfather, Carl Otto Teitzel, was a well-known and successful German pastoralist who pioneered a large grazing property and vineyard outside Warwick. In 1902, the Teitzel boys enrolled at the nearby Bony Mt Provisional School, where they completed their schooling.[5]

It was not until Ted was a young teenager that he returned to live with his parents. By then, his parents' Gympie life had improved substantially. His father alternated gold prospecting with a regular job as a carter,[6] and Ted's mother established a store in Alfred Street.[7] With astute savings, they purchased a dairy farm at Heyteys Pocket at

Chatsworth, outside Gympie. This 120 acre property with fine Mary River frontage provided a secure living plus employment for Ted.

While he worked the farm with his father, Ted also developed a passion for gold prospecting. He and his father obtained two Prospecting Areas (781 and 782) in granite rock country around Mothar Mountain, about 25 kilometres from the farm. After months of unsuccessful prospecting, in 1908, they traced the source of fine gold found in nearby gullies and made a significant discovery.[8] However, establishing a mine required a large amount of capital. Teitzel Gold Mines Ltd. was formed and substantial money was borrowed. Unfortunately, there were many costly delays and, when the mine finally went into operation in 1911, it struggled to deliver gold in payable quantities. To continue operations, the family sold their dairy herd and many possessions, including their buggy and harness.[9] With debts continuing to grow, in September 1911, the mine went into liquidation.[10] Six months later, the Teitzel farm at Chatsworth also had to be sold.[11] The family lost everything.

During these heartbreak years, the local football team and local citizen militia became welcomed distractions for Ted. In September 1912, he joined B Company of the Wide Bay Battalion, 4th Infantry Regiment, and enthusiastically embraced military life. Every Friday, he took part in the afternoon parade at the Drill Shed in Duke Street and on the weekends, he enjoyed military camps with his mates. He also diligently completed every training course that was offered. When Australia entered the war, Ted rushed to enlist. He was one of the first 33 men from Gympie to volunteer. Although the prospect of adventure and overseas travel was a powerful motivator, there was a more troubling reason for his enthusiasm. Ted's family was German and, in the weeks leading up to the outbreak of war, such families faced suspicion and hostility. With disbelief, he watched as the German culture he proudly grew up with become poisonous. German churches were closed, German music banned, food was renamed, German place names were given British names, and some German people were interned. As blind patriotism replaced rational thought, it became a dangerous time for German families. Patriots, looking for ways to display their loyalty, found them an easy target. Although Ted was Australian born, his grandparents were German and, to most people, his surname labelled him German. By rushing to enlist, Ted was proving his Australian identity. He was sending a message to the community that his family was loyal and that he was willing to fight against Germany and share the sacrifice of war.

The local newspaper described Ted and Gympie's first 32 volunteers as *'the cream of Gympie, boys to be proud of.'* The community farewelled them with a magnificent gathering at the Gympie Town Hall. After many patriotic speeches, there was song singing and, later, much drinking at the Mining Exchange Hotel. At 6.30 a.m., the next morning, with blurry heads, Ted and the other recruits gathered at the Drill Shed in Duke Street to prepare for their departure for Enoggera camp. After the raucous celebrations of the previous night, they expected a quiet leave-taking. However, as the volunteers marched through empty streets towards the railway station, local bands suddenly appeared to lead their way. By the time they reached the junction of Mary and Mellor Streets, hundreds of spectators were following behind and, at the station, a crowd of 2000 was waiting. A report in the Gympie Times described an unprecedented scene. *'Each man was practically mobbed by friends bidding farewell as he made his way to his place. The crush round the (train) carriage was intense ... "Rule Britannia" was sung and cheer after cheer was given. The train steamed out of the station to the accompaniment of the explosion of detonators, tumultuous cheering and the waving of hats and handkerchiefs.'*[12]

After only four weeks at Enoggera camp, on 24th September, the Gympie volunteers departed Brisbane with the 9th Battalion aboard HMAT "Omrah", the first troopship to leave Queensland for war. Their destination was the desert camp at Mena, 12 miles from Cairo where, for over three months, a tough regime of intensive military and physical training was endured. Ted's fitness, skills and confidence as a soldier grew immensely. On 1st January, his F Company amalgamated into D Company, and on 21st February, he proudly received promotion to Lance Corporal.

Two weeks later, the Battalion moved to Lemnos Island, off the Turkish coast. Battle orders remained sealed, but furtive preparations were earnestly made. In each battalion, soldiers were carefully selected from various companies to form scout contingents.[13] The scouts' task at the Gallipoli landing was to move forward first to locate and quickly destroy Turkish artillery and sniper positions so that the main body could follow.[14] Ted's expertise as a rifleman ensured his selection as a 9th Battalion scout.

On the 25th April, in pre-dawn darkness, Ted disembarked from his troopship, "HMS Queen" into the crowded leading boat of No. 1 Tow with Lieutenant Duncan Chapman's No 3 Platoon. In order to give them the best opportunity to reach shore first, he and some other well-chosen scouts were positioned near the front of the boat. Seated by Ted was Scout Sergeant Coe, Lieutenant Haymen and another scout, Private Frank Uden.[15]

About 50 yards from the beach, the steamships cast off their tows, and the men manned the oars for the last short distance. With every oar stroke, their excitement and anxiety grew more intense. The anticipation of the enemy's fire made the surrounding silence seem more deafening. Lieutenant Chapman gave the order, "All OUT!" and Ted and his mates scrambled for shore in water up to their waists. Ted and almost half of the men were on shore when it began. They felt almost relieved when suddenly the sand and water exploded under a deadly hail of bullets.

On that first day, the 9th Battalion suffered severely. When they mustered four days later, 419 casualties were recorded. Five of the seven mates who Ted enlisted with, from Gympie's Wide Bay Regiment's B and H Companies, were casualties on the first day. The loss devastated Ted, but this was only the beginning. For six dreadful months, he remained on the Peninsula facing the constant threat of Turkish artillery and sniper gunfire while taking part in numerous raids, counter-attacks and trench battles. One of the most unfortunate enemy encounters occurred on 28th June.[16] Its purpose was to distract the Turks from sending reinforcements against the British at Helles. Battalion historian, N.K. Harvey concluded this action *'had been so hurriedly arranged that the platoon commanders did not have very full particulars of what they were to do, nor did they know where the enemy trenches were. Worse still, the Turks were practically notified that the attack was coming.'*[17] As the 9th moved into position, their intention was clearly visible to the enemy. As a result, before the raid began, Ted and his mates came under heavy shrapnel and machine gun fire. When the order to leave the trenches was given, at about 1 p.m., they bravely ran across the open bed of Cooee Gully to begin their climb to the enemy positions on Sniper's Ridge. Shrapnel and machine gun fire rained upon them but, incredibly, by 1.25 p.m., a line was formed about 10 yards from the Turkish trenches. Despite heavy casualties, they heroically held this position for two hours. However, their effort and sacrifices were futile. At 3.25 p.m., orders were given to withdraw. Bewildered and frustrated, Ted and his platoon returned reluctantly to the line. The seemingly pointless operation had cost the lives of 37 Queenslanders, with 62 others wounded and six taken prisoner. To Ted, it seemed men were being sacrificed needlessly.

As the months wore on, worsening conditions in the trenches caused morale to further decline. No gains were made, and each day there were more casualties. Illnesses such as dysentery were also spreading at an alarming rate. By November, lack of sleep and constant exposure to danger was taking a toll on Ted's health. After reporting sick on 2nd November, he was immediately transferred to the hospital ship, "Nervaso" for transport to Egypt. The diagnosis was 'debility', the broad term used to describe physical and mental exhaustion.

Ted's removal from the battlefield was long overdue. Very few other 'original' Anzacs survived such a long period of continuous service on Gallipoli. From the 1000 men who landed on 25th April and the 500 reinforcements who arrived in the first few weeks, only Ted and 93 others could boast they survived six or more consecutive months.[18] He remained in hospital for almost two months. When finally discharged on 7th January 1916, the Gallipoli campaign had ended and his Battalion was back in the Egyptian desert. He re-joined them, energized and eager to get on with the job of war. Promotion to Temporary Corporal on 24th January further bolstered his spirits.

From Egypt, the Battalion moved to the battlefields of France. Their first destination was a relatively quiet area known as the Nursery, south of Armentieres. It was here that the Battalion's scout section reformed. Ted was again selected and, on 17th April, he also received his full promotion to Corporal.[19] He was pleased and proud to be a scout again, but soon discovered their missions on the Western Front were far more dangerous than those he experienced at Gallipoli. At night, the scouts were sent from the trenches on missions to survey and identify enemy positions. The risk was high, but these regular night patrols provided crucial intelligence. For instance, when the Battalion was first given responsibility for part of the front line at Fleurbaix, the information provided by the scouts enabled authority to be quickly asserted over No-man's-land.

While at Fleurbaix, in early July, Ted also took part in one of the 9th Battalion's most brilliantly executed operations. Volunteers were called for and carefully selected. Although Ted had just returned from a week in hospital, his experience as a scout assured his inclusion. The Battalion's Captain Wilder-Neligan meticulously planned the operation which became known as Neligan's Raid. Organized into three parties–right, centre and left, Ted joined the right flank party as a Corporal under Captain C.E. Benson.[20] While previous raids usually began with a preliminary artillery bombardment of enemy lines, Captain Neligan insisted this had to be a "silent raid." Surprising the enemy was crucial. He also gave strict orders that all wounded men were to be ignored. Any soldier who left the attack to tend a wounded colleague would be court martialled.

At 11 p.m., on the evening of 1st July, with his face and hands blackened and a supply of chewing gum to suppress any coughing, Ted quietly moved with his right flank party into No-man's-land. Their objective was an enemy sector 300 metres away. By 1.30 a.m., the three raiding parties had reached within 100 metres of the German line without being detected. Then, at precisely 2.03 a.m., Neligan gave the order. An artillery bombardment commenced and signalled the three parties to rush the German position. Bitter and close fighting followed. Ted's right flank quickly entered their sector of the trench, killed many Germans, and took four prisoners.[21] As well, a machine gun was captured and carried back to Australian lines. By 2.17 a.m., all parties had successfully withdrawn to their own lines. The operation was a triumph, but, as always, there was a bloody cost. Nine 9th Battalion men lost their lives, 21 were wounded and five went missing. Ted received a wound to his knee and was admitted to No.1 Casualty Clearing Station at Estaires. However, his injury was slight. Eight days later, he re-joined his unit as they moved to take part in one of the war's fiercest battles, the Battle of the Somme.

Their first engagement was the capture of the small village of Pozieres. It seemed an impossible task. Three previous British attempts to take this important high ground had failed with great losses. When the 9th arrived at 2 a.m. on the 20th July just south of Pozieres, Ted was exhausted, but he found sleep was impossible. An overpowering smell of unburied dead pervaded the night air, and the Germans welcomed the Queenslanders with a heavy bombardment of gas shells.

The next night, to prepare for the upcoming attack, Ted and the scouts were sent into No-man's-land to survey an area south of the village. Their task was to determine if the enemy had put out wire. It was a dangerous operation that went badly. Despite moving under the cover of darkness, German flares sighted the scouts. As one of the party expressed it, 'hell broke loose.' With bombs and heavy machine gun fire targeting them,[22] there was no option but to make a dangerous retreat. Two at a time, they crawled from shell-hole to shell-hole. Incredibly, no casualties were incurred. Ted returned to the line safely but with nerves severely tested.

The Australian attack on Pozieres began on 23rd July. Just after midnight, the 9th rushed forward with great daring and quickly secured the first trench. Fierce fighting continued and, by midday, they captured the village. However, the Germans launched fierce counter-attacks and the horrific battle continued for four days. A relentless enemy artillery bombardment created a hell on earth. Men were literally driven mad. 57 members of the 9th lost their lives, 271 were wounded and 65 went missing. Ted's scouts, in particular, suffered severely. From a contingent of 28 scouts, 22 became casualties.

Ted was one of these. While advancing on the village, he received a gunshot wound to his left hand. The injury was severe and, fortunately, removed him from the horrors of Pozieres. He was evacuated to England and spent the next seven weeks at Norfolk War Hospital. The bullet had severely fractured the metacarpal bones in his hand, leaving him with restricted thumb movement and the loss of power in his first finger. He slowly healed but, being left-handed, Ted could no longer effectively use a rifle. As a result, on 15th September, doctors declared him fit only for light duties. Ted received a transfer to No. 1 Command Depot at Perham Downs in south England.

Before being discharged from hospital, he developed a friendship with a local girl, Florence Mossendew, from the nearby small rural village of Castor. Their relationship quickly blossomed into romance and, just three months after his transfer south, on the 8th January, 1917, the couple married. They wed in Castor's beautiful historic church. A short honeymoon followed but, regrettably, Ted then returned to duty at the Perham Downs Depot while Florence remained in Castor, living in her parents' home in the High Street.[23]

Desperate to establish a home for his wife, Ted sought promotion. Six months after the wedding, he achieved the position of Acting Sergeant in the Overseas Training Brigade at Perham Downs. Unfortunately, his propensity to go AWOL caused the promotion to be short-lived. After absenting himself from duty for seven days, as punishment, Ted forfeited eight days' pay and was demoted to Corporal. Despite his recurring absences, he remained in England for over 12 months. On 21st October, 1917, the newlyweds' first child, Louisa Mary, was born.

Their daughter was almost one-year-old when Ted received his dreaded orders. He sadly bid farewell to his young family and, with much trepidation, returned to the frontline in France in August 1918. The timing of his return was extremely fortunate. He arrived as his Battalion began an overdue rest period. Weeks later, his good luck continued. Ted was selected in the first draft of soldiers to be granted "Anzac Leave" that gave the original 1914 volunteers two months' long service leave in Australia. Although overjoyed by this extraordinary opportunity to leave the war, for Ted, there was also a painful cost. Three weeks before the war ended, he embarked on the troopship, "Durham" from England, not knowing when he would see his wife and child again.

By the time his ship arrived in Australia, the war was over. Australia was still celebrating and when the 52 Queenslanders on-board arrived in Brisbane on Christmas Day, they received an extraordinary welcome. For the Teitzel family, there was much to celebrate and be proud of. Three days later, Ted's younger brother, Henry, a member of the Light Horse, also arrived home. Both sons had served gallantly and returned home safely. The small local community of Chatsworth welcomed them as heroes and, on New Year's Eve, gathered at the local hall to celebrate the Teitzel boys' return. A Gympie newspaper reported, *'at 8 o'clock the returned men marched into the hall, where they were right royally welcomed as guests at a banquet.'*[24] After many speeches, toasts and renditions of songs, they presented each boy with a gold medal inscribed with 'from their friends of the Chatsworth.' The hall piano then provided music for a lively evening of dancing.

Although overjoyed to be home, Ted feared the challenges ahead.

Separation from Florence and his daughter caused him much anguish, and the application process for their migration and free passage to Australia was painfully slow. As he waited, he worried about how he would support a family. His 50% disability pension was grossly inadequate and his damaged hand made him unsuitable for most manual jobs. With poor health and increasingly severe bouts of rheumatism, his employment opportunities were scarce. He applied to join the Brisbane Tramways, where many 9th Battalion mates were already working, but they refused him on medical grounds.

With few other options, Ted took a block of land in the Soldier Settlement Scheme at Beerburrum. The Scheme, one of the largest in Australia, promised discharged soldiers a 'fair go' by providing them with cheap 20 to 30 acre blocks of virgin bush. Unfortunately, for veterans with war disabilities, the work was incredibly difficult. Clearing the bush, building a residence and cultivating the land require enormous energy and effort. When Flo and Louisa finally arrived in June, 1919, Ted moved his family immediately to Beerburrum. They joined approximately 175 other soldier settlers and their families valiantly attempting to establish farms. When, after ten months of backbreaking work, their farm remained unproductive, Ted made a desperate plea to the Repatriation Board for help.

'Just these few lines to ask you for more pension as I get 17/- a week now, but it is not enough as I am on the Soldier Settlement and on account of a shortage of suckers for planting I am no further advanced than when I came up here 10 months ago and it means I have to go and work out for other people and as my left hand is just about useless and being a left-handed man in my work, it makes things very awkward for me and also having a couple of severe attacks of rheumatism. I did 4½ years in Egypt, Gallipoli and Flanders ...... I am not nearly the man I was before I went away from Australia in 1914 with the 9th Battalion.'[25]

Although Ted and Florence's small farm produced almost no income, they bravely stuck it out for another 20 months. When their second child, Florence, arrived in 1920, their financial struggles grew more acute. By 1921, they realized it was futile to carry on. Newspapers in November reported, *'Beerburrum is finished as far as settlement on a large-scale is concerned....There are now about 40 empty houses.'*[26] That week, Ted and sixteen other soldiers and their families walked off the land.

The First Ashore

Ted and Flo returned to Brisbane to live with Ted's parents at Coorparoo. Unable to find work, they survived on Ted's meagre war pension of 17/-. With two young children to provide for, their situation became increasingly desperate, and Ted soon found himself in trouble with the law. In March 1922, he and his youngest brother, Robert, were charged with stealing a log of bloodwood. Whether intentionally or unknowingly, the brothers felled and removed a log from an unattended property near Beaudesert. The court found them guilty of stealing and sentenced them to three months' jail, suspended to 12 months good behaviour.[27]

The incident shocked and humiliated the family and prompted Ted to make some hasty and drastic decisions. Just months after the court case, he moved his young family to New Guinea.[28] The League of Nations had just given Australia a mandate to govern the former German colony, and the government had appropriated all German property. This included 268 plantations which they offered for sale to returned soldiers. Ted did not have the capital nor desire, after his experience at Beerburrum, to become a plantation owner, but with the help of other returned Anzacs living in New Guinea, he gained a position as a plantation overseer for the Australian government.

The family's new home was at Kopoko, a harsh, isolated location on the northern tip of the island of New Britain. Although challenging and sometimes dangerous, the next two years were happy ones, full of adventure and new experiences. The family left Kopoko in 1924 when Ted got a better position as Native Police Master for the Home and Territories Department at Talasea, on the mid-north coast of New Britain. Unfortunately, this isolated outpost with the nearest doctor over 40 miles away soon proved an unsuitable posting for a veteran with declining health. Another move eight months later took them to Witu on Garove Island, north of New Britain, but again, distance from medical services was a problem. In 1926, Ted transferred to the larger settlement of Kavieng on the island of New Ireland. However, by then, his bouts of rheumatism, malaria and his general ill-health were making it increasingly difficult for him to carry out his duties. Eventually, Ted had no option but to resign from his position.[29]

The family returned to Australia in 1931 during the Great Depression. With over 30% of the Queensland workforce unemployed, Ted had little chance of finding work. His left hand had withered further, and he now had much less use of it. Also, the persistent cough that he had carried since the war had developed into serious chest and lung trouble. A medical report in 1932 referred to episodes of him spitting blood.

Yet Ted was desperate for work. Without a job and the ability to provide for his family, he felt robbed of his dignity. Ignoring his disabilities, he applied to join a government relief scheme that placed unemployed workers in banana cultivation. At the end of 1933, it allocated him a five acre block at the Mount Mee Settlement. Optimistically, Ted hoped the high altitude and fresh mountain air would be good for his chest, but he underestimated the amount of work required to bring a block into production. Ted pushed himself beyond his capabilities and, to make ends meet, he took extra work as the Mt. Mee Settlement's storekeeper. The strain weakened his already frail health. Mr Gower, the inspector from the Department of Labour admired Ted's efforts and made the following observation.

'I met him at the Settlement on about 4.3.36 and he was in very bad health.... While Tietzel felt that he had the energy to do some work he did it, but that trait in his character was the cause of his then state of health. Tietzel ranked in my personal records as a good citizen and father.'[30]

By March 1936, with the heavy workload falling on his wife and daughters, Ted and the family left Mt. Mee and again moved back to live with Ted's parents. The next 18 months were a struggle. His war pension was now only 25%, a meagre £1-16-11 ($3.69) per fortnight, less than a quarter of the basic wage. The local relief work programme for the unemployed offered some irregular labouring jobs, but Ted often was physically unable. His boss reported, *'He was that sick at times he would collapse on the job.'*[31]

The family's financial woes deeply distressed Ted. He believed his only option was to return to New Guinea where he was well known and his work had been valued. After receiving three job offers, he took a position offered by long-time family friend and renowned pioneer, Doris Booth, at her gold mine, "Cliffside" in the Morobe Province.[32] (Doris and her husband were neighbours at Kopoko in the 1920s.)

Ted arrived at "Cliffside" in 1937. It had only been six years since he left New Guinea and his old acquaintances barely recognized him. His thin and haggard appearance shocked them. It was obvious to all that his decision to return was ill conceived, but, as always, Ted battled on. He ignored his health issues and worked beyond his capabilities. Unsurprisingly, months after arriving, an acute attack of gastric malaria placed Ted in hospital. His condition deteriorated rapidly because of his already weakened state of health and, on the 19th May 1938, he drifted into a coma. The next day, Ted passed away. He was just 46 years of age. Officially, the cause of death was kidney damage and blackwater fever.[33] His death certificate failed to mention his extensive war service, which damaged his body irrevocably and plagued most of his post-war life with disability.

Ted had lived as a true Anzac. On the battlefields of Gallipoli and the Western Front, the bravery of this 9th Battalion scout was beyond doubt. At home, he displayed immense courage and also a steely determination to provide for his family. Without complaint, Ted battled sickness and the legacy of war. Toughness, determination, self-sacrifice and service were hallmarks of his brief life.

Corporal Edward Teitzel was buried at Bulolo, Papua New Guinea.

Private William Cleaver

No. 627, C Company, 9th Battalion
(later Sergeant, 1st Machine Gun Battalion)

On Christmas Eve, 1909, with high aspirations and a steely determination to succeed, 15-year-old William (Bill) left England to start a new life in Australia. He had no idea that four years later, world events would change his life so dramatically. As an enthusiastic volunteer in Australia's new army, Bill Cleaver fought gallantly at Gallipoli and endured over two years of active service on the Western Front. War left deep scars but also created a proud Queensland Anzac.

Born in 1894 in the inner London suburb of Lewisham, his childhood was challenging. His father, Alfred, a house painter, '*was not a sober man*'[1] and for four years was mainly unemployed. With five children to provide for, money was always scarce. In 1900, tragedy worsened the family's plight when Alfred Cleaver died from an opium overdose.[2] Bill was just 6 years old.

As Bill grew into adolescence, he desperately wanted to escape his life in Lewisham. He dreamt of following in the steps of his older brother, Roderick, who had migrated to New Zealand. An application to join an immigration scheme was successful but, instead of New Zealand, it granted him an assisted passage to Queensland. Migrating alone to the other side of the world was a daunting venture for the teenager, but Bill was resilient. He departed London on the "Osterley" with 743 other immigrants[3] and arrived in Brisbane on 10th February, 1910.[4]

Without family support and with few work skills, the prospect of establishing a new life in Australia was tough. He found a job as a sawmill worker at Mt Binga, a small, isolated and remote timber-getting settlement in the Blackbutt Ranges.[5] The pay was poor, and the work was exhausting. While adjusting to the challenges of his new life,

The First Ashore

in 1913, awful news arrived from New Zealand that his brother Rod, while working alone in the Waikaia bush, had suicided.[6] The tragedy caused Bill enormous grief, which he faced alone.

The following year, when Australia declared war, he was quick to volunteer. The army offered an adventurous alternative to the drudgery of the timber yard and also an opportunity for Bill to reconnect with his family in England. He travelled to Gympie and signed his enlistment papers less than four weeks after the declaration. 20 days later, he was on the troopship, "Omrah" leaving with the 9th Battalion for war.

He hoped their destination would be England. Instead, upon disembarking in Egypt, his Battalion moved to the desert camp at Mena where, for the next four months, they engaged in an intensive programme of mock battles, bayonet practice, endless drills and monotonous lectures. Although Bill loathed the gruelling regime, it transformed him into a fit and capable soldier. His confidence quickly grew, and by March, he was more than eager to leave the desert and join the war.

However, his enthusiasm for battle was quickly dispelled. As a 9th Battalion scout, Bill was one of the first Anzacs to touch shore at Gallipoli on 25th April, 1915, and also one of the first casualties. After the landing, perhaps during the heroic charge up the cliffs, or at one of the desperate attempts to hold ground on the plateau, he received a bullet wound to his hand. At day's end, he lay in pain on the beach with 1700 other wounded Anzacs waiting to be taken aboard a hospital ship.

The overcrowded hospital ship "Seong Choon" transported Bill to Cairo, where he was admitted, on 30th April, to the equally overcrowded No.1 Australian General Hospital. For six weeks, he remained in hospital, each day observing the growing tragedy of Gallipoli as wounded soldiers filled the wards and corridors. While his hand slowly mended, Bill's eagerness for war quickly evaporated.

When he re-joined his Battalion on 17th June, it was the height of summer. A plague of flies rose from the bloated and rotting corpses in no-man's-land. The stench of death was everywhere. Bill was alarmed by the stress that he saw etched into the faces of his mates. With neither side gaining ground, the Peninsula had become a stalemate of trench warfare. Instead of large scale frontal assaults, small sharp offensives were being carried out. Ten days after his return, at midday on 28th June, Bill's company was ordered out. That day's sad outcome was recorded in the diary of Lieutenant Ross, '*B & C Company take part and lose over 100 men in half an hour ... the job was rather hurried, no-one seemed quite certain what to do ... when met by a crossfire of shrapnel and machine guns were forced to retire leaving many men behind.*'[7] Bill was a fortunate survivor.

He served almost five continuous months on the Peninsula. Survival became a huge test of endurance. Every day, the strain of battle remained constant. Even when in reserve, or washing a shirt, or taking a bath, Bill was in range of the Turk's large guns and sniper fire. There were no safe places to go. Anxiety and tension were his constant companions.

He finally left Gallipoli on 16th November. The 9th Battalion was sent to the island of Lemnos for an overdue period of rest and, mercifully, weeks later, the Campaign ended. Bill then moved with his Battalion to Egypt, where a period of recuperation was expected. Instead, with a train of 80 camels, the Anzacs were marched through the desert to the sand ridge of Gebel Habieta near the Suez Canal. Their new mission was to consolidate the Canal's eastern defence by building a series of trenches in the sand. It was exhausting work, but Bill was pleased to be out of the firing line.

While at Gebel Habieta, he reluctantly left the 9th Battalion and transferred to the newly formed 3rd Machine Gun Company. The machine gun was gaining prominence as an integral strategy for winning the war and, in early March 1916, special machine gun companies were created. In order to ensure their success, competent soldiers, like Bill, were carefully selected. Although he deeply regretted leaving his mates and giving up his proud identity as an 'Original' 9th, Bill also looked forward to new challenges. Machine-gun units were highly trained and well organized. Gunners were arranged in groups of six, with two men to carry the gun and its tripod, two men to carry ammunition and another two kept in reserve. They were trained to use the Vickers Machine Gun, one of the war's most effective killing machines capable of firing 500 rounds per minute. Their mobility was also crucial, as the Germans' priority was to target these deadly guns.

After a month of training, on 29th March, Bill and the 3rd Machine Gun Company eagerly left the desert for what they regarded as the 'real battle' in France. They moved to the frontline in the Petillion area, south of Fleurbaix, where, from the 17th May, for eight weeks, their role

The First Ashore

was to support a series of infantry raids that aimed to annoy the enemy and distract attention from preparations for the upcoming Battle of the Somme. The most significant and daring of these raids took place on 2nd and 3rd July. Led by Captain Wilder-Neligan, Bill's machine-gun company played a crucial role by providing effective cover. During the raid they delivered over 20,000 rounds of ammunition. 24 German prisoners were taken and the operation was hailed as a great success. The praise that the gunners received boosted Bill's confidence and his enthusiasm for battle.

Two weeks later, this new passion for war quickly dissolved. The 3rd Machine Gun Company proceeded from Albert, on 19th July, to a position a kilometre south of the ruined farm village of Pozieres. Their mission was to support the 9th Battalion's attempt to take the village. When the gunners began firing at 2.30 a.m. on the 22nd July, the infantry soldiers moved forward to attack and the battle for Pozieres became a fiery hell. Bill's Company's diary recorded the gunners managed only eight hours sleep over the next six nights. By daybreak of the first morning, success was achieved, but the battle continued as the Germans responded with fierce counterattacks and an unrelenting heavy artillery bombardment. The noise was deafening as the ground trembled and trenches collapsed. Many men were buried alive and the nerves of the strongest were shattered. The 9th Battalion's size was reduced by a third. Bill's Machine Gun Company suffered 38 casualties. He lost many mates.

A short rest period followed but, less than four weeks later, the machine-gunners marched back to the front. Their new mission was to provide support for an attack on vital high ground, just north of the ruined village of Pozieres, at Mouquet Farm. A position was taken about 1500 yards south of the farmhouse and, on 19th August, the gunners entered a battle just as ferocious as Pozieres. In the first hour of the main assault, 36,500 rounds of ammunition were expended. The heavy shelling and artillery bombardment continued almost without pause. Bill's Machine Gun Company lost another ten men.

From Mouquet Farm, the exhausted gunners moved north to Flers in the Ypres area of Flanders, arriving at the beginning of an extremely severe winter. It was the coldest and wettest weather Bill had ever experienced. Weeks of rain turned the battlefield into a dangerous bog with mud in many trenches reaching a depth of 30 centimetres. In the deplorable conditions, many soldiers suffered frostbite and trench feet. Bill's only relief came on 16th December when he received two weeks' leave in England. At last, he could re-unite with his sister, Elizabeth and brother, Alfred. Their Christmas together was joyous but, regrettably, on New Year's Eve, Bill returned to the front to face what would be Australia's bloodiest year.

A seemingly endless series of horrific battles marked 1917. Bill fought in the Battle of Lagincourt in April, Second Battle of Bullecourt in May, the Battles of Menin Road and Polygon Wood in September, and the Battle of Broodseinde Ridge in October.[8] In each operation, the gunners were heavily targeted. Casualties were high but, fortunately, Bill survived without injury, although the mental stress of such continuous service was leaving a lasting impact. A small respite came in November with another two weeks' leave in England.

The last year of the war brought change and extra responsibilities for Bill. As the machine gunners' dominant influence on the battlefield increased, a new Battalion, the 1st Machine Gun Battalion, was formed. Bill joined this new Battalion and, in April, he was promoted to Lance Corporal. Weeks later, after another promotion to Sergeant (Cook), the 24-year-old became the Gun Battalion's Senior Cook.[9] This new role brought heavy responsibility, as the supply of meals was crucial to soldier morale. Moving food across the battlefield was also often a hazardous and often dangerous enterprise.

Yet, throughout 1918, Bill's good fortune continued. As the year dragged on, his battle weariness increased, but remarkably, he survived without injury. By war's end, Bill had served over 2½ years on the Western Front and was desperate for respite. He was entitled to two months special 'Anzac Leave', but it was not granted until a month after the war ended. By then, the repatriation of thousands of troops to Australia was in full swing. Exhausted soldiers, eager to return home, were frustrated by the long queues and the lack of transport ships but, Bill was not dismayed. He relished his two months' leave in England visiting family and friends.

When it ended on 24th February 1919, to avoid returning to his unit in Belgium, he applied to join 'Non-Military Employment'. This was a job training scheme devised to occupy the thousands of Australian soldiers idly biding their time in England. It also aimed to provide young soldiers with employment skills that would be useful for their return to civilian life. Bill was eager to exchange his military uniform for civilian clothes. For four months, from 11th June to 31st October 1919, he enthusiastically undertook a 'high class cooking and catering' course at Station Hotel, Princes Street, Edinburgh.[10] This work contrasted starkly with his wartime role as a cook. Adjusting to the frivolous demands of restaurant patrons was sometimes difficult, but he completed the training course diligently. His final report read, *'During the period, Sergeant Cleaver made good progress and gained experience which should be of value to him on his return to Australia.'*[11]

With 1200 other Anzacs, Bill left England for Australia in December 1920 on the steamship "Aeneas". Although he had only lived in Queensland for a few years before the war and regretted leaving his family in England, he felt optimistic about the future. The ordeals he experienced at Gallipoli and in the trenches of France had forged strong mateships, and these bonds created a proud Queensland and Australian identity.

Unfortunately, Bill's transition to civilian life was not as he imagined. Like most veterans, he faced many frustrations and disappointments. Finding employment in post-war Brisbane was not a simple task. He soon discovered his training in Scotland as a high-class cook and caterer was useless in Brisbane. Opportunities for work in this field were rare in provincial towns. With few options, Bill took a job as a fireman. Although it was well-paid and secure, this occupation was not conducive to a soldier's psychological healing. The sirens, smoke, flames and everyday dangers of a fireman's job triggered war memories that Bill desperately struggled to suppress.

Yet, he persevered. He had fallen in love with a country girl, Emily Rodhe, from Oakey. In order to marry, start a family and fulfill their dreams, job security and an adequate income were imperative. Therefore, Bill carried on. He fought to suppress the trauma his job created, and the young couple married on 20th January 1921. Twelve months later, their daughter, Gwendoline Marie, was born. Within two years, they saved sufficient money to put a deposit on a home in Gibb Street, Kelvin Grove.

Bill was proud of his achievements but, regrettably, the mental scars from war became increasingly difficult to deal with. He craved solitude and became desperate to escape the city and his job. Before 1927, he chose a dramatic lifestyle change. Bill left the stress of firefighting to become a lighthouse keeper. The remoteness and isolation of this occupation suited him well and, for the next 25 years, it became his life and livelihood.

Bill worked at some of Queensland's most beautiful and isolated coastal locations. His first posting was to Cape Capricorn Lighthouse on Curtis Island, 24 kilometres north of Gladstone. Emily joined him there, but for a young wife and infant child, the harsh, remote conditions proved too difficult. Mother and daughter returned to the family home at Gibb Street[12] and, for the next four years, Bill lived alone. He missed his family, but was consoled by the island's isolation and beauty.

Later, he took an even more difficult and remote posting at North Reef Lighthouse, over 100 kilometres off Gladstone's coast. A team of three manned this lighthouse, embedded in a reef, on a small island that sometimes would disappear and reappear. They lived in extremely cramped quarters with almost no outside recreation area.[13] In these extremely harsh living conditions, no women were allowed.

While at North Reef, Bill's mental health suffered a severe decline. On the night of 19th May 1932, the lighthouse's Morse lamps flashed an SOS alarm to a passing steamer. Bill was in a critical condition and urgently required medical attention. A launch was sent immediately, but it took almost 24 hours to reach North Reef. Ted was eventually evacuated in an extremely poor state to the hospital in Gladstone. His condition was diagnosed as the severe effects of insomnia.[14]

Upon recovery, he transferred to Cape Cleveland Lighthouse, an inhospitable piece of rock, with no natural water and little vegetation, 40 kilometres east off Townsville. Concerned for her husband's health after the incident at North Reef, Emily left Brisbane and joined Bill. They found a boarding school for their daughter at St Anne's in nearby Townsville,[15] and, for almost six years, the couple lived at remote Cape Cleveland. It was a way of life that Emily also came to enjoy immensely.

Their next posting was to the less isolated Double Island Point Lighthouse.[16] With easier access to the mainland and better facilities, this lighthouse provided a happy home and idyllic lifestyle. Unfortunately, by 1942, the threat of a Japanese invasion became very real and, in response, the government decreed all women and children were to be evacuated from Queensland's lighthouses. Emily and Gwen reluctantly left Bill perilously alone at Double Island Point and returned to the safety of Brisbane. For Bill, the troubling memories and trauma from the First World War returned as he suddenly found himself on the frontline of another war. For the next three years, it was his duty to ensure the lights kept burning.

As soon as war ended, Emily and Gwen eagerly returned to Double Island Point. Fortunately, conditions on the lighthouses during the post-war years were gradually improving. Kerosene fridges were installed and cottages gained electric lights.[17] The family's last posting, in 1947, was to Cape Moreton Lighthouse,[18] perched on Moreton Island's northern tip. There, they continued to relish their romantic lifestyle. After seven years at Cape Moreton, in 1954, at 60, Bill retired. He ended a 25 year career that included service on five spectacular heritage lighthouses.

Bill and Emily returned to Brisbane to enjoy their retirement years at their home at Gibb Street, Kelvin Grove. A grandson and great grandchildren soon enriched their lives. For Bill, reading also became a favourite pastime and escape. He and Emily also enjoyed travel, returning to England to visit family. As an 'Original Anzac', Bill became a respected member of Brisbane's RSL community and the 9th Battalion Association. The comradeship and reunions of 9th Battalion and 3rd Machine Gun Battalion mates were highly valued.

On 25 July, 1986, Sergeant William Cleaver passed away. He was 92 years old.

Private Frederick Thomas Uden

No. 718, D Company, 9th Battalion

In 1914, Fred Uden, a 20-year-old English farm labourer, left England to start a new life in Australia. Four months later, war was declared and his plans for the future suddenly ended. Without hesitating, Fred joined Australia's new army. After serving gallantly at Gallipoli and on the Western Front, he returned intensely proud of his role as a 9th Battalion Scout, with a strong new identity and a firm belief in the Anzac tradition of mateship and service.

Fred was born in January 1894 in the small farming village of Stourmouth in Kent. With 14 children in the Uden family, their life was sometimes a struggle. His father, William Uden, was a very capable farm labourer and an ambitious man. By the time Fred was 11, his father had attained the position of farm bailiff on Great Pett Farm[1] at Bridge, near Canterbury. The family's circumstances improved markedly and, as head of Pett Farm in charge of its workers, he could assure jobs for his sons, Fred, William, Alfred and Walter.

However, Fred did not aspire to be an English farm worker. He possessed an adventurous spirit and devised various schemes to secure a different future. He first took the more genteel job as groom at Great Pett House, the home of retired Rear Admiral Henry Kingsford,[2] and, later, he joined the British Army as soldier in the 3rd Buffs, Kent County's infantry regiment, garrisoned in Canterbury. After two years' army service, the army was not to his liking. His family purchased his discharge[3] and Fred migrated to Canada.[4] However, this also proved to be a mistake. After arriving in Saint John, the 18-year-old found there were very few jobs available for agricultural workers. Without an income and with the onset of a bitter Canadian winter, Fred became one of thousands of disgruntled immigrants who returned each year to England.[5]

The First Ashore

Despite this setback, Fred believed emigration was his best path to a better future. Soon after returning to England optimistically, he signed up with the Kentish Emigration Office. £2 fares, payable from wages, were available for young lads between 16 and 20 to work on farms in New South Wales and Victoria.[6] The government's Dreadnought Scheme also promised farm jobs at a pay rate of 10/- to 15/- per week plus free board and lodging.[7] Fred was accepted. He left England on 5th March 1914 with 318 other immigrants, including 28 agricultural labourers and 20 Dreadnought lads. When their ship, "Miltiades", docked in Sydney, Immigration Officers were waiting to place the young lads at various positions throughout the state.[8]

They sent Fred north to Ballina to be employed as a dairy farm worker. He rented a small room at Ballina's Exchange Hotel and enthusiastically set about adjusting to his new way of life. He envisaged a prosperous future, but months later, all his hopes abruptly ended.

Fred's patriotism and connection to England and the Empire were unshakeable. When war was declared, without hesitation, he gave up his new life up and headed to the nearest recruiting office at Lismore. On Monday 24th August, he took the oath of allegiance and the next day, with 119 other local volunteers, he marched to Lismore's railway station to catch the 5.30 a.m. train for Brisbane's military camp. It was a morning which Fred would never forget. The Northern Star newspaper reported the unprecedented spectacle that unfolded.

'In the dark and early hours of yesterday morning one of the most impressive scenes took place that has ever been enacted in Lismore. While the day was yet in its infancy with no sound to disturb the sleeping city... a din broke forth that never before was heard.... The quaint old river steamer howled from its siren, a noise to wake the gods... mills and works piercing whistles blew. Fire bell clanged and even the aged city canon was charged again...... The shrieking sounds had not echoed away ere the patter of feet were heard. The town was alive with hurrying steps. From every conceivable street and lane, the people still came... Verily it was an inspiring sight...

When the banner bearers reached the Terminus Hotel, there were still many civilians to cross the bridge.... In all, there were fully between 3 or 4000 people present.'[9]

On arrival at Brisbane's Enoggera camp, training began and events moved quickly. Only two weeks later, as a member of the 9th Infantry

Battalion's F Company, Fred embarked on the troopship, "Omrah" for overseas service. He left eager to do his part and bring the war to a speedy end, but, like others, he was to be disappointed. Australia's Expeditionary Force disembarked in Egypt rather than England and, for the next four months, in the hot sandy desert, they endured a daily rigorous and repetitive routine of military training. Another wearisome seven weeks of training followed on the Greek island of Lemnos near the Turkish coastline.

When operational orders were finally received on 24th April, Fred greeted the news with enormous relief. At last, he and his mates would do what they enlisted for. His recent appointment to the Battalion's scout contingent also added to his excitement. While on Lemnos,[10] soldiers with previous military experience, or superior qualities or skills, had been selected as scouts and tasked with special responsibilities. Their role in the upcoming operation was to precede and clear the way for the main covering force by dealing with snipers, and by locating and destroying Turkish artillery.[11] Success of the early stages of the landing would depend on their effectiveness.

At about 2.30 a.m., the 9th Battalion's A and B Companies and the scout contingent silently left the battleship "Queen". With well-rehearsed precision, they disappeared down rope ladders into rowboats. Each group of three boats was then towed by a steam pinnace slowly towards the shore. Anxiously, Fred sat with other scouts at the front of the lead boat of No. 1 Tow. Desperately, he searched the darkness for signs of the enemy. Beside him were Lance Corporal Teitzel and Scout Sergeant Coe, and at the bow was Scout Officer Lieutenant Haymen with the No.3 Platoon commander, Lieutenant Duncan Chapman.[12]

When their small life-boat reached the pebbly shore, the silence was eerie. For a moment, Fred thought the Turks may not be there. His recollection was that at least seven or eight men from the boat were already on the shore when the Turkish alarm was raised. In a letter to the Department of Army, Fred affirmed he was standing on the beach when the Turks fired the first shot.[13]

In a further recount of the landing, written by Fred in 1933, some controversy was fuelled. In a letter to the newspaper, he loudly disputed the claim made by war historian, Dr Charles Bean, that Lieutenant Chapman was the first man ashore.

The First Ashore

'Mr F. Kemp whom I knew as Sergeant Coe says that Lieutenant Chapman was the first man ashore. I imagine if Mr Kemp thinks back he will see that he made a mistake. It was Lieutenant Hayman, our scout officer, who was the first ashore. Those in the bows of the boat were Lieutenant Hayman, Sergeant Coe, Lance Corporal Titzal (Tietzel) and myself.'[14]

Unfortunately, Lieutenant Haymen, killed on the first day, could never verify Fred's assertion. However, this eyewitness testimony, from a man well known for his meticulous attention to detail, warrants consideration.

With Turkish bullets raining down, the landing at Anzac Cove quickly descended into chaos and confusion. While some men hesitated, unable to move from behind the cliff that gave them protection, the scouts stayed true to their orders. They were to push forward, no matter what, in order to clear the way for others to land safely. As Turkish fire intensified, Fred quickly scrambled up the sheer slopes.

Unfortunately, the wild charge from the beach caused the men from the first boat to become separated. Scattered into small groups and fuelled with adrenalin, they rushed across Plugge's Plateau in a rapid advance. Some tracked to the left to the slopes of Baby 700, but Fred moved towards the right across 400 Plateau. His Scout Officer, Lieutenant Haymen, followed a similar path. Perhaps, together, they attempted to follow the 9th's original orders to secure the rise on the 3rd Ridge, Anderson's Knoll and the guns at Gaba Tepe.

Fred recalled he reached an area on the right of Lone Pine, well ahead of the rest of the landing force. He re-confirmed this location many years later when he adamantly asserted a blue enamel bottle, retrieved from this area, on display at the Australian War Memorial,[15] was the one he lost while retreating late in the day.[16] The bottle had been found near the site where Lieutenant Haymen's small, isolated advance group fought desperately throughout the afternoon. This group, which also included Frank Loud, another member of the first boat, bravely held on to an area forward of the Cup, near Lone Pine. Outnumbered, they maintained their position but, after suffering huge losses, at sunset, the Turks forced them to retreat. During this desperate move, Fred was critically wounded. A severe gunshot wound dislocated his left shoulder. In enormous pain and with much blood loss, he incredibly found his way back to the safety of the beach.[17]

After evacuation to a hospital in Egypt, it took seven weeks for his wound to heal. When he re-joined his unit on the 17th June, the conditions on the Peninsula were horrendous. In the summer heat, an overpowering stench of death pervaded the air. Also, because of poor diet, a scarcity of clean water and a lack of sanitation, there was much sickness. The threat of Turkish shrapnel and snipers was constant. However, Fred's timing was fortunate. Two days after returning, his Battalion was withdrawn from the front line for 'rest' in Brigade Reserve. Over the next weeks, while 'resting', he and his mates worked to build an important sunken road from Shell Green to Shrapnel Gully.

On the 1st July, they returned to the firing line on Bolton's Ridge. The dreaded stalemate of trench warfare continued, with occasional raids and diversionary strikes being made. These were often ill-planned operations that resulted in high casualties. The most frightful was the charge at Lone Pine on 6th August. Although the 9th Battalion did not take part directly, Fred and his mates provided important support by laying heavy fire on the opposing trenches before the attack began. When finished, they sat on the parapet and observed the disaster unfold. Helplessly, Fred watched as waves of men were needlessly sacrificed. The carnage he witnessed was difficult to forget.

By August, morale was extremely low. Added to the heat, flies and deplorable conditions in the trenches, diarrhoea, dysentery and enteric fever were now rampant. During August, almost 30% of the 3rd Brigade were evacuated. Fred left the battlefield on 8th September suffering severe influenza. However, two weeks after being admitted to Cairo's No.3 Auxiliary Hospital, a new diagnosis of 'rheumatism' was made. During the Gallipoli campaign, this diagnosis was often used to cloak medical ignorance and could describe a variety of conditions associated with physical injury or mental trauma.[18] It took four months for Fred to recover. For the first 10 weeks, he remained bedridden, suffering severe sciatica pain in the right leg and rheumatic fever. He did not return to Gallipoli.

When he re-joined his unit on 6th January, 1916, the 9th had moved from Gallipoli to the desert camp of Tel-el-Kebir in Egypt. Their new mission was to construct trenches on the sandy frontier near the Suez Canal. Although Fred's health had improved, strenuous work was still beyond his capability. At Tel-e-Kebir, he was put on light duties and assigned to the transport unit, but the pain in his hip, knee and ankle remained constant. Even this work proved difficult.

The First Ashore

In March, orders finally came for the Anzacs to join the 'real' war against the Germans in France. Medical records show Fred's physical condition was poor, but he was determined not to miss out. Ignoring medical advice, Fred volunteered to go.[19] This eagerness proved to be a mistake. After serving only two months in the trenches, he again fell severely ill. Bronchitis and worsening sciatica caused him to be evacuated from the battlefield. He was admitted on 11th June to the 13th General Hospital in Boulogne and a few days later moved to England.

At the military hospital in Birmingham, doctors noted Fred had difficulty sleeping and could not stand upright or walk without limping. He suffered severe pain in his back, right thigh and leg, with marked tenderness along the entire length of his right sciatica. Over two months of hospital treatment failed to improve his condition. At the end of August, the Medical Board declared him unfit for active service and recommended his return to Australia. Fred left the war on the 17th October, 1916. His troopship, "Ajana" with its cargo of wounded and sick soldiers, reached Melbourne on 8th December. From there, Fred and the 40 members of the 9th Battalion, on board, left by special train for Brisbane. An extraordinary welcome greeted them. Friends and family crowded Central Station's No. 5 Platform as the sound of cheering almost drown out the military band's tumultuous rendition of "See the Conquering Heroes Come." In the surrounding streets, throngs of well-wishers pushed and shoved to get a glimpse of their Anzac heroes. Regrettably, amid so many happy and emotional reunions, Fred felt alone. He was returning to a country he knew only briefly before the war, and there were neither family nor friends to greet him.

Also, much of his youthful strength was lost. The 22-year-old now walked with a limp and would require a stick for the rest of his life. The Medical Board in Brisbane deemed he had a 50% disability and recommended his immediate discharge from the army. A disability pension of £3 per fortnight (a year later reduced to £2 and 5 shillings) was awarded, but this was far below the average wage. Without family to support him, Fred needed to find work quickly. He returned to the only place he knew, Ballina, and again rented a room at the Exchange Hotel on River Street. With dogged determination, he set about obtaining labouring jobs on surrounding farms.

In the small Ballina community, Fred's war service, outgoing personality and tenacity won much admiration. He soon became a well-known and popular identity. In May, four months after his discharge, the small farming community at Meerschaum Vale, about 30 kilometres from Ballina, honoured him with a late welcome home. They organized a social evening at the Meerschaum Hall at which Fred was awarded a citizen-funded 'Shire of Tintenbar War Service Medal'. The Northern Star newspaper reported, *'The attendance was large, the hall being crowded with friends of the returned soldier ... On entering the hall he was applauded ... Refreshments were served and the presentation made ... Several other gentlemen spoke ... The chairman then presented the medal to Private Uden. On rising to speak, the recipient was given an ovation. He thanked his many friends for the medal and their kind remarks. This medal, he said, would always be one of his most treasured possessions... The rest of the evening was spent in dancing.'*[20]

While working on dairy farms in the district, Fred met Isabella Clair Stone, whose parents ran a dairy farm at North Creek, north of Ballina. Their friendship blossomed into romance and, after a brief courtship, the couple wed on 12th April, 1918, at North Creek Church of England. As with all aspects of life, the shadow of war hung over the celebrations. Isabell's three brothers were still serving overseas and, to honour them, the small country church was decorated in pale blue and white ribbon streamers, the colours of their battalion.

Two years after marrying, Fred fulfilled the dream that brought him from England to Australia in 1914. He gained his own farm. On 1st April 1920, the Soldier Settlement Scheme allotted him 93 acres of undeveloped land near Emerson's Road at Rosebank, about 20 kilometres from Byron Bay.[21] Fred was elated and determined to make his small dairy farm a success. He and Isabell moved to Rosebank shortly before the birth of their son. They faced enormous challenges and worked many long and arduous hours. The block lacked fences, roads, buildings and even a house, and the farm's small size made its viability difficult. Also, the lack of access roads hampered their ability to sell milk. Three years after taking up the land, Fred protested to the Shire Council that, although he paid £30 in rates, he remained without an access road to his property.[22]

For the next six years, he and Isabell struggled at Rosebank. Finally, in 1926, exhausted and frustrated, they gave up. Their farm was sold and, fortunately, the sale produced sufficient funds for Fred to fulfill his long held dream to visit England once more. He was desperate to reunite with his aging parents and also eager to introduce his wife and 5-year-old son to his English family. An extended holiday was enjoyed at Great Pett Farm.

The Udens returned to Australia in November 1926 at an opportune time. The government was recruiting staff for a massive new programme to eradicate and control the spread of ticks among cattle in northern N.S.W. Fred's farming experience, plus a policy of preferential employment for returned soldiers, assured him a position as a 'tickie'. Over the next three decades, he worked at various locations throughout northern N.S.W. and built a very successful career.

Although Fred enjoyed the work immensely, there were some aspects of the job that were challenging. For instance, the maintenance of cattle dips, yards, and boundary fences tested the physical abilities of a war veteran with disabilities. Also, Fred regretted the job required his family to lead a very transient lifestyle. Quarantine and tick-infested areas were constantly changing and, during his 30 year career with the Tick Board, the Udens lived in seven different towns. Their first posting was to Nimbin, then Macksville, and later Bellingen. In 1935, when Fred transferred to Urbenville, the family lived at nearby Acacia Creek. In 1941, after his promotion to Senior Assistant Inspector of Stock, they made a new home in the small town of Lawrence. Three years later, another promotion to Inspector of Stock caused the family to move to Ballina. A final transfer in 1951 sent the Udens to Byron Bay.

In each town, Fred's dedication to public service and his genial nature ensured a close connection to the community. He and Isabell were active members of the Church of England in the various parishes they lived. Fred also became a prominent member of each local RSSILA branch. In Urbenville, he was elected to the Troopers Welfare Committee,[23] which provided food relief to returned men passing through the district. Close to Fred's heart was the work of the Red Cross and, in 1942, he served as Secretary of the Red Cross branch in Lawrence.[24] At Ballina, he became a member of the Executive Committee of the Ballina R.S.L.[25] and, also, served on the Parochial Council of the local Church of England. As well, he was a Justice of the Peace and a board member of the Ballina Hospital, taking the important role of Treasurer.[26] During World War 2, he also took on the duties of Police Reservist.[27]

Throughout his post-war life, Fred's involvement in community service was extensive and extremely time-consuming. However, he always found a place for his favourite leisure-time pursuit, lawn bowls. At the Nimbin Club, Maclean Club, Ballina Club and later the Murwillumbah Bowls Club, he was an A-grade competitive player.

World War 2 brought much anguish for Fred and Isabell. Their only child, Fred junior, enlisted as a member of the 20th Battalion and, in February 1942, became one of the many Australian soldiers captured by the Japanese at the fall of Singapore. They worried incessantly as the months and years passed and their son's fate remained unknown. During these uncertain years, Fred directed his anxiety into energetic fundraising for the Red Cross. In the small town of Lawrence, in June 1942, he organized a community Carnival and Sports Day, and evening dance, to raise funds for the organization's POW Appeal. This gala event was a spectacular success, raising approximately £130. The local newspaper praised Fred for his hard work and dedication. *'The greatest credit must be accorded the hon. Secretary, Mr. F. Uden whose untiring efforts were responsible for all details.'*[28]

After nine years' work at Ballina as stock inspector, Fred transferred to Byron Bay. He and Isabell enjoyed a wonderful beach lifestyle in their large Queenslander home at 56 Carlyle Street,[29] close to Clarkes Beach. It was Fred's last government posting. At the age of 65, he ended his long and successful career with the Tick Board and retired to Woy Woy and later Belmont North, near Lake Macquarie. During retirement, he continued his busy involvement in the activities of the local RSL, bowling club and church.

In the final years of his life, Fred returned to his beloved Ballina, the town that gave him his first start in Australia. He became a resident at the Ballina Ex-Serviceman's Rest Home and passed away there on 27th August, 1980, aged 86 years. The town and wider community honoured their popular resident at a very large funeral held at St Mary's Anglican Church. Family and many friends remembered him for his service, courage and fortitude and his firm belief in the Anzac spirit of mateship.

Private Fred Uden was cremated and his ashes interred at Lismore Memorial Gardens.

Private Alexander Kyle Wilson
No. 616, A Company, 9th Battalion

Alex Kyle Wilson arrived in Australia in 1911 with high hopes. After serving eight years in the British Army in South Africa and India, the 31-year-old Scotsman was tired of military life and ready to settle down, perhaps even get married, and raise a family. He saw Australia as a land of opportunities where a prosperous life might be achieved. Sadly, the Great War stole his dreams.

Alex, born in 1880 in the picturesque Scottish village of Dunoon[1] on the banks of the Firth of Clyde, grew up in Maryhill, an affluent area of west Glasgow. His father, Robert Wilson, was a well-regarded confectioner whose very successful grocery and confectionery business afforded the family a comfortable lifestyle and home at 255a New City Road.[2]

While most of his brothers followed the traditional family occupation of grocer, Alex learned his father's specialist trade. By the age of 20, Alex had become an accomplished confectioner and artisan making delicious sweetmeats, biscuits and ices. Regrettably, his career choice proved to be a poor one. Throughout Europe, at the turn of the century, the once highly regarded and skilled handcraft was being quickly replaced by mass production. Rapid industrialization of the confectionery business caused his father's business and the family's fortune to suffer.

Faced with unemployment and few options, Alex desperately sought a new career. As Boer aggression intensified in South Africa, there was a surge in patriotism throughout Britain, resulting in 90,000 men enlisting in the British Army in 1900. Alex became one of these new recruits. On 1st May, 1900, he joined the highly respected Argyll and Sutherland Highlanders regiment.[3]

After five months of rudimentary military training, he was dispatched to the war in South Africa. Arriving on the 18th October, 1900, his first action was west of Pretoria where his Regiment helped guard the towns of Rustenburg, Oliphant and Megato Neks, and provided escorts for convoys. In April 1901, they moved to Eastern Transvaal, where they successfully took over the railway between Erstefabrihin and Balmoral, and later were involved in the big drive to the Vryburg line.[4] Alex fought for 14 months in this dangerous guerrilla war and, for his service, he was awarded the Queen's South Africa Medal with clasps "Cape Colony", "Orange Free State" and "Transvaal", plus the King's South Africa Medal with clasps "South Africa 1901 1902."

When the War ended in 1902, he moved with the Highlanders to India. They were stationed at Kolkata (formerly Calcutta) and then at Poona.[5] Although it was mainly peacetime garrison duty, the posting was not without its dangers. The graves in the Scottish Cemetery at Kolkata reveal that during his first year, 26 members of Alex's regiment lost their lives because of disease.[6]

Garrison soldiers like Alex also faced the unusual danger of free time. Gambling and drinking were popular and often problematic pastimes for idle British soldiers in India. At first, Alex used his time wisely by completing necessary courses and training. As a consequence, he received a promotion to Lance Corporal on 24th May 1904. However, the Scotsman's youthful exuberance caused him to sometimes stray. He gained an arm tattoo of a Bengal lance on one misadventure and, two years after his promotion to Lance Corporal, his propensity for 'misconduct' resulted in demotion to Private.[7]

At the end of four years' garrison duty in India, on 29th December, 1906, his unit was transferred back to South Africa. 15 months later, on 31st March, 1908, the Highlanders returned to Scotland.[8] Alex was pleased to be home and ready to leave military life. When his eight years' service contract ended, he hastily vacated the military barracks at Stirling and headed home to his family in Glasgow.

Disappointedly, civilian life was not as he expected. Jobs were hard to find and Alex left the army with few work skills. Fortunately, his brother Andrew had secure employment as a grocer and could provide him support. Together, they rented a room in the home of Mrs Margaret Philips and her daughter Hannah at 137 Statefield Street, Glasgow.[9]

Alex desperately searched for work and eventually gained a lowly paid job as a warehouseman at a clothing factory. It was a tedious job, without prospects, and not the future he envisaged for himself. As his discontent grew, Alex earnestly searched for an escape from life in Glasgow. Newspaper advertisements promoting Queensland as 'a land of sunshine and plenty' with 'unrivalled climate … good wages, plenty of work and assisted passages' captured his imagination. Two years after leaving the army, Alex departed Scotland, on board the newly built "Morialta," for Brisbane.[10]

Upon disembarking in Brisbane in January 1912, he moved immediately north to Bundaberg and took up residence at Lynwood, a small sugar cane growing area on the road to Childers.[11] Recent laws prohibiting South Sea Islanders from working in Queensland meant there was an acute shortage of cane-cutters for the local industry. For fit enterprising men, there was an abundance of well-paid work. Although cane-cutting was hard and exhausting work, Alex persevered, as he had big plans and dreams. With sufficient savings, he hoped one day to be self-employed like his father. In the Bundaberg district, there were many opportunities for grocery businesses and maybe his brother would join him.

Sadly, Alex's many aspirations ended suddenly. When war was declared, without hesitation, as a true Empire man, he joined the rush to enlist. His army service in India and Africa had instilled a fierce pride in Empire and Alex firmly believed it was his duty to serve.

The only obstacle was his age. Alex was about to turn 35, the cut-off age for enlistment in 1914. He feared, because of stringent recruitment regulations, he would not be accepted. (Over 33% of volunteers were rejected in the first year of the war.)[12] However, Australia's new army needed soldiers with war experience. Without delay, Bundaberg's recruitment office processed Alex's enlistment on 28th August, 1914.

From Bundaberg, Alex travelled to Brisbane where he joined 1289 other volunteers who were pitching tents in Bell's Paddock, Enoggera. He became a member of the newly formed 9th Battalion's C Company (later moved to A Company) and, less than four weeks later, left with them on the troopship "Omrah" as part of Australia's First Expeditionary Force. Coincidentally, while Alex embarked for war, his brother Andrew in Scotland enlisted in the King's Own Scottish Borderers Regiment. In different armies and Regiments, the brothers would land at Gallipoli on 25th April, 1915.

On the day before the landing, with some foreboding, Alex prepared for his fate. Stoically, he drew up his will. His last wishes were that his savings of £20 and his Boer War army decorations be given to his brother. Any remaining money was to go to Miss Hannah Philips, the daughter of the landlady from whom they rented their room in Glasgow. Alex was unaware that his brother, Private Andrew Wilson, would not survive the war. Andrew would die the following year on the battlefields at Ypres.

In Australia's official war history, Alex is referred to as 'Wilson of the Scouts.'[13] Shortly before the landing, while on Lemnos Island, he was assigned to the scout contingent, *'put together again under Sergeant Coe'*[14] with Lieutenant Haymen as scout officer.[15] In each battalion, scouts were carefully selected to carry out important responsibilities at the landing. General Birdwood, in his instructions to the 3rd Brigade, referred to them as "special groups to deal with snipers" who would precede the landing force.[16] They were to reconnoitre and clear the way for the landing force to follow.

At the bow of the first boat of No.1 Tow, Alex was positioned with Scout Sergeant Coe, Lieutenant Haymen and Lieutenant Duncan Chapman. Their small crowded craft approached the coast in the early morning darkness and was the first to touch shore. Momentarily, it seemed the Turks were not there. Overwhelmed with anxiety, Alex scrambled onto a silent beach. When the gunfire began, almost half his boat was already ashore. It was reported Alex was standing alongside Sergeant Coe. Sergeant Coe recalled, *'We touched shore, and Lieutenant Chapman was the first ashore. I followed him and we all got ashore. Wilson of the Scouts (Private A.K. Wilson) was taking my pack off when the first shot rang out, a pause, then seven more....'*[17]

As boat after boat of the first wave followed, the scene on the narrow beach quickly descended into chaos. Battalions, companies and platoons became hopelessly mixed. In the mounting confusion, the scouts valiantly attempted to remain true to their orders. Packs were thrown off, bayonets fixed, and, with speed, they climbed the steep hill towards Plugge's Plateau. Unfortunately, in the rugged terrain, communication was quickly lost, and the men became scattered into small groups. Upon reaching the Plateau, rather than pause to re-group, they continued their rapid advance inland. It is probable that Alex moved with Sergeant Coe.

Recorded evidence shows he and Coe remained closely together on the beach. The fate of this group was tragic.

By 10 o'clock, they had cleared the north end of the 2nd Ridge and moved into the vicinity of Baby 700 and Battleship Hill where, for the rest of the day, they joined a valiant attempt to control the strategically important high ground on the left flank. Sergeant Coe recounted that *'at 2 o'clock we got it heavy'* when at least two Turkish battalions swamped across the main range towards them. Despite the mounting threat, further retreat became no longer an option *for if they beat us back they could have enfiladed the centre and right, so there was no retiring where we were.'* Major Robertson of the 9th Battalion ordered Sergeant Coe's group to hold *'a Turkish trench on the extreme left of Second Ridge.'* It was his last order. Soon after, in the intense fire, the Major *was bowled over by a burst of shrapnel, and died a brave gentleman.'* Fred wrote, *'At half-past 5, out of the 33 we had in the trench on the left, only two were left, and we were forced to retire, expecting death at any moment.'* At the end of the day, *'Of our original 70, under Major Robertson, I think only 6 are left.'*[18] Regrettably, Alex was not one of those six. It is probable his life was sacrificed for the defence of the left flank.

A few days after the landing, the exhausted remnants of the 9th Battalion, bearded men in ragged uniforms, returned to the beach. One of these men carried the identity disk that he had removed from Alex's lifeless body. With his other personal effects, including photos and letters, this disk was later sent to his brother's address in Glasgow.

Alex's body was never recovered. Like thousands of other Anzacs, the grave of Private Alexander Kyle Wilson remains unknown. His sacrifice is remembered on Panel 32 of Gallipoli's Lone Pine Memorial.

Endnotes

Identification
1. Stanley (2014), p.104
2. Bean (1941), p.250
3. ibid, p.xi
4. *Courier Mail* (Brisbane), 11 Jun 1915, p.8
5. AWM: PR89/132, Loud, Frank Thomas, Diary
6. *Telegraph* (Brisbane), 18 Jan 1934, p.10
7. *Courier Mail* (Brisbane), 9 Feb 1954, p.2
8. Harvey (1941) p.40
9. Private Bostock identified Chapman's boat belonged to No.1 Tow, *Daily Telegraph* (Brisbane), 24 Jan 1934, p.12. Lance Corp Loud stated it was first in the tow directly behind the steam pinnace, *Loud, Frank Thomas, Diary* AWM: PR89/132
10. Winter (1994) p.94
11. *Sydney Morning Herald*, 26 Apr 1939, p.12
12. Harvey (1941), p.40
13. 'First Ashore' Available at: http://www.9bnassoc.org/9th_battalions/9bn_AIF/first_ashore/
14. *Courier Mail* (Brisbane), 8 Feb 1954, p.2
15. Colonel A G Butler, 'Gallipoli Report' cited in Hancock (2016), p.101. p.97
16. Hancock (2016), p.97
17. *Brisbane Courier*, 3 Jul 1915, p.6
18. Inclusion supported by Bostock 'Letters to Editor' *Telegraph*, 18 Jan 1934, p.10
19. Supported by 1) P. Pedersen, Head of Research AWM in Anzac Treasures, Murdoch, 2014, p.136. 2) Gallipoli Diary, AWM PR89/132 30
20. Supported by F. Uden in Sun (NSW), 1 Dec 1933, p.11
21. Supported by F. Uden in Sun (NSW), 1 Dec 1933, p.11
22. Supported by Sgt F. Coe and Dr Bean in Bean (1941), p. xii
23. Supported by 1) letter to Secretary, Dept. of Army Canberra, 1967 in NAA: B2455, Uden, Frederick Thomas. 2) Letter to editor *Sun* (Sydney), 1 Dec 1933, p.11. 3) acknowledged by Private Spiers, *Telegraph*, 18 Jan 1934, p10 & D. Suller, Secretary of 9th Battalion Assoc., *Telegraph*, 11 Jan 1934 p.10

24. 'Anzac Day Ninth Battalion Mr R.S. Davies of Ubobo.' Unidentified newspaper clipping, Family scrapbook of Mrs Evelyn Davies
25. *Independent* (Deneliquin), 27 Aug 1915, p.2
26. *Courier Mail* (Brisbane), 25 Apr 1947, p.2

Lieutenant Duncan Kenneth Chapman
1. *Maryborough Chronicle*, 8th June 1887, p.1
2. Australia Electoral Rolls, Qld. 1903-1909
3. *Maryborough Chronicle*, 11 Mar 1919, p.3
4. Oral tradition, told by Fred Chapman, Duncan's brother to his daughter
5. *Maryborough Chronicle*, 30 Aug 1889, p.3, & 8 Jul 1899, p.3
6. NAA: B2455, Chapman, Duncan
7. *Maryborough Chronicle*, 9 Dec 1896, p.3 & 16 Dec 1899, p.2
8. ibid, 4 Feb 1903, p.2
9. ibid, 18 June 1904, p.3
10. ibid, 14 Nov 1905 & 28 May 1906, p.3
11. ibid, 31 July 1906, p.3
12. *Queenslander* (Brisbane), 2 Sept 1916, p.38
13. *Maryborough Chronicle*, 24 Oct 1907, p.2
14. *Northern Miner* (Charters Towers), 6 Feb 1909, p.6
15. ibid, 9 Sep 1910 & 2 Dec 1910, p.3
16. ibid, 27 Oct 1910, p.5
17. *Sydney Morning Herald*, 27 May 1915, p.8
18. Grey (2008), p.80
19. *Brisbane Courier*, 11 Jul 1913, p.8
20. *Sydney Morning Herald*, 27 May, 1915, p.8
21. *Brisbane Courier*, 22 Sept 1913, p.7
22. ibid, 22 Jun 1915, p.12
23. ibid, 22 Sept 1913, p.7
24. *Brisbane Courier*, 5 May 1917, p.15
25. *Queenslander* (Brisbane), 16 Nov 1912, p.6
26. Lieutenant Harry Ker was 34 years old, 7 years older than Duncan
27. Wilson (2012), p.55
28. NSW State Archives: NRS 12189, Convict Indents 1788-1890

29. AWM: IDRL/0428, Major Duncan Chapman
30. *Telegraph* (Brisbane), 24 Jan, 1934, p.12
31. Extract from Lt Chapman's letter to brother, Fred from Gallipoli, July 8, 1915, published in *Fraser Coast Chronicle* (Maryborough), 25 Apr, 2012
32. *Courier Mail* (Brisbane), 9 Feb, 1954, p.2
33. William Fisher, 'Letter to Anna Kruze', 3 May 1915, published in *Sunday Mail* (Brisbane), 23 Apr 1995, p.66
34. AWM: PR89/132, Ford, Thomas Walter (Corporal) Diary
35. *Telegraph* (Brisbane), 18 Jan, 1934, p.10
36. ibid, 24 Jan, 1934, p.12
37. *Maryborough Chronicle*, 17 Aug 1915, p.5
38. Lowndes (2011), p.120
39. Harvey (1941) p.61
40. *Maryborough Chronicle*, 17 Aug 1915, p.5
41. *Courier Mail* (Brisbane), 9 Feb, 1954, p.2
42. Letter to Fred Chapman published in *Fraser Coast Chronicle* (Maryborough), 25 April, 2012
43. *Brisbane Courier*, 13 July, 1915, p.7
44. Harvey (1941) p.135
45. AWM: 1DRL/0428, Major Duncan Chapman

Sergeant Walter Edward Latimer
1. 1911 Census for England and Wales, Chilbolton
2. 1891 Census for England and Wales. Pentridge
3. 1881 Census for England and Wales. Corfe-Mullen
4. Recollection of Roger and Bruce Latimer reported in 'History of Walter Edward Latimer' compiled by Kieth Latimer, unpublished (personal communication 1 Oct 2019)
5. 1891 Census for England and Wales. Pentridge
6. NA, UK: British Army Service Records, Walter Edward Latimer
7. NA, UK: Anglo-Boer War Records, C. Holder
8. ibid
9. *Graphic* (London), 17 Nov 1900, p.25
10. NA, UK: British Army Service Records 1899-1902, C. Holder, 708

11. Australian Electoral Roll, Queensland
12. *Brisbane Courier*, 22 Sept 1908, p.3
13. *Daily Standard* (Brisbane), 29 Sept 1914, p.7
14. NAA: C138 C70810 Part 2, Latimer, Walter Edward- Lieutenant
15. *Telegraph* (Brisbane), 24 Jan 1934, p.12
16. Testimony of J.D. Bostock and J.R. Speirs in *Telegraph* (Brisbane), 24 Jan 1934, p.12
17. NAA: C138 C70810 Part 2, Latimer, Walter Edward- Lieutenant (Medical Report)
18. ibid
19. *Brisbane Courier*, 27 Dec 1915, p.7
20. NAA: C138 C70810 Part 2, Latimer, Walter Edward- Lieutenant
21. ibid
22. AWM 4 23, Australian Imperial Force Unit War Diaries – 42nd Infantry Battalion
23. NAA: C138 C70810 Part 2, Latimer, Walter Edward-Lieutenant. Summary
24. ibid
25. ibid
26. 'Casualties of War' Available at: www.awm.gov.au/wartime/article2
27. NAA: C138 C70810 Part 2, Latimer, Walter Edward- Lieutenant
28. Seigfried Sassoon, *The Complete Memoirs of George Sherston*; P. Barker, *The Regeneration Trilogy*; *Regeneration*, film; S. McDonald, *Not About Heroes*, stage play
29. Sassoon (1936), p.54
30. NAA: C138 C70810 Part 2, Latimer, Walter Edward- Lieutenant
31. ibid
32. *Daily Standard* (Brisbane), 21 Sep 1917, p.7
33. NAA: C138 C70810 Part 2, Latimer, Walter Edward- Lieutenant
34. ibid
35. Latimer (1995)
36. NAA: C138 C70810 Part 2, Latimer, Walter Edward- Lieutenant
37. ibid
38. Recollections of Roger and Bruce Latimer reported in Latimer (1995)
39. NAA: C138 C70810 Part 2, Latimer, Walter Edward –Lieutenant
40. ibid
41. ibid

Lance-Corporal James Claude Henderson

1. Queensland Government Gazette, 16 June 1920
2. NAA: B2455, Henderson J C
3. *Brisbane Courier*, 4 Oct 1910, p.4
4. *Telegraph* (Brisbane), 24 Jan 1934, p.12
5. ibid
6. Private Stuart cited in *Morning Bulletin* (Rockhampton), 21 Jun 1915, p.5
7. *Telegraph* (Brisbane), 10 Dec 1915, p.2
8. *Daily Standard* (Brisbane), 24 Feb 1916, p.4
9. Hills (1927), Appendix V
10. *Brisbane Courier*, 24 May 1916, p.7
11. ibid, 4 Oct 1916, p.7
12. ibid
13. *Telegraph* (Brisbane), 25 Feb, 1916, p.2
14. QSA: ID 16748, Queensland Council Minute Books
15. ibid
16. ibid
17. ibid
18. ibid
19. ibid
20. *Telegraph* (Brisbane), 23 Feb, 1917, p.3
21. *ibid*, 25 Feb 1916, p.2
22. *Daily Mail* (Brisbane), 14 Jul 1917, p.6
23. *Daily Standard* (Brisbane), 20 Sep 1916, p.6
24. ibid
25. ibid
26. *Brisbane Courier*, 8 Jun 1916, p.5
27. *Daily Standard* (Brisbane), 13 Jul 1916, p.8
28. *Brisbane Courier*, 10 Aug 1916, p.5
29. *Telegraph* (Brisbane), 9May 1922, p.6
30. ibid, 17 Mar 1917, p.14
31. *Daily Standard* (Brisbane), 1 Feb 1917, p.5
32. *Sydney Morning Herald*, 5 Mar1917, p.6
33. *Telegraph* (Brisbane), 1 Aug 1916, p.9
34. *Daily Mail* (Brisbane), 12 Apr 1917, p.9
35. *Warwick Daily News* (Qld), 26 Apr 1945, p.2
36. *Telegraph* (Brisbane), 13 Oct 1917, p.14

37. *Daily Mail*, (Brisbane), 23 Jul 1922, p.8
38. *Brisbane Courier*, 1 Nov 1922, p.12; 16 Feb 1923, p.8
39. ibid, 27 Aug 1926, p.6
40. *Telegraph* (Brisbane), 21 Jan 1926, p.13
41. *Telegraph* (Brisbane), 9 May 1940, p.11
42. *ibid*, 11 Jun 1940, p.7
43. *Warwick Daily News* (Qld), 26 Apr 1945, p.2

Lance-Corporal Frank Loud

1. AWM: PR89/132, *Ford, Thomas Walter; Loud, Frank Thomas Diary*
2. *Geelong Advertiser*, 19 Jul 1907, p.2
3. *Telegraph* (Brisbane), 19 Jul 1913, p.2
4. *Western Star and Roma Advertiser* (Roma), 16 Dec 1914, p.2
5. ibid, 29 Aug 1914, p.3
6. Gunson (1997), p.33
7. Gammage (1990) p.66
8. Gammage (1990) p.66
9. Broadbent (2015), p.66
10. ibid, p.67
11. Wrench (1985) p.63
12. *Western Champion* (Barcaldine), 25 Apr 1925, p.18
13. Hancock (2016), p.113
14. NAA: B2455, Kendrick, Benjamin Hugh
15. NAA: B73, M54364, Loud, Frank Thomas
16. NAA: B2455, Loud Frederick Leslie
17. NAA: B73, M54364, Loud, Frank Thomas
18. AWM: 4 24/8, AIF Unit War Diaries, Third Australian Machine Gun Company, January 1918
19. ibid, March, 1918
20. *Australasian* (Melbourne), 7 Dec 1918, p.35
21. ibid
22. NAA: B73, M54364, Loud, Frank Thomas
23. Gunson (1997), p.34
24. ibid
25. Gunson (1997), p.34

26. NAA: B73, M54364, Loud, Frank Thomas
27. ibid
28. NAA: B4218 Loud Frank Thomas (Civil Constructional Corps), CV38907
29. NAA: B73, M54364, Loud, Frank Thomas
30. ibid

Private James Dundee Bostock

1. 'Genealogy of the Bostock and Bostwick Families' Available at http://www.bostock.net/tree/bostgen/trees/
2. *Queensland Times* (Ipswich), 5 Aug 1915, p.6
3. *Morning Bulletin* (Rockhampton), 19 Nov 1903, p.4
4. *Brisbane Courier*, 3 May 1905, p.4
5. ibid, 11 Dec, 1908, p.6
6. *Queensland Times* (Ipswich), 19 Apr 1913, p.13
7. *Brisbane Courier*, 26 Sept 1913, p.7
8. *Daily Telegraph* (Brisbane), 24 Jan 1934, p.12
9. ibid
10. 'James Dundee Bostock Diary 1915', SLQ, Brisbane
11. NAA: B1015 M4747, Bostock James Dundee
12. *The Farmer and Settler* (Sydney), 5 May 1916, p.3
13. *Queensland Times* (Ipswich), 6 May 1916, p.10
14. NAA: B1015 M4747, Bostock James Dundee
15. ibid
16. *Brisbane Courier*, 24 Aug 1918, p.15
17. Diary, Alfred Leslie Crisp, 1918. Available at https://ehive.com
18. *The Age* (Melbourne), 25 Nov 1918, p.8
19. *The Telegraph* (Brisbane), 26 May 1933, p.11
20. *Maryborough Chronicle*, 21 May 1938
21. *Cairns Post*, 8 Apr 1935, p.6
22. NAA: BP 1015/1, M4749, Bostock, James Dundee
23. *Courier Mail* (Brisbane), 14 Apr 1934, p.10
24. ibid, 16 Apr 1938, p.3
25. *Sunday Mail* (Brisbane), 19 Jun 1938, p.26
26. ibid, 23 Apr 1938, p.4
27. *Northern Miner* (Charters Towers), 12 Mar 1934, p.2

28. *Courier Mail* (Brisbane), 3 Feb 1939, p.7
29. *Courier Mail* (Brisbane), 6 Aug 1935, p.12
30. ibid

Private Eli Coles

1. *Brisbane Courier*, 3 Feb 1883, p.7
2. *Telegraph* (Brisbane), 23 Jan 1893, p.4
3. ibid, 17 Apr, 1913, p.11
4. *Brisbane Courier*, 11 May 1915, p.7
5. ibid, 2 Aug 1913, p.12
6. *Telegraph* (Brisbane), 18 Dec 1918, p.7
7. Lowndes (2011) p.201
8. AWM 089255: 'In Great Spirits: The WW1 diary of Archie Barwick'
9. Harvey (1941), p.153
10. ibid, p.273
11. *Courier Mail* (Brisbane), 26 Apr, 1954, p.1
12. ibid, 26 Apr, 1954, p.3

Private Andy Fisher

1. Letter by Andy Fisher reprinted in *Sunday Mail* (Brisbane), 23 Apr 1995, p.66
2. FishMan (30 Dec 2005), Topic: Death (discussion post) Available at: https://www.rootschat.com/forum/index.php?topic=115777.msg508631#msg508631
3. GRO, London: 'William Henry Fisher', Certified copy of Death Certificate, 5 Jun 1898
4. 1901 Census for England and Wales
5. 1911 Census for England and Wales
6. *Telegraph* (Brisbane), 15 Jul 1933, p.13
7. *The Queenslander* (Brisbane), 31 Jul 1915, p.41
8. *Brisbane Courier* (Brisbane), 18 Aug 1915, p.7
(Sgt Coe reported similar times and events. At 2 o'clock he came under heavy fire and, by 4 pm, was forced to retreat.)
9. Butler (1938), p.407
10. *Telegraph* (Brisbane), 17 May 1916, p.7

11. *Daily Standard* (Brisbane), 1 Feb 1917, p.5
12. Brisbane Courier, 10 Nov 1917, p.5
13. Hills (1927)
14. *National Leader* (Brisbane), 1 Nov, 1918, p.3; *Darling Downs Gazette* (Toowoomba), 22 Nov 1919, p.8;
Brisbane Courier, 25 Apr 1919, p.7
15. Vamplew (1987), p.412
16. Evans (1988), p.24
17. *The Daily Standard* (Brisbane), 8 Aug 1918, p.6
18. Evans (2004), p.34
19. ibid
20. *Darling Downs Gazette* (Toowoomba), 1 Dec 1919, p.5
21. *Daily Standard* (Brisbane), 22 Mar 1920, p.5
22. ibid, 2 Jul 1921, p.1
23. *Brisbane Courier*, 15 Aug 1922, p.9
24. ibid, 17 Jul 1923, p.6
25. *Telegraph* (Brisbane), 12 Apr 1923, p.4
26. *Queensland Times* (Ipswich), 16 Nov 1936, p.8
27. *Brisbane Courier*, 8 Apr 1924, p.12
28. *Telegraph* (Brisbane), 15 Jul 1933, p.13
29. ibid, 27 Aug 1934, p.5
30. *Courier Mail* (Brisbane), 13 Aug 1947, p.7
31. *Telegraph* (Brisbane), 16 Dec 1927, p.11
32. ibid, 25 Apr 1938, p.12

Private Frederick Young Fox

1. Fox (1923), p.580
2. Norman Fox, *'Frederick Fox II'*, 1987, Available at: https://www.foxfamilyhistory.com.au/wheeler/fyfox.htm
3. *The Queenslander* (Brisbane), 26 Sep 1903, p.36
4. *Maryborough Chronicle*, 27 Jun 1910, p.3
5. Fox, (1923), p.581
6. *Morning Bulletin* (Rockhampton), 21 Jun 1915, p.6
7. ibid
8. Fox (1987)

9. *Morning Bulletin* (Rockhampton), 21 Jun 1915, p.6
10. Fox (1987)
11. *The Capricornian* (Rockhampton), 10 Jul 1915, p.12
12. ibid
13. Wrench (1985) p.76
14. Peter F M Stuart Diary. 1915-1916, M493, John Oxley Library, Brisbane
15. ibid
16. Fox (1987)
17. *Morning Bulletin* (Rockhampton), 21 Jan 1919, p.10
18. AWM: 281/184, Honours and Awards (Recommendations), Frederick Young Fox
19. *Morning Bulletin* (Rockhampton), 5 Dec 1916, p.5
20. AWM 4: 23/66, AIF Unit War Diaries - 49th Infantry Battalion
21. *Morning Bulletin* (Rockhampton), 21 Jan 1919, p.10
22. NAA: B2455, Stuart, Peter Fitzallan MacDonald
23. *Morning Bulletin* (Rockhampton), 'Death of Lieutenant P.Stuart', 21 Sep 1916, p.6
24. *The Capricornian* (Rockhampton), 16 Nov 1916 and 13 Jan 1917, p.11
25. 'WW1 Mother of Queenslanders Lauded 0n International Women's Day', Queensland State Library Blog, Available at: http://blogs.slq.qld.gov.au/ww1/2015/03/06/wwi-mother-of-queenslanders-lauded-on-international-womens-day/
26. *Morning Bulletin* (Rockhampton), 29 Mar 1918, p.6
27. NAA: B2455, Frederick Young Fox
28. *Newcastle Sun* (Newcastle), 27 Dec 1918, p.5
29. *Morning Bulletin* (Rockhampton), 10 Jan 1919, p.5
30. Fox (1987)
31. *The Queenslander* (Brisbane), 25 Jan 1919, p.15
32. *The Queenslander* (Brisbane), 15 Nov, 1919, p.15
33. *The Capricornian* (Rockhampton), 20 Dec 1919, p.5
34. *Morning Bulletin* (Rockhampton), 31 Jul 1920, p.8
35. Fox (1987)
36. ibid
37. Hamilton (2008), p.289-291
38. *Longreach Leader,* 4 Apr 1924, p.26
39. Fox (1987)
40. *Morning Bulletin* (Rockhampton), 5 Mar 1927, p.8

41. Fox (1987)
42. ibid
43. ibid
44. NAA: BP709/1, M12595, Fox, Frederick Young

Private Harold Hansen
1. Seal (2004), p.174
2. Qld BDM: 'Jens Peder Hansen', Certified copy Death Certificate, 15 Aug 1901
3. Qld BDM: 'Ann Catherine Hansen', Certified copy Death Certificate, 14 Nov 1903
4. *Telegraph* (Brisbane), 29 Jun 1906, p.5
5. *Truth* (Brisbane), 24 Apr 1904, p.1
6. NAA: B2455, Harold Reginald Hansen
7. *Morning Bulletin* (Rockhampton), 26 Dec 1912, p.5
8. ibid, 18 Oct 1913, p.12
9. ibid, 10 Dec 1913, p.3&4
10. *Brisbane Courier*, 6 Aug 1914, p.8
11. *The Queenslander* (Brisbane), 16 Nov 1918, p.28
12. Harvey (1941), p.40
13. NAA: M4728 BP709/1, Harold Reginald Hansen
14. *Telegraph* (Brisbane), 19 Apr 1918, p.5
15. NAA: M4728 BP709/1, Harold Reginald Hansen
16. ibid

Private Cecil Holdway
1. Holdway Family History (unpublished) in possession of Mrs L G Holdway, Brisbane
2. *Brisbane Courier*, 26 Dec 1904, p.6
3. NAA: J26, M10946, Holdway, Cecil. (Report by Dr Perkins)
4. NAA: B2455, Holdway, Cecil, (Letter to Central Army Records)
5. Fitzsimmons (2014) p.241
6. AWM: 315 419/048/018, Cecil Holdway, Letter to Australian War Memorial, 1965
7. ibid
8. Harvey (1941), p.59

The First Ashore

9. 'Improvised Postcard from Gallipoli' Available at: https://www.awm.gov.au/collection/C1074502
10. NAA: J26, M10946, Holdway, Cecil
11. *The Road to Gallipoli*, 9th Battalions Association, Queensland, 2015, p.26
12. Harvey (1941), p.277-278
13. Bean (1941), p.710
14. *Townsville Bulletin*, 9 Nov 1917, p.4
15. NAA: B2455, Holdway, Cecil 295
16. V Kevern, 'Postcard to Cecil Holdway', 7 Feb 1918 (possession of daughter-in-law, Mrs L G Holdway, Brisbane)
17. NAA: J26, M10946, Holdway, Cecil
18. ibid
19. ibid
20. ibid
21. *Daily Standard* (Brisbane), 23 Jan 1926, p.6; 3 Feb,1933, p.4; 15 Dec 1934, p.1
22. ibid, 29 Aug 1923, p.4
23. *Courier Mail* (Brisbane), 1 May 1965
24. NAA: J26, M10946 Holdway, Cecil
25. ibid

Private William Jarrett
1. Commonwealth Electoral Roll (Qld) 1903
2. Lance Corp Jarrett mentioned in *Telegraph* (Brisbane), 7 Oct 1907, p.8
3. *Telegraph* (Brisbane), 13 Mar 1907, p.3
4. *Brisbane Courier*, 11 Jun 1915, p.8
5. *Courier Mail* (Brisbane), 11 June, 1915, p.8
6. Lowndes (2011) p.174
7. Harvey (1941) p.135
8. NAA: BP709/1, M4951 Jarrett, William
9. ibid
10. Dunbar (2014)
11. AWM: AIF Unit War Diaries 1914-1918 War - No.1 Australian Dermatological Hospital Bulford, March-July 1917
12. Ibid 1
13. NAA: BP709/1, M4951, Jarrett, William

14. *Census Returns of England and Wales, 1911*, Kew, Surrey
15. *Daily Mail* (Brisbane), 14 Sep 1920, p.1; 13 Nov, 1920, p.1
16. *Daily Standard* (Brisbane), 17 Feb 1920, p.5; 1 Mar 1920, p.5
17. *Telegraph* (Brisbane), 4 Aug 1930, p.15
18. *Brisbane Courier*, 22 Sep 1927, p.19
19. NAA: BP709/1, M4951, Jarrett, William
20. ibid

Private David Kendrick

1. *Census* Returns of England and Wales, *1901 & 1911*
2. Census Returns of England and Wales, 1891
3. England & Wales, Civil Registration Marriage Index, 1837-1915
4. *Daily Standard* (Brisbane), 17 Apr 1913, p.5
5. Commonwealth Electoral Roll (Qld) 1914
6. NAA: B2455: David Kendrick
7. Harvey (1941), p.40
8. SLQ: M493, Peter F Stuart Diary
9. ibid
10. Harvey (1941), p.213
11. NAA: B2455, David Kendrick
12. *West Australian* (Perth), 26 Nov 1918, p.5
13. *Brisbane Courier*, 26 Nov 1918, p.7
14. Commonwealth Electoral Roll (Qld) 1920
15. NAA: BP384/1, Queensland Passports Index, 1915-1925
16. *Australia, City Directories, 1845-1948, Qld PO Directory*
17. ibid
18. Commonwealth electoral roll (Qld) 1934-1943
19. UK, Commonwealth War Graves, 1914-1921 & 1939-1947
20. *Telegraph* (Brisbane), 16 Nov 1942, p.6
21. *Australia, City Directories, 1845-1948, Qld Post Office Directory*
22. NAA: B2455 David Kendrick
23. Commonwealth Electoral Roll (Qld) 1954
24. Qld BDM: 'David Kendrick', Certified copy of Death Certificate, 16 Jan 1957

Private Benjamin Hugh Turner Kendrick

1. Queensland Railway Employees 1889-1940, Queensland Historical Society, 2004
2. *Brisbane Courier*, 2 Feb 1909, p.3
3. *The Queenslander* (Brisbane), 23 Aug 1913, p.44
4. *Brisbane Courier* (Brisbane), 5 Mar 1906, p.7
5. *Queenslander* (Brisbane), 23 Apr 1936, p.10
6. *Telegraph* (Brisbane), 21 Sep 1914, p.8
7. *Brisbane Courier*, 21 Jul 1915, p.8
8. Harvey (1941) p.275
9. *Brisbane Courier*, 3 Jun 1916, p.12
10. Harvey (1941) p.275
11. *Brisbane Courier*, 21 Jul 1915, p.8
12. *Western Champion* (Barcaldine), 25 Apr 1925, p.18
13. Broadbent (2015), p.77
14. AWM: PR89/132, Diary, Ford, Thomas Walter (Corporal); Loud, Frank Thomas (Private)
15. Harvey (1941), p.143
16. NAA: BP709/1, M19188: Kendrick, Benjamin Hugh
17. AWM: RCDIG1064166, 113 Private Quinton John Hunter, 9th Battalion
18. New York, Passenger Lists, 1820-1957
19. NAA: B2455, Kendrick, Benjamin Hugh
20. 'Editorial', *Canadian Medical Association Journal*, Vol 50 (4) Apr 1944, p.362-363
21. *Daily Mail* (Brisbane), 5 Feb 1923, p.7
22. NAA: BP709/1, M19188, Kendrick, Benjamin Hugh
23. ibid
24. *Brisbane Courier*, 10 Aug 1927, p.10
25. *Courier Mail* (Brisbane), 6 Mar 1937, p.25
26. NAA: BP709/1, M19188, Kendrick, Benjamin Hugh

Private Samuel Aubrey McKenzie & Private Robert McNeil Crawford McKenzie

1. 1891 Census for England and Wales
2. 1901 Census for England and Wales
3. War Memorials Register, UK, Item 20163, Liverpool Institute School

4. NAA: B2455, Samuel Aubrey McKenzie
5. New York Passenger Arrival Lists
6. NAA: B2455, Samuel Aubrey McKenzie
7. United Grand Lodge of England Freemason Membership Registers, 1751-1921
8. NAA: B2455, Robert McNeil Crawford McKenzie
9. Inward Passenger Lists NRS13278
10. ibid
11. *Adelaide Advertiser*, 1 Nov 1917
12. *Sydney Morning Herald*, 14 Aug 1914, p.12
13. Harvey (1941), p.61
14. NAA: B2455, Samuel Aubrey McKenzie
15. NAA: B2455, Robert McNeil Crawford McKenzie
16. AWM: 4 23/26/2, AIF Unit War Diaries – 9th Infantry Battalion
17. NAA: B2455, Robert McNeil Crawford McKenzie
18. SLQ: M493, Peter F Stuart Diary
19. Wrench (1985), p.432
20. R.M.C. McKenzie, 'Letter to Daisy Davis', 19 Apr 1916
21. Private Abell, Harold, AWM: RCDIG1062913 (Statement by Private J. Thompson, C Company)
22. AWM: 281/1, 'Recommendation File for Honours and Awards, AIF, 1914-1918', 21 Apr 1916
23. NAA: B2455, Samuel Aubrey McKenzie
24. ibid
25. R.M.C. McKenzie, 'Letter to Daisy Davis', 15 Jul 1916
26. ibid
27. ibid
28. ibid, 20 Aug 1916
29. ibid
30. AWM: RCDIG1062913, Sergeant Denis Rowden Ward
31. *Queensland Times* (Ipswich), 26 Sep 1916, p.6
32. R.M.C. McKenzie, 'Letter to Daisy Davis', 1 Nov 1916
33. ibid
34. ibid, 25 Apr 1917
35. ibid, 18 Aug 1917
36. ibid, 4 Jul 1917

Private William Alexander Pollock

1. *Derry Journal* (Ireland), 28 Sep 1894, p 7. *Londonderry Sentinel* (Ireland), 5 Apr 1898
2. NA: Militia Service Records, WO 96, William Pollock
3. ibid
4. NA: British Army Service Records, William Pollock
5. 'Imperial Units Royal Inniskilling Fusiliers' Available at https://www.angloboerwar.com/unit-information/imperial-units/563-royal-inniskilling-fusiliers
6. Passenger Lists Leaving UK 1890-1960
7. NSW Passenger Lists, 1913, "Wyandra"
8. Australia Electoral Rolls, Queensland, 1915
9. *Daily Record* (Scotland), 14 Oct 1914, p.2
10. Harvey (1941) p.38
11. ibid, p.61
12. William Alexander Pollock, NAA: B2455
13. ibid

Private Archibald Henry Reynolds

1. *Mercury* (Hobart), 11 Jan 1901, p.3
2. Reynolds, Archibald. 'Album' (manuscript) RAHS, Sydney
3. ibid
4. ibid
5. *Telegraph* (Brisbane), 20 Aug 1914, p.12
6. *Brisbane Courier*, 1 Sep 1914, p.6
7. Reynolds, Archibald. Album (manuscript) RAHS, Sydney
8. ibid
9. ibid
10. ibid
11. ibid
12. ibid
13. ibid
14. Winter (1994), p.155
15. Reynolds, Archibald. 'Album' (manuscript) RAHS, Sydney

16. Harvey (1941) p.48
17. Reynolds, Archibald. 'Album' (manuscript) RAHS, Sydney
18. ibid
19. Reynolds, Archibald. 'Album' (manuscript) RAHS, Sydney
20. *The Age* (Melbourne), 23 Jan 1919, p.8
21. *Telegraph* (Brisbane), 25 Jan 1919, p.7
22. NAA: C138, M99653, Reynolds, Archibald Henry
23. *Western Champion* (Parkes), 12 Feb 1920, p.5
24. 'Letter to Prime Minister' NAA: C138, M99653, Reynolds, Archibald Henry

---

Private William James Rider
1. Queensland Assisted Immigration, 1848-1912
2. 1891 Census Returns of England and Wales
3. *Telegraph* (Brisbane), 24 Oct 1881, p.2
4. ibid
5. *Toowoomba Chronicle & Darling Downs Gazette*, 30 May 1929, p.5
6. QSA: ID28009, 'Toowoomba South Boys State School Admission Register, 1870-1908'
7. *Toowoomba Chronicle*, 20 Dec 1887, p.3
8. NAA: B2455, William James Rider
9. Australia Electoral Rolls 1912 to 1915
10. Qld BDM: Mary Jean Hanson, Certified copy of Marriage Certificate
11. Qld BDM: William James Rider, Certified Copy of Marriage Certificate
12. Wrench (1985) p.432
13. Howie-Willis (2019), p.11-22
14. Kinloch (2016), p.85
15. Howie-Willis (2019), p.11
16. 'Mutiny at Etaples Base in 1917', Available at: http://www.militarian.com/threads/mutiny-at-etaples-base-in-1917.7050/
17. NAA: B2455, William James Rider
18. Smith (2016), p.133
19. NAA: B2455, William James Rider
20. *West Australian* (Perth WA), 26 Nov 1918, p.5

21. Queensland Electoral Roll 1919, 1921,1922
22. Qld BDM: Certified copy of Death Certificate, William Rider, 1932
23. Noonan, D (2016) 'War Losses (Australia)' International Encyclopaedia of the 1st World War. Available at: https://encyclopedia.1914-1918-online.net/article/war_losses_australia

---

Private James Roy Speirs
1. *Brisbane Courier*, 24 Jul1915, p.5
2. 1891 Census England, Scotland and Wales
3. *Capricornian* (Rockhampton), 11 Aug 1900, p.45
4. *Brisbane Courier*, 21 Sep 1901, p.12
5. ibid
6. Australia Electoral Roll, Port Curtis, 1901,1912
7. *Morning Bulletin* (Rockhampton), 4 Sep 1914, p.8
8. *Telegraph* (Brisbane), 18 Jan 1934, p.10
9. *Brisbane Courier*, 24 Jul 1915, p.6
10. NAA: B2455, Spiers, James Roy
11. ML SLNSW: MS1493, Archie Barwick Diary
12. AWM: 1RDL/0428, Private Robert George Henderson Proudfoot
13. AWM: 4 19/3, AIF Unit War Diaries— 1st Australian Division Salvage Company, December 1917
14. ibid
15. ibid
16. *Daily Mail* (Brisbane), 26 Dec 1918, p.5
17. Australia Electoral Roll, 1922, Port Curtis
18. UK and Ireland Incoming Passenger Lists 1878-1960
19. Australia Electoral Roll, 1930, Port Curtis
20. *Morning Bulletin* (Rockhampton), 27 Jan 1941, p.8
21. ibid, 6 Feb 1920, p.10
22. *Morning Bulletin* (Rockhampton), 20 Feb 1941, p.10; *Courier Mail* (Brisbane), 16 Mar 1939, p.9

Private Frederick Thomas

1. *Western Star & Roma Advertiser* (Roma), 27 Aug 1904, p.3
2. *Brisbane Courier*, 14 Dec 1914, p.8
3. 'Mitchell War Memorial', Available at https://apps.des.qld.gov.au/heritage-register/detail/?id=600038#
4. Fitzsimmons (2014) p.241
5. NAA B2455, Frederick Thomas
6. Wrench, (1985), p.432
7. Harvey (1941), p.115
8. Harvey, (1941), p.142
9. Keating (1963), p.29
10. Harvey (1941), p.227
11. *Queenslander* (Brisbane), 'A Joyous Homecoming' 30 Nov 1918, p.10
12. *Brisbane Courier*, 'Appreciation of Soldiers' 9 Dec 1918, p.9
13. *Brisbane Courier*, 'Appreciation of Soldiers' 26 Dec 1918, p.6
14. Australian Electoral Rolls, Qld 1919
15. Australian Electoral Rolls, Qld 1922
16. *Daily Standard* (Brisbane) 22 Jan 1921, p.8
17. Australian Electoral Rolls, Qld 1939
18. *Courier Mail* (Brisbane), 20 Feb 1935, p.19
19. *9th Battalion News*, No.1, Dec 1947., No 2, Jan, 1949, p.8., No.3 Mar 1950, p.1
20. ibid, 'Notes of the Day', No.1, Dec 1947, p.5

Lieutenant Frank Haymen

1. *Who's who in Australia*, Crown Content, Melbourne, 2003
2. *Brisbane Courier*, 19 Oct 1894, p.6
3. ibid, 18 Oct 1902, p.14
4. ibid, 27 Jul 1907, p.5
5. *Brisbane Grammar School Magazine*. Vol VIII 1906 and Vol IX 1907
6. *Brisbane Grammar School Magazine*. Volume IX November 1907
7. *Brisbane Courier*, 13 Nov 1912, p.6
8. *Warwick Examiner and Times*, 13 May 1912, p.3
9. *Telegraph* (Brisbane), 28 May 1912, p.2

10. *Brisbane Courier*, 3 Nov 1913, p.10
11. ibid, 29 May 1914, p.4
12. *Telegraph* (Brisbane), 3 Jul 1913, p.6
13. *Brisbane Courier* (Brisbane), 'Intelligence Corps', 27 Mar 1913, p.7
14. *Brisbane Courier*, 22 Sep 1913, p.7
15. *Telegraph* (Brisbane), 26 Nov 1913, p.2. (Frank seconded to the 7th Infantry Moreton Regiment for 12 months)
16. *The Queenslander* (Brisbane), 21 Mar 1914, p.40
17. *Daily Mercury* (Mackay), 5 Aug 1914, p.4
18. Telegraph (Brisbane), 5 Aug 1914, p.3
19. *The Evening Telegraph* (Brisbane), 22 Aug 1914, p.5
20. Private F. Uden identified Lt Haymen as his scout officer. *Sun* (Sydney), 1 Dec 1933, p.11
21. Private G. Preston wrote: 'The Scouts who have been got together again under Sgt Coe'. *Queenslander* (Brisbane), 3 Jul 1915, p.8
22. 'Infantry Training Manual 1905' cited in Winter (1994) p.186
23. ibid, p.154
24. *Sun* (Sydney), 1 Dec 1933, p.11
25. Harvey (1941) p.51
26. *Western Champion* (Barcaldine), 25 Apr 1925, p.18
27. ibid
28. ibid
29. AWM: PR89/132, *Ford, Thomas Walter; Loud, Frank Thomas Diary*
30. Broadbent (2015), p.66

Scout Sergeant Frederick Charles Coe (aka Fred Kemp)

1. 1891, 1901 Census for England & Wales
2. *Cairns Post*, 23 Aug 1912, p.7;
3. NA, London: British Army Service Records, Frederick Charles Coe
4. ibid
5. *Cairns Post*, 23 Aug 1912, p.7
6. ibid
7. ibid
8. *The Queenslander* (Brisbane), 20 Jan 1912, p.37
9. *Cairns Post*, 14 May, 1912, p.2

10. ibid, 3 Oct 1910, p, 5
11. ibid, 7 Oct 1910, p.7
12. Australia Electoral Rolls, Qld. 1913
13. *Cairns Post*, 23 Aug 1912, p.7
14. *Cairns Post*, 1 Mar 1918, p.1
15. *The Queenslander* (Brisbane), 3 Jul 1915, p.8
16. Winter (1994) p.186
17. ibid, p.154
18. Account by Private E. Gandy, 9th Batt. in *Brisbane Courier*, 3 Jul 1915, p.5
19. Sun (Sydney), 1 Dec 1933, p.11
20. Bean (1941) p.xii
21. Bean (1941) p.293 (footnote)
22. *Brisbane Courier*, 18 Aug 1915, p.7
23. Bean (1941) p.310
24. NAA: BP709/1, M149, Coe, Francis Charles (aka Frederick)
25. Bean (1941), p.290
26. Lowndes (2011), p.144
27. *Brisbane Courier*, 18 Aug 1915, p.7
28. *The Queenslander* (Brisbane), 31 Jul 1915, p.41
29. Bean (1941), p.292
30. *The Queenslander* (Brisbane), 31 Jul 1915, p.41
31. *Brisbane Courier*, 18 Aug 1915, p.7
32. Bean (1941), p.293 (footnote)
33. *The Queenslander* (Brisbane), 31 Jul 1915, p.41
34. *Brisbane Courier*, 18 Aug 1915, p.7
35. *The Queenslander* (Brisbane), 31 Jul 1915, p.41
36. *Brisbane Courier*, 18 Aug 1915, p.7
37. ibid
38. ibid
39. *Cairns Post*, 14 Oct 1916, p.7
40. ibid
41. GRO: Marriage Certificate, 23rd Nov, 1916, M14843
42. Memo for Public Curator, 24 Jan 1945 in NAA: B2455, 3266382, Frederick Charles Coe
43. *Cairns Post*, 1 Mar 1918, p.1
44. NAA: BP709/1, M14.9, Coe, Francis Charles (aka Frederick)
45. *Queenslander* (Brisbane), 6 Sept 1919, p.29

46. *Brisbane Courier*, 9 Mar 1929, p.28
47. NAA: BP709/1, M14.9, Coe, Francis Charles (aka Frederick)
48. ibid
49. QSA: ID ITM2309498, Coe (Kemp) Frederick Charles

Corporal Edward Teitzel

1. NAA: BP709/1, M12588 – Teitzel, Edward
2. Queensland State Electoral Roll 1896
3. Gladstone State School: Admission Register, 11 May 1896
4. *Gympie Times and Mary River Mining Gazette*, 13 Apr 1899, p.3
5. Bony Mountain State School Admission Register 1902-1971
6. Queensland State Electoral Roll 1900
7. ibid, 1906
8. *Truth* (Brisbane), 6 Sep 1908, p.8
9. *Gympie Times & Mary River Mining Gazette,* 10 Dec 1910 p.2; 15 Dec 1910, p.2; 6 Apr, 1911 p.2; 9 Nov 1911 p.2
10. ibid, 28 Sep 1911, p.2
11. ibid, 12 Mar 1912, p.2
12. ibid, 25 Aug 1914, p.3
13. 'The scouts were put together again under Sergeant Coe.' *The Queenslander* (Brisbane), 3 Jul 1915, p.8
14. Winter (1994) p.154, p.186
15. *Sun* (Sydney), 1 Dec 1933, p.11
16. NAA: B2455, Teitzel, Edward. Statement by Corp E. Titzel, 25/7/16
17. Harvey (1941), p.83
18. Ibid, p.278
19. NAA: B2455, Teitzel, Edward
20. Harvey (1941), p.115
21. Holmes (2014) p.79
22. Harvey (1941) p.125
23. NAA: B2455 – Edward Teitzel
24. *Gympie Times Mary River Mining Gazette*, 7 Jan 1919, p.1
25. NAA: BP709/1, M12588, Teitzel, Edward
26. *Bowen Independent*, 19 Nov 1921, p.3
27. *Beaudesert Times*, 3 Mar 1922, p.8

28. Genealogical Index to Australian and other Expatriates in Papua New Guinea
29. *Pacific Islands Monthly*. 22 June, 1938
30. NAA: BP709/1, M12588, Teitzel, Edward
31. ibid
32. ibid
33. ibid

Private William Cleaver

1. *Kentish Mercury* (London), 25 May 1900, p.2
2. ibid
3. *Argus* (Melbourne), 4 Feb 1910, p.7
4. William departed using his birth name, Ulric Cleaver (Passenger Lists Leaving UK 1890-1960, NA, London). On arrival, he is 'William Cleaver' (Victoria Inward Passenger Lists 1839-1923, PRO, Victoria)
5. Pugh's Almanac and Queensland Directory 1911-1915
6. *Mataura Ensign* (Gore, NZ), 2 Dec 1912, p.2
7. Wrench (1985) p.76
8. ibid, April to October 1917
9. NAA: B2455, William Cleaver
10. ibid
11. ibid
12. *Brisbane Courier*, 21 Sep 1929, p.27; 26 Jul 1930, p.25
13. *Time and Place*, Issue 17, 2007, p.6
14. *Brisbane Courier*, 20 May 1932, p.12; 23 May 1932, p.10
15. *Townsville Bulletin*, 29 Nov 1934, p.4; 6 Feb 1936, p.6
16. *Brisbane Courier*, 2 Dec 1942, p.6
17. *Courier Mail* (Brisbane), 22 Feb 1947, p.2
18. ibid, 25 Mar 1948, p.1

Private Frederick Thomas Uden

1. 1911 Census for England and Wales
2. ibid
3. NAA B2455, Uden, Frederick Thomas

4. Passenger Lists leaving UK 1890-1960
5. *Daily Telegraph* (Sydney), 3 Aug 1914, p.12
6. *Folkestone, Hythe, Sandgate & Cheriton Herald*, (England), 21 Jun 1913, p.10
7. *Sydney Morning Herald*, 10 Sep 1914, p.9
8. *Daily Telegraph* (Sydney), 24 Apr 1914, p.2
9. *Northern Star* (Lismore), 29 Aug 1914, p.5
10. *The Queenslander* (Brisbane), 3 Jul 1915, p.8
11. Winter (1994), p.154, p.186
12. *Sun* (Sydney), 1 Dec 1933, p.11
13. NAA: B2455, Uden, Frederick Thomas, Letter from F.T. Uden
14. *Sun* (Sydney), 1 Dec 1933, p.11
15. AWM: REL/15961.002
16. Peter Uden. "Re: Gallipoli Water Bottle." Message to P.Burgess, 18 Oct 2017. E-mail. (Recollection of Fred's grandson)
17. NAA: B2455, Uden, Frederick Thomas
18. Butler (1938), p.364
19. NAA: B2455, Uden, Frederick Thomas
20. *Northern Star* (Lismore), 23 May 1917, p.2
21. NSWSA: Government Gazette, 3 Jun 1921, No 80, p.3297
22. *Northern Star* (Lismore), 12 May 1923, p.15
23. *The Kyogle Examiner*, 6 Aug 1935, p.8
24. *Daily Examiner* (Grafton), 30 Oct 1942, p.1
25. *Northern Star* (Lismore), 3 Feb 1945, p.7
26. ibid, 20 Jun 1952, p.5; 14 Apr 1950, p.4
27. *Port Macquarie News and Hastings River Advocate*, 20 Aug 1948, p.2
28. *Daily Examiner* (Grafton), 24 Jun 1942, p.4
29. Australian electoral rolls, 1901-1936

Private Alexander Kyle Wilson

1. NA, UK: British Army Service Records, Alexander Wilson
2. 1871 & 1881 Scotland Census, Glasgow
3. NA, UK: British Army Service Records, Alexander Wilson
4. 'Argyll and Sutherland Highlanders' at www.angloboerwar.com/unit-information/
5. https://www.britisharmedforces.org/i_regiments/argsuthhigh_index.htm

6. Memorial plaque to Argyll and Sutherland Highlanders, 1902-03, St Andrews Church (Church of Scotland), Kolkata
7. NA, UK: British Army Service Records, Alexander Wilson
8. ibid
9. 1911 Census, Glasgow
10. Passenger Lists Leaving UK 1890-1960
11. Queensland Commonwealth Electoral Roll 1913
12. AWM: Enlistment Standards
13. Bean (1941), p xii
14. *Brisbane Courier*, 23 Jun 1915, p.7
15. '*Lieutenant Haymen, our scout officer*' quoted in letter by Private F. Uden: *Sun* (Brisbane), 1 Dec 1933, p.11
16. Winter (1994) p.154
17. Bean (1941) p. xii
18. *Brisbane Courier*, 18 Aug 1915, p.7

Bibliography

ACRONYMS:

AWM	Australian War Memorial
GRO	General Register Office, England
ML	Mitchell Library, Sydney
NAA	National Archives of Australia
NA	National Archives of UK
NLA	National Library of Australia
NSWSA	New South Wales State Archives
PRO	Public Record Office, UK
QSA	Queensland State Archives
RAHS	Royal Australian Historical Society
SLNSW	State Library of NSW
VPRS	Public Record Office, Victoria

RECORDS:

Australian War Memorial:
   AWM 4 Australian Imperial Force Unit War Diaries, 1914-1918 War
   AWM 8 Unit Embarkation Nominal Rolls
   AWM 281 Recommendation files for Honours and Awards, 1914-1918 War
   AWM RCDIG Red Cross Wounded and Missing Enquiry Bureau Files, 1914-1918

National Archives of Australia:
   NAA B2455, 1st AIF Personnel Dossiers, 1914-1920
   NAA BP709/1, Repatriation Medical case Files
   NAA J26, Medical Case Files
   NAA C138, Personal Case Files

BOOKS:

Armitage, Richard, *Robert McNeil an Interesting Tale*, self-published, 2016
Bean, C.E.W., *Anzac to Amiens*, AWM, 1946
Bean, C.E.W., *The Official History of Australia in the War 1914-1918* Vols. 1, 3 & 4, Angus & Robertson, 1941
Broadbent, H., *Defending Gallipoli. The Turkish Story*, Melbourne University Press, 2015
Brown, L & Le Moal, M., *The Australian Soldier*, OREP, 2017
Butler, A G, *The Official History of the Australian Army Medical Services, 1914-1918*, Vol.1, 1938
Cameron, David, *25 April 1915*, Allen & Unwin, 2007
Caulfield, Michael, *The Unknown Anzacs*, Hatchette, 2013
Chambers, Stephen, *Anzac the Landing*, Pen & Sword, 2008
Coombes, David, *A Greater Sum of Sorrow: The Battles of Bullecourt*, Big Sky, 2016
Cranston, Fred, *Always Faithful: A History of the 49th Infantry Battalion*, Boolarong Press, 1983
Dunbar, Ray, *The Secrets of the Anzacs*, Scribe, 2014
Evans, Raymond, *Radical Brisbane. An Unruly History*, Vulgar Press, 2004
Evans, Raymond, *The Red Flag Riots, A Study of Intolerance*, University of Qld Press, 1988
FitzSimons, Peter, *Gallipoli*, Heinemann, 2014
Fox, Matthew, *History of Queensland*, States Publishing, 1923
Grey, J., *A Military History of Australia*, Cambridge University Press, 2008
Gunson, Neil, *Reminiscences of the Loud Family in England and Australia*, N.Gunson, 1997
Hamilton, John, *Gallipoli Sniper: The Life of Billy Sing*, Macmillan, 2008
Hancock, Richard, *Such a Noble Man was He*, self-published, 2016
Harvey, Norman, *From Anzac to the Hindenburg Line*, Naval & Military Press, 1941
Hills, Loftus, *The Returned Sailors and Soldiers Imperial League of Australia*, Southland Press, 1927
Holmes, Peter, *A Magnificent Anzac: the Untold Story of Lieutenant Colonel Maurice Wilder Neligan*, Peter Lloyd Holmes, 2014
Kinloch, Lieutenant Colonel, *Echoes of Gallipoli*, Exisle, 2016
Lowndes, Chris, *Ordinary Men Extraordinary Service*, Boolarong Press, 2011

Pedersen, Peter, *Anzac Treasures*, Murdoch, 2014
Sassoon, Seigfried, *Sherston's Progress*, Faber & Faber, 1936
Seal, G., *Inventing Anzac*, University of Qld Press, 2004
Smith, G., *A Family that went to War*, Lulu Press, 2016
Stanley, Peter, *Lost Boys of Anzac*, NewSouth, 2014
Taylor, J. (ed.), *The Derniere heure*, L. Wolf, Rouen, 1919, p.5
Vamplew, W. (ed), *Australians Historical Statistics*, Fairfax, 1987
Wilson, G, *Bully Beef and Balderdash: some Myths of the AIF examined and debunked*, BigSky, 2012
Winter, Denis, *25 April 1915. The Inevitable Tragedy*, University of Queensland Press, 1994
Wrench, C.M., *Campaigning with the Fighting Ninth*, Boolarong Press, 1985

DIARIES:

Loud, Frank Thomas, Diary. AWM: PR89/132
James Dundee Bostock Diary 1915. SLQ, Brisbane
Diary, Alfred Leslie Crisp, 1918. Available at https://ehive.com
WW1 diary of Archie Barwick. AWM: 089255
Peter F M Stuart Diary. 1915-1916. M493, John Oxley Library, Brisbane
Reynolds, Archibald. Album (manuscript) RAHS, Sydney

NEWSPAPERS:

Adelaide Advertiser
The Age (Melbourne)
Argus (Melbourne)
Australasian (Melbourne)
Cairns Post
Capricornian (Rockhampton)
Courier Mail (Brisbane)
Daily Examiner (Grafton)
Daily Standard (Brisbane)
Darling Downs Gazette (Toowoomba)
Derry Journal (Ireland)
Farmer and Settler (Sydney)
Geelong Advertiser

Gympie Times
Graphic (London)
Independent (Deneliquin)
Maryborough Chronicle
Mercury (Hobart)
Morning Bulletin (Rockhampton)
Mataura Ensign (New Zealand)
Newcastle Sun
Northern Miner (Charters Towers)
Northern Star (Lismore)
Port Macquarie News
Sydney Morning Herald
Sun (Sydney)
Sunday Mail (Brisbane)
Telegraph (Brisbane)
Townsville Bulletin
Truth (Brisbane)
Warwick Daily News
West Australian (Perth)
Western Champion (Barcaldine)
Western Star (Roma)

PERIODICALS:

9th Battalion News, No.1, Dec 1947, No 2, Jan, 1949, p.8., No.3 Mar 1950, p.1

Gammage, Bill, 'Collection Notes. A New Gallipoli Diary', *Journal of the Australian War Memorial*, 16, April 1990

Howie-Willis, Ian, 'The Australian Army's Two 'Traditional' Diseases: Gonorrhoea and Syphilis,' *History*, Journal of Military & Veterans Health, Vol 27, No 1, Jan 2019

Keating M.T., 'Unofficial History, Lagnicourt, 17th April, 1917' *Journal of the Fighting Ninth*, 16, 1963

Roberts, C., 'The Anzac Landings. A Failure in Command.' *The Gallipolian*. No 137, Spring, 2015

The Road to Gallipoli, 9th Battalions Association, Queensland, 2015

The Road to Pozieres, 9th Battalions Association, Queensland, 2016

www.ingramcontent.com/pod-product-compliance
Lightning Source LLC
Chambersburg PA
CBHW031308150426
43191CB00005B/128